ROYAL FLYING CORPS KITBAG

Per ardua ad astra – Through adversity to the stars

The Royal Flying Corps motto which was approved by King George V on 15 March 1913, and confirmed by Army Order No. 111

ROYAL FLYING CORPS KITBAG

AIRCREW UNIFORMS AND EQUIPMENT FROM THE WAR OVER THE WESTERN FRONT IN WWI

Mark Hillier

FRONTLINE
BOOKS

ROYAL FLYING CORPS KITBAG
Aircrew Uniforms and Equipment from the War Over the Western Front in WWI

Mark Hillier

First published in Great Britain in 2020 by Frontline Books,
an imprint of Pen & Sword Books Ltd, Yorkshire - Philadelphia

Copyright © Mark Hillier, 2020
ISBN: 978-1-52675-299-4

The right of Mark Hillier to be identified as Author of this work has been asserted by him in accordance with the Copyright, Designs and Patents Act 1988. A CIP catalogue record for this book is available from the British Library All rights reserved.

No part of this book may be reproduced or transmitted in any form or by any means, electronic or mechanical including photocopying, recording or by any information storage and retrieval system, without permission from the Publisher in writing.

Typeset by Aura Technology and Software Services, India.
Printed and bound in India by Replika Press Pvt. Ltd.

Pen & Sword Books Ltd incorporates the imprints of Pen & Sword Archaeology, Air World Books, Atlas, Aviation, Battleground, Discovery, Family History, History, Maritime, Military, Naval, Politics, Social History, Transport, True Crime, Claymore Press, Frontline Books, Praetorian Press, Seaforth Publishing and White Owl

For a complete list of Pen & Sword titles please contact
PEN & SWORD BOOKS LTD
47 Church Street, Barnsley, South Yorkshire, S70 2AS, UK.
E-mail: enquiries@pen-and-sword.co.uk
Website: www.pen-and-sword.co.uk

Or

PEN AND SWORD BOOKS,
1950 Lawrence Road, Havertown, PA 19083, USA
E-mail: Uspen-and-sword@casematepublishers.com
Website: www.penandswordbooks.com

CONTENTS

Acknowledgements	vii
Introduction	viii
Chapter 1: Flying Clothing	1
Chapter 2: Flying Equipment	101
Chapter 3: Uniforms	127
Chapter 4: Rank, Badges, Insignia and Buttons	181
Chapter 5: Paperwork and Documents	214
Chapter 6: RFC to RAF Transitional Arrangements	237
Appendix I	257
Appendix II	258
Appendix III	260
Notes	262
Bibliography	265
Index	267

ROYAL FLYING CORPS KITBAG

This book is dedicated to the memory of those members of my family who served during the First World War: Second Lieutenant George Stephenson of the Royal Flying Corps, an engineer and inspector of rotary Le Rhone aircraft engines; his brother, 3784 Rifleman John Alfred Stephenson of 'B' Company, 1st/9th Battalion London Regiment, Queen Victoria's Rifles, who was killed on the first day of the Battle of the Somme in 1916; their sister and my great-grandmother, Nurse Memie Gwendolin Stephenson of the Red Cross, a volunteer ambulance driver; my great-grandfather, Private Albert Church of the Middlesex Regiment, who was gassed during the war; and his father, who served in the Royal Engineers. They will not be forgotten.

Second Lieutenant George Stephenson RFC. (Mark Hillier Collection)

ACKNOWLEDGEMENTS

Many people have been instrumental in helping to bring this massive project together and it has been a real team effort. First and foremost, thanks to Simon Lannoy, who has inspired me and encouraged me with all the titles I have published in the Kitbag series. Phil Phillips, who has bent over backwards to help me with providing kit and information. Mick Prodger, a fount of all knowledge whose invaluable help and assistance is much appreciated. Collector Scott Rall, who allowed Rainer and Maura Stephens to photograph some of his collection for me. David Farnsworth of Historic Flying Clothing, for helping with text and photos. Carlo and Elizabeth Marogna of Constructive Heritage, for access to photos of their collection. Malcolm and Roberta 'Bobbie' Webb (née Saunders), for sparing their time and memories, mementoes and photos of a very special RFC Pilot, Samuel Saunders. Adrian Kilby, for access to some of his collection. Tangmere Military Aviation Museum, for access to their archive of information and photographs. Mark Khan, for help with the firearms information and flare pistols. Additional thanks must go to Adrian Roberts of Cross & Cockade for his constructive comments. Martin Mace at Frontline Books, for assisting me with all my projects. Once again, I am very grateful to my lovely family for supporting me. My final thanks go to 'the silent man', who knows who he is.

NOTE ON IMAGES

Please note that all the items of uniform and equipment illustrated are in the hands of private collectors and are 100 years old. In some instances, the quality and display of the items is not as clear as I would have liked due to the need for preservation and conservation. Also, the conditions were not always conducive to the best photography.

INTRODUCTION

My passion has always been open cockpit biplane flying, and this has entailed dragging myself out in all seasons, not just the warmer summer months, to fly. Being at one with the elements and with the view from the cockpit, spectacular scenery framed by the aerofoils, as well as the noise from the engine and the wind whistling through the struts and bracing wires makes it all extremely rewarding.

However, the stark reality is not as romantic; 100mph slipstream tearing at your goggles, engine oil in your face, cold penetrating your every extremity the higher you go, the engine noise invading your senses. You must be dedicated to want to fly in all seasons, al fresco.

It was no hobby for those who flew on active service during the First World War, choice was not a luxury they possessed and operational necessity dictated their need to fly. The difficulties faced by the first Royal Flying Corps pilots and observers who met the challenges of early aviation in open cockpit machines can only be imagined. Not only flying and navigating, but also fighting for survival in this raw, unforgiving theatre of war, battling archie (anti-aircraft) and machine-gun fire from enemy aircraft.

Aircraft and engine serviceability were not great, and the risk of being shot down by the enemy either by ground fire or by return fire was high. On top of this coping with the invasion of the senses, unpleasant smell and taste of oil on your face from the aircraft engine, tossed about by the turbulence and extreme cold all in all lead to a rather unpleasant experience. It was altogether a far cry from the romantic notion of open cockpit flying we have now, but for many better than the reality of trench warfare.

In my mind the early pilots and observers were like explorers, pioneers blazing a trail for military aviation, battling against adversity. What makes these men so special is that, like the explorer, they not only had to face the elements and exhaustion, but also the additional risks resulting from aviation still being in the experimental stage and the dangers of warfare itself.

For those who mastered the air and made it their element, they had to learn on the job, testing and understanding the limits of their aircraft and gaining new skills. This included finding ways of keeping warm and alert whilst flying and adapting and adopting kit that was available at the time. It was clear that the pilot who remained responsive and focused would have the upper hand in combat. Keeping warm was not just about creature comforts, but maintaining alertness which meant the odds of surviving increased on long or high-altitude sorties.

Dressing to survive is now the norm for today's military aviators and even for pilots flying light aircraft over water or inhospitable terrain. The human factors side of aviation is much better understood. This encompasses, for example, such considerations as the effect of fatigue with regards to safety and its contribution to accidents and the lack of oxygen at altitude leading to hypoxia among others.

Parachutes, life jackets, hearing protection and immersions suits have all developed over the past century of aviation and are now readily available. However, in the early days of aviation before the First World War, pilots had no real concept of the environment and what they were up against. Their only comparison was with the automobile or motorcycle, meaning gloves to protect your hands from the elements and goggles to stop dust and grit getting in your eyes might be a good idea. Articles published in early editions of *Flight* magazine on flying clothing and associated adverts sprang from a developing industry of private-purchase options for jackets, goggles and helmets.

Early flights would be short hops, low level and low speed, often ending in a controlled crash – or sometimes uncontrolled! Little or no wind would be preferable for a safe sortie and good visibility. The intrepid aviator thought that a tweed jacket, flat cap worn backwards and goggles would be enough protection for their flights, and indeed many photos show pilots aviating with little or no thought about personal kit and safety. The idea of human factors, the role of protective clothing and pilot ability\skill and survival rates were not even a concern at this stage. The focus was on the art of flying, and it was an art form at this time rather than a science.

Indeed, Duncan Grinnell-Milne, a Royal Flying Corps (RFC) pilot of the First World War wrote, 'in aviation, a friend of mine was wont to say there is as much art as science', and he continues, 'and with aeronautics, in its earlier stages, art often seemed to be marching ahead of science that was in its infancy and waiting for the pilots whose progressive discoveries, be it said, were frequently the result of accident'.[1] The development of flying equipment was born out of necessity.

As aircraft developed, speeds and range increased and aircraft performance meant the ability to climb higher and this resulted in greater exposure to extreme cold, lack of oxygen and weather conditions for longer. Towards the end of 1917–18 the ceiling and range of the new varieties of aircraft had expanded. The Sopwith Pup had enough fuel for a flight of 3 hours' duration and a ceiling of just over 17,000ft, while the Spad VII managed 18,000ft. Patrols were flying regularly at 10 to 15,000ft and above with outside air temperatures often at -35 °C or lower.[2]

Some thought had to be given to the protection of the aviator as aircraft developed and the role of the aircraft moved from a new hobby to one of reconnaissance and then a fighting machine. The risks increased, and the frailty of the pilot also needed to be considered.

Early on, before the establishment of the RFC, during the days of the Air Battalion of the Royal Engineers (RE), there had been some thought about the choice of suitable clothing for officers employed on aeronautical work and the costs associated with it.

Although some kit was available, many would-be pilots during this time and after the establishment of the RFC looked to the automobile clothing manufacturers for protective equipment. Companies such Burberry's, Gamage's, Dunhill, Robinson & Cleaver and Gieve's among others produced aviator combination suits, fleece-lined boots, specialised goggles, rainproof gauntlets and leather coats.

The accident rate was inevitable as these aviators were learning on the job, although the rewards were great. A number recognised the possible benefits of having some head protection as in a crash the many wires, braces and struts within the structure of the plane increased the risk of being knocked senseless. Some pilots favoured helmets used by motorcyclists, but those who found these cumbersome could choose to fly with a leather helmet or just a balaclava.

Early manufacturers of specific aviation helmets included Dunhill in England and Roold in Paris. A helmet that is often seen in early photos was developed by a Mr Warren from Hendon and, with its excellent shock-absorbing qualities, was widely used by pilots in the training schools.

Prior to the establishment of the RFC, the RE had developed an air battalion which had operated with balloons and the first fixed wing aircraft. On 13 April 1912 the King issued a Royal Warrant for a new service and the battalion was replaced with the Royal Flying Corps, which had both a military wing and a naval wing with a joint Central Flying School. The uniform adopted for the military wing at this time was khaki and officers were seconded to the wing from existing regiments, initially retaining their uniforms and only adding RFC pilot's wings as a means of identification. The naval wing under the title of the RFC was not popular and became the Royal Naval Air Service (RNAS) from 1 July 1914; this is not discussed in this book, the topic deserving its own publication – although the flying equipment worn was of a similar nature to that shown.

For NCO and rank-and-file men enlisting in the RFC the service dress was the new approved maternity tunic, although images show that the 1902 Pattern service dress was also retained (see appendices for scale of provisions). For officers this style of maternity or plastron fronted jacket was subsequently adopted soon after, and jodhpurs, breeches or trousers worn with boots. RFC cap badges and collar badges were developed and shoulder titles for the enlisted and NCO aircrew. After the birth of the RAF in 1918, a specific uniform style developed in blue featuring RAF insignia and this is the forerunner of the uniform we know today. Throughout the First World War the uniform was khaki for operational use.

In 1914, the use of aircraft as a military tool was initially recognised as beneficial for reconnaissance, observing troop concentrations, fortifications, artillery and stores etc. It is clear that the formal issue of clothing to RFC and RNAS pilots was limited and often adapted from motoring garments used by army drivers and despatch riders.

However, there was some equipment on offer as issue and this was listed in the scale of provision of 1914, and included weatherproof coats, goggles, gauntlets, leather boots and leather caps. Aircrew still had the option to purchase their own clothing and commercial companies continued to develop their motoring ranges into more specialised flying clothing.

As the war progressed the exposure of the aircrew became starkly apparent with pilots suffering frostbite and chilblains, and the RFC looked to develop better kit for their aviators.

The 1915 *Training Manual RFC* lists the clothing expected to be worn by the aircrew as 'two pairs of thick long drawers, a woollen waistcoat, a British "warm coat" with a waterproof oilskin over it, a cap with ear pads, two balaclavas, a flying helmet, goggles, a warm scarf, and two pairs of socks and gloves'.[3]

The idea of using layering to preserve body heat was by now well established, and it would be important for the aircrew to dress only immediately before each sortie to prevent them sweating as the excess perspiration would then freeze at altitude. An often-overlooked fact is that many gunners and observers transferred to the RFC for duty with little or no experience, were issued flying kit and taken up for air experience while in the front line with training on the job. For this reason, the uniforms of both officers, NCO and air mechanic ranks, all of whom could have been employed on aerial duties during the First World War, are included here.

INTRODUCTION

Arthur Whitehouse (later awarded the Military Medal) was a gunner who had previously served in the trenches with the Northants Yeomanry and on arrival at his squadron witnessed at close hand an aircraft hit the ground minus its wings, killing its pilot:

'You the new aerial gunner. . . . Whitehouse. . . . No 1785, 3rd/1st Northants Yeomanry?' someone barked at me. 'Yes, Sergeant. . . .' 'Did you see that officer out there . . . killed?'

'Your new number will be 78563. Second class Ack Emma now, not trooper, lad. Remember that. And for God's sake, don't go pullin chaps out of crashes like that agayne. You're posted for flying you know. You'll get a vertical gust doin' things like that. Ere . . . ere's yer flyin-kit. . . . Over 'ere. . . . Come on. . . . One 'elmet, a bit dirty. Flying coat, leather, one. Goggles, flying, one; and you'd better clean them up a bit lad. That's blood on there. . . . Mister Aslett stopped one in the napper, the other day. . . . observer, yer know. They all come unstuck. . . . Nah then, flying boots, one pair, knee length; gloves, leather one pair . . .'[4]

This gives an idea of what sort of kit was being issued in the line to those seconded to the RFC in its hour of need for additional crew. As the aircraft became more capable and the operational heights increased, it was quite clear that better thermally insulated kit was required for aircrew.

In the winter of 1916 a small breakthrough was made with what really was the first flying suit, as described by Dr Graham Rood of the Farnborough Air Sciences Trust:

The first significant stride was made to providing effective protection for the pilot and this arrived from the brain of Sidney Cotton, an RNAS pilot with No. 8 Squadron. Cotton had been working on his own aircraft when a 'scramble' was called, and he flew in his dirty overalls for an hour or so and upon landing found that, unlike his fellow pilots who were shivering from the cold, he was quite unaffected. Having thought through this effect, he realised that it was the oil and grease soaked into the overalls that had retained the body heat. Picking up on the idea, he took leave and travelled to London, to Robinson & Cleaver, where he had a flying suit made for him to his design. The suit had three layers, a thin lining of fur, a layer of airproof silk, and an outside layer of light Burberry's material, all made into a one-piece suit, just like his overalls. Robinson & Cleaver were asked to register the design on behalf of Cotton and the flying suit took its name from the inventor and was called the Sidcot suit (Sidney Cotton). By late 1917, tests had shown that the Sidcot Flying Suit No 5 was regarded by pilots as the most suitable for operational use. Consequently, the manufacturers of the suit, Robinson & Cleaver, were asked to produce 250 suits per week, just fourteen days after the order. Deliveries were later expected to reach 1,000 per week just four weeks after the initial order. By December 1917 the orders for leather flying coats, some 3,000, were cancelled in favour of the Sidcot suit.[5]

Steps were also taken to introduce electrically heated waistcoats, gloves and boots, although these were designed to complement other items of kit and not to replace them. However, this equipment was not that successful and caused burns or the wires to the elements broke as they were fragile and therefore the items were often rendered useless.

When flying above 10,000ft hypoxia was an ever-present issue. Oxygen supplies and helmets that could be fitted with an oxygen mask didn't become available until late in the war. In August 1918 the Air Board issued a specification for the Mk 1 helmet with wireless telephony and fittings for an oxygen mask. However, this was not popular with many aircrew and one of the problems with the early masks was that exhaled moisture froze on the face and restricted oxygen flow.

Goggles would often fog up or become frosted and some chose not to fly with them due to the lack of peripheral vision. Some development of goggles by the RFC/RAF took place in 1918 but most were adopted from civilian patterns.

Fire was the aircrews' biggest fear and to a degree the leather helmets, goggles made of Triplex and leather flying coats gave some protection, but parachutes were still not issued and these may have saved lives. Sadly, some aircrew took to carrying pistols, not for self-defence but with which to take their own lives rather than face being burned to death. Some investigation into fire-rated flying clothing was carried out but those taking part in the tests suffered burns through the flying suit material and this was abandoned.

This has been an enjoyable project to research with evidence collated and relied on from photographs, limited first-hand accounts that talk about equipment and documentation, records available at The National Archives and other established texts. These sources are at times contradictory to say the least and a definitive record is difficult to establish. Certainly, from photographs, which are our best source of information, it's clear that there was a wide variety of kit used either private purchase, adapted, adopted or issued.

As it has been difficult to give a definitive account for all items, this kitbag is intended to be illustrative of the type of flying equipment and service uniforms used by the RFC pilot and observer and gunner from inauguration in 1912 to the birth of the Royal Air Force (RAF) on 1 April 1918 and the end of the First World War. The RAF is not covered in detail as this merits another volume in its own right, but there is a chapter about the transitional uniform and period to the end of the war. The role and equipment of the brave RFC balloon observers and crews of airships are not included in detail in this edition but are occasionally mentioned where appropriate.

Examples of types of uniforms, badges and equipment used by the enlisted man, NCO and officer aircrews of the RFC on day-to-day duties are detailed and illustrated with period photographs. The examples given are limited to uniforms worn on duty or used for aviation, not mess dress or full dress.

The following passage from *Into the Blue* by Norman Macmillan, a pilot with 45 Squadron in April 1917, illustrates the variety available. He comments specifically on the arrival of his new commanding officer taking in the scene in the mess on his arrival:

> He looked around the room at the faces intent upon his, all of them countenances of men used to the chances of flight, to the crack and the woof of Archie, to the crackle of machine guns about their ears. They were dressed in motley garb; regimental tunics, RFC tunics, sweaters; silk scarves, woolly scarves; leather flying coats wound tight about them, buttoned up, or falling loose, sheepskin thigh boots, knee length flying boots, slacks and shoes, or breeches and puttees.[6]

This extract sums up the variety of kit in use and the problem involved in trying to create a definitive handbook. The topic is vast and some of the equipment very rare and therefore difficult to locate or photograph, and so this book is intended as a handy, illustrative, guide to a wide-ranging and comprehensive subject.

Mark Hillier
Fontwell, 2020

Chapter 1
FLYING CLOTHING

Some of the first memos relating to the use of suitable clothing for officers employed on aeronautical work date back to 5 January 1911 and are held at The National Archives. The RE had experience of operating balloons, man flying kites and airships and was now starting to explore fixed wing aviation.

The series of letters, memos and minutes makes for interesting reading regarding the initial ideas for appropriate clothing and equipment for the early aviator. This predates the official establishment of the Aeronautical Battalion of the RE, although clearly relates to when it will be established. A letter written from the major general in charge of administration, Aldershot command, is in response to a minute from the director of fortifications and works dated 25 November 1910 asking a question about suitable attire for aviation. The following excerpt from his letter, No. 15077, to the secretary of the War Office is worth quoting:

> There is no difficulty as to the clothing when experimental runs from Aldershot or Salisbury plain are in question, because over their uniform officers could wear suits of workman's overalls, suitably lined for cold weather, the shape and fit being of no importance. These suits could be kept permanently at the Air Battalion Headquarters and could be used by any officer or man requiring them. Their cost including lining should not exceed £3 a suit and their life would be indefinite. A knitted balaclava helmet will keep the head warm in cold weather. In hot weather the ordinary blue dungaree overalls will suffice, costing less than the suits. Six suits of each should suffice.
>
> 2) On manoeuvres, however or when reconnoitring with troops, officers will be unable to wear workman's clothing, as their rank must be apparent as seen as they descend. Some costume then becomes necessary which will proof against cold and dirt, and at the same time allow the wearer to be recognized as an officer.
>   a) The fur cap, with ear flaps which can be tied under the chin, will keep the head warm and will not be liable to be blown off. It is proposed to issue an order that everyone in an aeroplane shall wear an aviator's protective

helmet. The cap can be carried strapped to the machine and assumed on descent. It will always be worn in dirigible balloons; a silver badge could be added to the front if smartness is desired.

b) The leather jacket should be large enough to allow for its being worn over the ordinary khaki serge, so that in the event of an officer having to walk after landing he may be able to remove his hot outer coat.

c) The leather breeches are a necessity, as they will not show grease. Moreover, no amount of underclothing will enable Bedford cord to keep out the wind when traveling at 40 miles per hour.

d) Field boots are specified because experience shows that Stohwasser leggings are apt to check circulation and produce cold fast.

e) Gauntlets are necessary to prevent the wind from blowing up the sleeving.

This costume should suffice for any weather and being of black leather will not be injured by oil, while an officer can if necessary, ride in it. Everything should fit very loosely, especially the boots. A pair of 'spatter dash' leggings lined with lamb's wool going over the boots and ending above the knee can be used for additional warmth when in the machine and their appearance is not bad. A knitted helmet may be needed to protect the nose and ears from frostbite.

3) The cost of such a suit is £10 and if approved perhaps it may be possible to make a grant to each officer on final appointment to the Air Battalion in order to defray the cost of purchase of leather equipment.[1]

This letter clearly lays out the beginnings of a pattern of clothing which changed little through the early years of the RFC with issue clothing becoming available but limited in quantities per squadron. However, it is interesting to note the suggestion of black leather. Eventually brown was chosen for the RFC, while the RNAS unofficially adopted black.

A memo of 5 November 1911 suggests that there is still much debate about what

LEFT: Second Lieutenant Harold Balfour (later Harold Harington Balfour, 1st Baron Balfour of Inchrye, MC and Bar, PC) in front of a Caudron G2/G3. Balfour transferred from the Army to the RFC in 1915. The image was probably taken in 1915, though Balfour is dressed in typical early flying attire. He is also wearing short boots and Stohwasser leggings, along with private-purchase goggles and a very simple lined leather cap. The latter is possibly an example of the earliest pre-war-issue style; note the little tab on the top of the cap which indicates an early flying cap with lappet-style ties. (Historic Military Press)

FLYING CLOTHING

is best to wear with a recommendation that brown coveralls, lined, would be better than leather. A suggestion is made that all officers adopt the 'Bleriot' helmet and that further trials be carried out on suitable footwear and gloves or gauntlets and that a grant of £5 be given to officers of the Air Battalion to enable them to purchase suitable attire.

What is not apparent and what is speculation is how much equipment was available on issue at the outset of the RFC, the best guess being that gauntlets, leather coat, trousers and an unlined cap were the basics. It is not until the Army Orders of 1914 were issued that a clearer idea of what was available is given (see Appendix I).

The prevalence of leather flying equipment and lined gloves springs from the early Air Battalion and is evident in many period photographs. Its development from that point onwards was borne out of necessity and driven by aircrew experience on the Western Front. As is known, at the outset of hostilities the aircraft types available meant that pilots were exposed to the slipstream around the aircraft, engine oil and fumes, and dust and bugs which could get in your eyes, hence motoring apparel was thought to be most suited to the rigours of aviation.

What is clear from the Army Orders of 1914 is that basic flying kit was available on issue but limited to each flying squadron and shared (see also Appendix I). This obviously led to many preferring to buy their own equipment and, as the early memos suggest, a £5 grant was available for a period of time to purchase flying kit. When this grant was stopped it is difficult to ascertain how clothing and equipment was supplied.

RIGHT: A typical combination of flying clothing worn by early RFC pilots. This includes a leather coat, which is basically a motoring jacket, simple leather flying cap with no wind deflectors and goggles, again probably produced for driving. The hands are protected by leather, blanket-lined, long gauntlets and there is a scarf to keep the draught out. Underneath the coat the flyer would wear uniform. Note the puttees and black boots indicating an enlisted man. (Constructive Heritage Collection)

One early RFC pilot, Denys Corbett Wilson, commented in a letter home that he had plenty of warm clothing for winter flying in November 1914:

> We have had frost and snow, lovely days, but very cold and high N.E wind at anything over 2000 feet. I've any number of warm things though, and today was as warm as toast all day, feet and all – quite a triumph. I wear galoshes [over boot made of rubber] over my ordinary boots with great success, also leather trousers and really I was warmer in the machine than out.[2]

The RFC-issue short leather jacket was available by then along with leather trousers, but the rest of his warm kit was probably private purchase including boots. Indeed,

"Instructions regarding the issue of Clothing and Necessaries during Mobilization," issued with Army Order 114 of 1915—Amendments.— *Add* new Table I.A— A.O. 155. 1915.

TABLE IA.
SCALE OF WORKING CLOTHING FOR AN AEROPLANE SQUADRON AND CENTRAL FLYING SCHOOL.

	Per squadron.	Central Flying School.
Boots, knee, R.F.C. ... pairs	25	25
Caps, fur-lined	25	25
Gauntlets, observers ... pairs	12	24
,, pilots ,,	12	24
*Gloves, chamois leather	12	...
Goggles, with triplex glasses	25	50
Glasses for goggles (light or dark-tinted) pairs	25	50
Helmets, aviation	8	50
Jackets, leather	27	40
Masks ...	25	25
Overshoes, gaitered ...	25	25
Trousers, leather	27	40
Jean clothing, or brown drill, combination suits.	2 per man biennially.	2

* For use in cold weather by men doping wings in the open.

ABOVE: This table has been extracted from the Army Orders of 1915. It details the scale of provision for aeroplane squadrons and the CFS (Central Flying School), and lists a selection of kit including flying helmets and fur-lined caps, leather jackets, trousers and leather face masks; the 'Boots, knee' are not the later fug boots. There are few changes in terms of types of equipment issued from the public clothing allowance of the Army Orders in 1914. However, 'Boots, knee' and 'Gloves, chamois leather' were an addition by 1915, as were the face masks and gauntlets for pilots and observers. This is probably when trigger-finger-style gauntlets were introduced as this is the first time they are split into two distinct types on the scale of provision. See Appendix I for the 1914 table. (Tangmere Military Aviation Museum)

FLYING CLOTHING

RIGHT: An aviator in front of his Caudron G3. As well as a leather flying coat and a scarf to keep out the draught, he is wearing a fur-lined leather cap typical of those mentioned in the 1915 scale of provision. (Historic Military Press)

as winter drags on, he writes home for a pair of gumboots to keep his feet dry at the airfield and asks for a .45 calibre pistol to be sent out for him.

As the war progressed and the demands of the aircraft and crews increased the practicality of some of the kit and its shortcomings soon became apparent. The RFC did get better at providing equipment and in early 1915 Denys writes home: 'They are doing us very proud as regards boots, furry high ones for flying and fur caps both very good articles.'³ The boots he mentions are not the well-known 'fug boots'. Officially termed 'Boots, thigh', this type of footwear was sealed as a pattern in the RFC in December 1916. Designed by Major Lanoe Hawker VC, DSO, they replaced earlier attempts at equipping flying personnel with footwear that was suitable for their special purpose. Initially Hawker had them made at Harrods, which christened them the 'Charfor' boot, however they soon became universally known as fug boots. The ones described in this account are possibly what was known as 'Boots, knee' and were fur-lined and had a square-looking toe.

The extreme cold soon highlighted the flaws in the issued kit when flying at altitude, as described by Duncan Grinnell-Milne, a pilot of 16 Squadron and operating the B.E.2c in 1915:

> At 14000 feet over, Northern France in November one realized how very exposed were the seats in a B.E. I was thoroughly chilled myself and I had a windscreen, whereas the observer's had been removed to make room for the forward gun mounting. With the engine running slowly it was possible to make oneself heard. I shouted to ask how he felt. He turned, trying to grin; but he could barely move his jaw enough to shout something back at me. I only got one word: 'awful'; sufficient to make me push the stick forward for a faster descent.
>
> One of the disadvantages of flying so high was that it seemed to take such a long time to come down, especially as I had to run the engine every now and then to make sure it was not getting cold. Had we met an enemy aeroplane during that glide we would have had to run for it; the observer could never have handled the gun with frozen fingers. It did not begin to be noticeably warmer until we were below 6,000 feet, but I went on down and did not flatten out until we were at three

thousand. . . . My hands and feet were aching from the recent freezing cold and I could imagine how the observer must be suffering from the way he kept bouncing about in his seat, stamping, clapping his hands and rubbing his face. Thawing out is agony, but I was glad to notice that his cheeks were no longer white.[4]

Despite the introduction of fur-lined flying caps as well as the use of layers of clothing, leather overcoats and gloves, the cold at this altitude for any period could be intolerable and indeed many aircrews suffered frostbite and the onset of hypoxia. If they were sweating after enemy action or the kit had become wet through rain on the climb up, ice started to form next to the skin which was particularly unpleasant.

Arthur Gould Lee eloquently describes his preparation for a high-altitude sortie at 18,000ft in late 1917 over the Western Front, and his efforts to reduce frostbite and extreme cold:

> Our orders are close offensive patrol at 18,000 feet. By now I know what kind of arctic temperatures to expect at these heights, even in June, and like my two companions I take elaborate precautions. We assemble in 'C' flight office, and while the patrol leader, Captain Pratt, speaks about his intentions and tactics, I pull on my sheepskin

ABOVE: The crew of a Royal Aircraft Factory F.E.2d in their positions. The pilot is furthest from the camera; his observer in front, in this case showing the use of the rear-firing Lewis gun which required him to stand. This photograph graphically illustrates the exposure to the elements that the crew would have faced. The gunner would have had to maintain his balance and keep up fire on the enemy while evasive action was being taken by the pilot, and all with no parachute. The gunner is wearing a long, leather flying coat, no doubt with several layers underneath. (Historic Military Press)

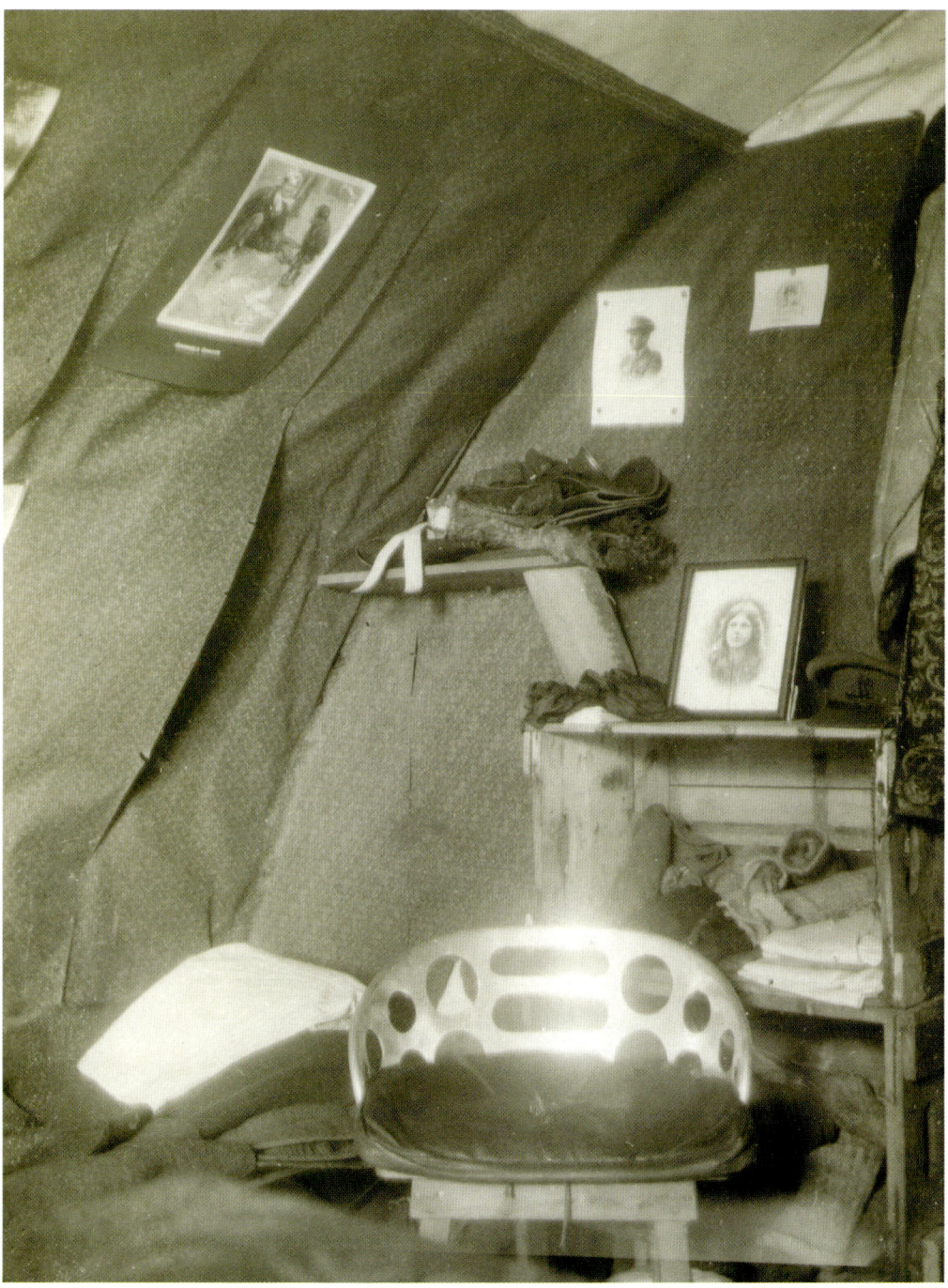

ABOVE: An aviator's home from home somewhere in France, with his kit stowed away on the makeshift furniture and shelving. His seat, positioned next to his campaign bed, is taken from a wrecked aircraft; the packing crate behind is modified and made into shelves to store his shirts and his officer's cap, badged to the Royal Artillery, sits on top. The airman's flying cap, gloves, goggles and what appear to be fug boots have been placed on the shelf top left. (Mark Hillier Collection)

ABOVE: A sheet of paper that serves as a poignant reminder of a brave man. This is a list of the personal effects and belongings of Second Lieutenant Robert Taylor (pictured top right on the opposite page) which were catalogued after the death. Serving in 41 Squadron, Taylor was shot down while flying in an Airco D.H.5 over the Western Front on 17 September 1917. He was a victim of Oberleutnant Ernst Udet of Jasta 37. The list provides a good insight into the kit bag of an aviator at this point in time. (Mark Hillier Collection)

FLYING CLOTHING

thigh boots (wool inside), having first put on my second pair of socks (thick ones), then a couple of sweaters under my tunic. I arrange my long muffler carefully around my neck and don my knee length, wool lined, fur collared, leather flying coat, beautifully stained and smelly with castor oil from many hours' exposure to rotary engines.

Next is the unpleasant job of applying a generous layer of whale grease to my face, especially the parts that will be exposed – the cheeks, lips and tip of the nose – if they are not protected, I can be sure of frost bite. The revolting aroma of grease will haunt me all through the patrol, but that is part of a high flyer's burden. Having wiped my hands-on cotton waste, I fit my oily, fur lined leather helmet, reeking even more than the coat of castor oil and my goggles in the fur lined mask, first making sure that the lenses are perfectly clean, for in the air the specks of dirt will appear to

be distant Huns. Then I draw on my leather, wool lined gauntlets, with a fold over mitten to keep my fingers less frigid when they are not manipulating controls or the gun. Most of us including me, wear fine silk under gloves as well.[5]

By 1917, Sopwith Camel pilots were flying patrols regularly at altitudes of 10,000–17,000ft and having to face extreme cold. They suffered from the effects of hypoxia; the lack of oxygen slowing down the decision-making process and rendering the poor victim almost a happy passenger. One pilot, Leonard H. Rochford DSC and Bar, DFC who flew with the RNAS and RAF, describes his experience of flying on oxygen when it became available:

During the evening of 17 July [1917] I took my new camel, B3807, up to 22,000 feet which was the greatest height I had ever reached. I was testing a new oxygen supply apparatus, a cylinder containing the oxygen and a tube leading from it and attached to a mask which could be clamped over the mouth and nose when desired. A valve controlled the supply of oxygen to the mask and this was operated by hand. It was a beautiful sunny evening as at this great height over the English Channel I had a wonderful view of the earth below which took in the French coast, well beyond Boulogne, the south coast of England beyond Bournemouth and the east coast to East Anglia. I did not experience any discomfort at this height of 22,000 feet but when I turned on the oxygen and breathed it into my lungs through the face mask, the effect was amazing. It was comparable to an overcast sky changing to brilliant sunshine and I felt very much more alert, it was unfortunate that the apparatus was heavy and clumsy to carry around in a small fighter aeroplane and I do not recall it being put into service in any of our fighter squadrons beyond the end of the war.[6]

However, this indicates that progress was being made in recognising the issues being faced by aircrew, although oxygen was not fully adopted apart from on the larger bombers due to weight issues.

The development of the thigh-length fug boot and the Sidcot suit to combat the cold were also a step in the right direction in helping the long-suffering aircrews. Appendices II and III feature two tables found in correspondence relating to flying kit and clothing that should be issued to student pilots dated 1917 and a table relating to stocks of equipment held that confirms all available issue kit in that year prior to the inception of the RAF on 1 April 1918.

Although parachutes of the Spencer type were provided for balloon observers, they were not issued to RFC airmen. These were mainly what are termed today as the static-line variety of parachute, and would not have been any use to the pilot or observer of an aircraft due to both the bulk and the mode of operation. Free-fall parachute designs are better suited to fixed-wing aircraft.

Elliot White Springs, an American pilot with the RFC, wrote about Calthrop and his thoughts on the parachute in his book *War Birds*. The subject of the book was his deceased best friend and fellow pilot John McGavock Grider while they were both on 85 Squadron in 1918:

> Information has been received that the Germans have developed a parachute that can be used from an aeroplane. Springs got all excited about it and went to see Calthrop the inventor of the Guardian Angel parachute that all the balloon-attics use. Calthrop is working on the idea. Springs offered him two thousand dollars if he would make one for him according to his idea. Calthrop said he couldn't do it as the War Office wouldn't let him work for individuals, but that he would be glad to have any assistance or ideas. Springs offered to test out Calthrop's and take it to the front for further tests and they are working on the same idea.
>
> Calthrop's idea is to have the parachute arranged in the trailing edge of the wing like an aileron.
>
> The trouble with that is that it is liable to foul on the tail and it would take some time for the pilot to get out of his seat and get the straps on. And he would have to get out in a spin or a steep dive. Calthrop is developing it primarily for the big planes where there is a crew and all of them could possibly get out except the pilot.
>
> Springs wants one made to fit on an S.E. where the streamline for the pilot's head is on the top of the fusilage. Then the pilot could wear the harness all the time and all he would have to do would be to unfasten his safety belt and jump. The objection to that again is the possibility of fouling. He figures on having a long cord between the parachute and the plane so that it would be free of the plane before it started to open. As the pilot fell away from the plane the cord would open the parachute and then the pilot could cut loose. It might be very difficult for the pilot to cut loose and Calthrop figures on doing it with a series of rubber bands or an unravelling device.
>
> I like the idea. It would certainly help at the front. Most pilots are killed by structural defects or by having the plane catch fire in the air. It would also be a great device for testing.
>
> Springs tried to get permission from the U.S. Headquarters to go ahead with it, but they said nothing doing.[7]

Looking at the information available in The National Archives at Kew it seems that parachutes were discussed at the Royal Aircraft Factory, particularly Calthrop's 'Guardian Angel' (AIR 1/1121/204/5/2073). Tests were successfully carried out on the Calthrop parachute in 1917 (AIR 5/1348). There was no British order for free-fall parachutes until September 1918, and by this time the RFC and RNAC had combined to form the RAF. Had parachutes been issued and developed at a suitable rate they may have saved lives. The Germans, however, issued static-line-type parachutes after the spring of 1918; at least two of the top ten German aces of the time were killed when their parachutes failed to open.

This chapter shows examples of the type of flying equipment available, either issue or private purchase.

FLYING HELMETS AND LEATHER FLYING CAPS

As the development of aircraft continued, speeds and heights attained increased and pilots pushed the boundaries, and the inevitable crashes racked up at an alarming rate. Training was initially rudimentary with a nervous student being given just a few hours' dual in a very basic machine. Cecil Lewis was one of those pilots with very few hours' experience, as he recalls: 'one and a half hours dual stood to my credit. I had trundled round the aerodrome with Sergeant Yates my instructor, doing left hand circuits, and made a few indifferent landings.'[8] At this point his instructor was happy that he flew solo in the afternoon if the wind was right!

Head protection was thought to be beneficial and initially motorcycle-style helmets or leather caps were worn. The earliest types of caps were made of unlined leather and secured by ties but these gave little protection. Pilots were surrounded by struts, wires and other bits of fuselage that would cause serious injury and even concussion to the hapless occupant. These early helmets were more about impact protection than warmth or practicality. *Flight* magazine, dating back to the early days of military aviation in 1912, often carried articles and adverts on the latest safety equipment that was thought best for aviation.

After training, operational aircrews often ditched the more cumbersome Roold and Warren helmets for balaclavas and leather helmets, as mentioned in the memoirs of William Urquhart Dykes: 'While we were pupils, we wore heavy crash helmets, which we were allowed to discard when we had passed out and got our RFC Wings.'[9]

The early helmets fell into two distinct types, those that gave some protection from abrasions\scraping of the head and those that kept out the cold. Leather flying caps were satisfactory but provided no resistance to impact or blunt trauma to the head. The biggest problem with the flying helmets was their bulk as they added to drag when flying and also meant that the aviator suffered with buffeting around the head, and needed strong neck muscles to hold his head out in the slipstream. Also, these helmets being quite broad meant that the flying goggles did not sit well on the helmet either and therefore the goggles didn't provide a good fit on the face.

What is clear from documents in The National Archives dated 3 May 1912 is that sample leather flying overalls and leather caps had been provided for RFC consideration from the quartermaster general. The reply discusses the kit provided for trial:

> The aviation helmet is the normal headdress for pilots and passengers when making ascents in aeroplanes, but they are not worn in airships, and only a limited number are available, we want every man to have a cap which is suitable for wear in an airship and in emergency, in an aeroplane should a helmet not be available. The universal pattern

service-dress cap is not suitable since it will not stay on in an aircraft and does not afford adequate protection from cold; it is however suitable for other occasions. The leather cap is suitable for wearing in aircraft and can be folded and placed in a pocket of haversack but is somewhat unsightly and so not suitable for wear with service dress.[10]

It is not clear from the 1914 scale of provision, that leather flying caps were issued as it only lists flying helmets. However, this could just be broad terminology as it is felt that issue caps were available in 1914, although what pattern these were is not clearly defined. Included in this book is a 1914 dated unlined example which, in my view, is almost an issue variety. It is known that the RFC sealed as patterns 'Caps, fur-lined, temporary' (Pattern No. 8150) in November 1914 and, as a replacement, 'Caps, leather' in May 1915 (Pattern No. 8402). These were also fur-lined, and a dated example of the correct style is depicted here.

As there were so many private-purchase caps on the market telling the difference between issue and non-issue is sometimes difficult. Some helmets and cowl helmets often have a WD mark or 'A' over a broad arrow but similar styles were available for private purchase.

What is clear is that they were all of a similar construction with chrome leather outer, often with buckle fastening under the chin. Early examples can be found with lappet-style tape fastening, as seen in the photographs here, and these still appear in contemporary photographs until quite late on in the war.

Some leather flying helmets have wind deflectors on the side and press-studded flaps. Some have peaks and are fur-lined, others have neck flaps. On 6 February 1917 two further caps, 'Caps, leather, winter' (Pattern No. 9302) and 'summer' (No. 9303), were approved having been sealed as a pattern, as all army equipment was required to be. These caps were sealed as patterns on 18 December 1916 and it is though that the winter version was probably the cowl type helmet and the summer variant being what was later to become known as the Mk I Flying Helmet by the RAF, both with fur lining.[11]

The RFC stock table in Appendix III gives all the types of cap available to the aircrew in 1917 as: 'Caps, fur-lined, summer', 'Caps, fur-lined, winter' and 'Helmets, aviation (Roold or Warren)'.

Safety Helmets

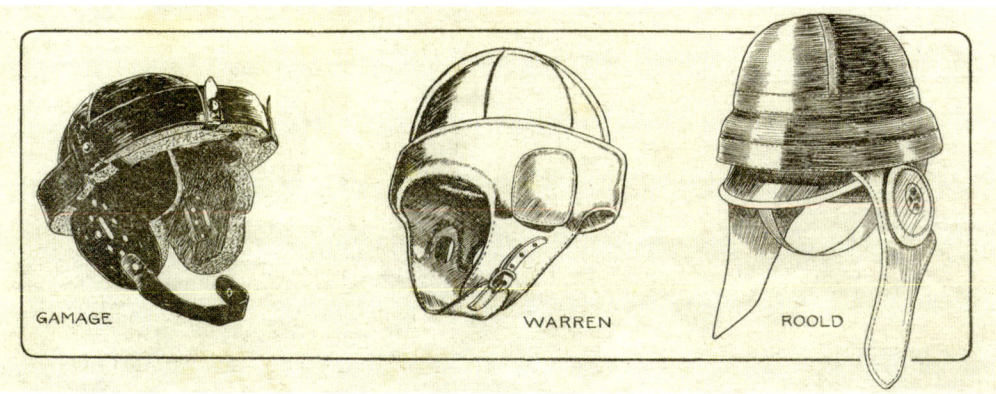

ABOVE: An advert that appeared in *Flight* magazine in October 1912 illustrating the three main types of full protective safety helmet which were commonplace at the time – the Gamage, the Warren and the Roold helmets. All three were available for private purchase, and the latter two were also available on issue to RFC aircrew. (Historic Military Press)

FLYING CLOTHING

ABOVE: This crashed Royal Aircraft Factory R.E.8 illustrates the fact that even a slow-speed ground loop on landing can still be quite terrifying and result in injuries. At this stage in aeroplane development, head protection was bulky. (Mark Hillier Collection)

BELOW: Sat in the nose of a Maurice Farman Longhorn, this pilot is wearing a Warren Helmet. During the early days of the RFC, these flying helmets were often more commonly seen at training schools than in the front-line units. Goggles were not easy to wear on the outside of this helmet as they did not then sit correctly against the eyes. If worn under a helmet with the elastic round the airman's head, the goggles regularly fogged up as they couldn't be lifted up. (Historic Military Press)

ABOVE: An RFC aviator pictured in a Royal Aircraft Factory B.E.2b, 1914. In August 1914, on the outbreak of the First World War, three squadrons equipped with this reconnaissance and light bomber were immediately sent to France. The early B.E.2a and 2b aircraft remained in operational service into 1915. When withdrawn from squadron service they were transferred to flying training establishments. This pilot is wearing a Gamage Helmet and RFC short, leather coat with map pocket. The Gamage Helmet was not adopted by the RFC for issue but is regularly seen in early RFC photos. (Mark Hillier Collection)

The Roold Helmet

Adverts for the Roold Helmet appeared in *Flight* in 1912. Originally a French design, it had a high, domed appearance, wide brim and ear flaps with a round metal perforated disk at the ear positions. It was constructed from cork and gutta-percha. The lightweight cork shell was covered with loreid and painted light brown, the inside often had a pale-gold-coloured lozenge-quilted satin lining while the narrow peak was lined with green satin. There was no means for size adjustment but a black elastic strap prevented the helmet from being blown off the wearer's head when the ear flaps were not buttoned up.

The large ear flaps, made of oilcloth and lined with soft brown fabric, were also painted light brown. This is the most common type of helmet seen in period photographs and was mainly in use at training schools.

In 1914 the officer commanding the RFC wrote to the quartermaster general's offices suggesting the adoption of the Roold-type helmet with certain modifications. At this time, it was supplied by the General Aviation Company at Regent Street London. On 1 January 1914, a letter was sent from the lieutenant colonel commanding the military wing at South Farnborough, RFC to the General Aviation Company requesting certain modifications to be incorporated. This included recommendations for an inflatable bladder to the inside crown, further padding and another chin strap, all of which were advised against by the manufacturer. Further amended samples were provided and the type was sealed under

FLYING CLOTHING

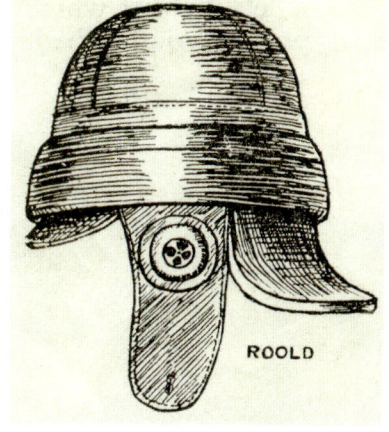

"ROOLD"
SAFETY HELMETS, AVIATION SUITS, UNBREAKABLE GLASS GOGGLES.
"EVERYTHING FOR THE AVIATOR."
SOLE CONCESSIONAIRES FOR THE BRITISH EMPIRE:
THE GENERAL AVIATION CONTRACTORS, LTD.,
30, REGENT STREET, PICCADILLY CIRCUS, LONDON, S.W.
WIRE "Santochimo, London."   'PHONE 980 Gerrard.

ABOVE: An advert for the Roold Helmet which appeared in the edition of *Flight* magazine published on 12 October 1912. (Historic Military Press)

RIGHT: A drawing of the Roold Helmet which appeared in *Flight* magazine in March 1913. (Historic Military Press)

pattern in May 1914 (Pattern No. 8061), although photographs exist from as early as 1913 featuring RFC pilots wearing this type of helmet but these were most probably privately purchased.

One unit that clearly wanted the Roold Helmet on issue was the Aeronautical Inspection Department at Farnborough, which, after seeing the Army Orders of April 1915 relating to scale of provision of flying equipment, wrote to the War Office to suggest the scale of provision for officers testing aircraft should be considered:

> With reference to revised scale of flying clothing no provision has been made for officers testing machines for Aeronautical Inspection department. I would suggest that the issue of the following items to Chief Inspector, Aeronautical Inspection Department be approved.

Boots, knee, RFC pairs	20
Caps, fur lined, RFC	20
Jackets, leather RFC	20
Overshoes, gaitered	
Gauntlets, observers	10
Gauntlets, pilots	10
Goggles with triplex glass	20
Helmets, aviation, Roold	20
Mask, RFC	20
Trousers, leather, pairs	20

ABOVE and OPPOSITE: A 1915 dated Roold Helmet. The Roold was made from oiled fabric stretched over cork, and has an oiled fabric sweatband and a padded silk-lined crown. The type's unique design featured a double cork-walled shell with coiled horsehair in between the cork walls to cushion any knock or impact. Though superficially similar in appearance to the Tautz Aviator Safety Helmet No. 2, the Roold range of helmets was quite different in design and principle. The Tautz featured a leather suspension liner with a drawstring. Similarly, the Roold had a more rounded appearance and more tapered crown, whereas the Tautz was squat and square. Also, the Roold is buttoned, while the Tautz has a buckle. Both helmets can be seen being worn by RFC students. Note the brass wheel inserts normally marked 'DBF Paris' in the ear flaps are missing in this photograph. (Mick Prodger Collection)

FLYING CLOTHING

ROYAL FLYING CORPS KITBAG

ABOVE and RIGHT: A Tautz Aviator Safety Helmet No. 2, seen here by way of comparison with the Roold. As already mentioned, the construction was different to that of the Roold, the Tautz being made from leather and leatherette and featuring a leather suspension liner with a drawstring. Note also the helmet is secured by a buckle. This one also has the brass-wheel-style inserts, again marked 'DBF Paris', which can make you think this helmet is a Roold. (Phil Phillips Collection)

BELOW LEFT and RIGHT: The inside of a Tautz Helmet showing the various labels and markings. (Phil Phillips Collection)

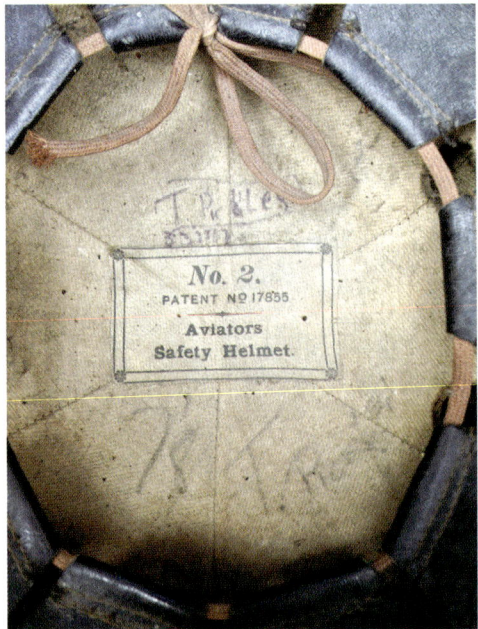

FLYING CLOTHING

RIGHT: An early Royal Flying Corps pilot, who, in one source, is named as W.L. Brock, pictured holding a Tautz Helmet. The image is dated 1912. (Historic Military Press)

Although this scale was downgraded to more or less five of each in subsequent correspondence, the Aeronautical Inspection Department clearly valued having this helmet and flying training units continued to use the Roold, however those who completed training and were sent to front-line units soon discarded it.

The Warren Helmet
Sealed as a pattern in August 1914 (Pattern No. 8115), the Warren Helmet was often seen being worn by both RFC and RNAS trainees. Many images exist of ab-initio pilots wearing these helmets, which were available from the early days of the RFC as private purchase and later as issue.

The helmet was advertised and discussed in magazines such as *Flight* as early as 1912. Examples often feature the manufacturer's label 'Tautz & Co.', which produced it exclusively. Easily identifiable from the other types available, it was a well-padded helmet with no perforations or round vents at the ear. Keen to illustrate the benefits of his design, Mr Warren himself demonstrated its attributes by hurling himself headfirst at a wall and also letting others strike his head with hammers!

ROYAL FLYING CORPS KITBAG

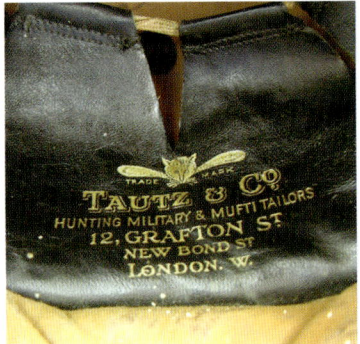

LEFT and ABOVE: An early safety flying helmet designed by Mr Warren of Hendon. Manufactured exclusively by Tautz & Co. of Grafton Street, London, it comprised a double-skin shell of cork and thin, steel plate separated by horsehair padding. The lower part of the helmet crown is surrounded with a wide padded band that extends to form a chin strap. The outside of the helmet is covered in a proofed brown cloth with the appearance of leather. The crown is lined with leather and has an adjustable leather 'harness', while the lower padded section is lined with chamois. It was fitted with earflaps for use with Gosport-type communication tubes. This safety helmet had excellent shock-absorbing qualities in case of accidents. It was possible to wear goggles with this helmet but they did not fit well due to the width of the helmet at the sides. (David Farnsworth Collection)

BELOW: The inside of a Warren Helmet showing the padding and liner. (David Farnsworth Collection)

ABOVE: An advert for the Warren Safety Helmet which appeared in *Flight* magazine on 28 September 1912. (Historic Military Press)

FLYING CLOTHING

The Gamage Helmet

Samuel Cody used this style of helmet which was to his own design and sold by Gamage's of Holborn as the 'Farnborough'. The ugliest and least popular of the safety flying helmets, the Gamage was advertised in *Flight* in January 1912. This type is seen in very few RFC photographs and often only very early on in its formation. This type of helmet was not adopted by the RFC as issue equipment.

RIGHT: On display in the Museum of Army Flying at Middle Wallop, this particular Gamage Helmet was worn by Staff Sergeant Richard Wilson. Known as 'Bert', Wilson was one of the early entries into the RFC; he earned his RAeC certificate, No. 232, in a Bristol of the CFS on 18 June 1912. He was only the second NCO pilot in the RFC. Wilson was the passenger in a 70hp Nieuport which, flown by Captain Eustace Broke Lorraine, crashed on the Plain on 5 July 1912. Wilson was the first Other Rank casualty of the RFC. (Mark Hillier Collection)

ABOVE: A postcard depicting the crash site of the first RFC casualties. Captain Eustace Lorraine (33) and Staff Sergeant Richard Wilson (29) were killed after their aircraft crashed from 400ft while undertaking a steep turn near Stonehenge. To commemorate their colleagues, the squadron unveiled The Airman's Cross, a Celtic cross made of Cornish granite, at Stonehenge on 5 July 1913. (Historic Military Press)

ROYAL FLYING CORPS KITBAG

Leather Flying Caps

The most favoured and regularly seen item of headwear in period photographs is the leather flying cap, which gave some protection against the slipstream and, to a certain degree, kept the head warm. These started as simple caps without peaks which were often tied under the chin with simple cords and the early ones were not fur-lined. The photographs

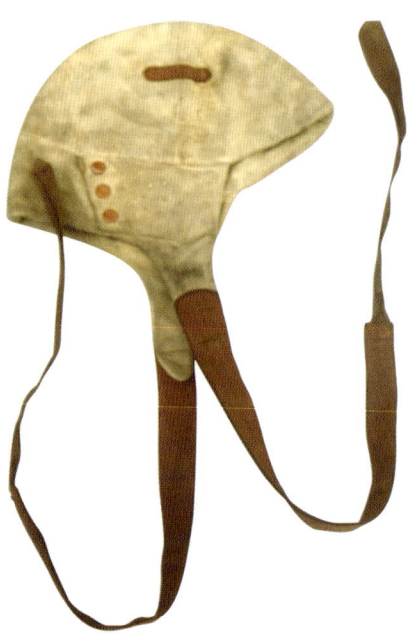

ABOVE and LEFT: A very early leather cap dating to about 1912 or 1913. Manufactured by Gieves, this private-purchase example was used by a RNAS pilot. Note the lappet tie ribbons which pass through each other under the chin, go up around the ears and are tied at the top. Note also the flaps over the ears, with three studs for fastenings, which remained a feature of issue caps throughout the First World War. Some of these early caps were not well lined, in many cases being little more than blanket-lined. They were eventually given up as they provided little protection against the cold. Note the very early private-purchase Triplex motoring goggles. (Mark Hillier Collection)

FLYING CLOTHING

RIGHT: A RFC veteran, Samuel Saunders, pictured wearing his early issue leather flying cap. The lappet-style ties and the leather loops on the cap, which helped retain the ties up around the ears, dates this item of headgear to about 1914 or 1915. Saunders joined the RFC in 1914 as an air mechanic and was posted to 1 Squadron as an observer. Having served on the Western Front, in late 1916 he undertook pilot training and gained his Royal Aeronautical Certificate, No. 4175, at Brooklands while still a 1st class air mechanic. Saunders was later promoted to sergeant as a flying instructor at Netheravon. (Courtesy of Mrs Roberta 'Bobbie' Webb, née Saunders)

RIGHT: Sergeant Samuel Saunders with his wife during the period he was instructing at Netheravon. (Courtesy of Mrs Roberta 'Bobbie' Webb, née Saunders)

seen here give an idea of the evolution and changes in date order. They developed into leather caps with wind deflectors at the ears, stud-fastened ear covers to allow for speaking tubes, flaps to cover the neck and a buckle or popper fastening. Balaclavas had been often worn as a layer underneath but eventually in 1916 this idea was developed into a cowl helmet along similar lines. The leather cap was lightweight and allowed ease of movement of the head, essential for keeping watch for the enemy.

As aircraft started to fly faster, the security of flying equipment became more important to the pilot as the slipstream was tugging at every item, waiting to snatch it away. Lappet-style ties under the chin became less favoured and gave way to buckles and straps to ensure security at critical moments. Latterly these caps were fur-lined for extra warmth, as shown in the 1915 kit lists.

The idea of the wind deflectors, the stuffed rolls of leather in front of the ears, was literally to disrupt the air flow and help the wearers hear any shouts of warning or instruction from their crew, although in reality were of little value as the wind noise still drowned out voices. The ear covers behind would be perforated to allow sound in. Early communication between crew members was more effective by writing on a notepad. There are many variations on the flying cap theme, too many to include every one.

ABOVE: An early issue leather flying cap with a very typical government contract label and a broad arrow in the peak, dating to 1914. Note that this example is not fur-lined and pre-dates the 'Caps, fur lined', as detailed in the 1915 scale of provision. At this point in time the RFC was moving away from the lappet-style tie to a buckle connection. This one has a peak and ear flaps with the typical castle-stud arrangement. This particular cap is known to have belonged to 269 Air Mechanic William Percy Parker who enlisted in the RFC on 18 July 1912. He gained his Aviator's Certificate, No. 850, in July 1914. The cap was accompanied by Parker's goggles, which are also seen, as well as his gloves. The cap is broad-arrow marked, which helps place it in the issue lineage – see the section on gloves on pp. 60–8. (Simon Lannoy Collection)

FLYING CLOTHING

ABOVE and RIGHT: Dated 1915, this fur-lined flying cap is an issue example. It is stamped with the letter 'A' over a broad arrow which indicates air use. This cap is shown on the 1915 scale of provision as 'Caps, fur lined', and is the same as one that was issued to Major Edward Corringham 'Mick' Mannock VC, DSO and Two Bars, MC and Bar – he can be seen in some archive pictures wearing his cap with the ear flaps buckled up, as here, and also, in his cockpit, with the sides down. This particular flying helmet was issued to 859 Air Mechanic Charles Albert Cordeaux who joined the RFC in 1913 and occasionally flew as an observer, being a wireless expert. It still retains its leather loops which confirms its lineage from the lappet style, a conversion of the earlier type. In terms of flying, these caps were the next step on from the unlined examples and were typical of the period 1915–16, at which point the Mk I flying helmet and cowl helmet started to be issued. The 'A' over arrow marking was initially thought to stand for 'Air Board', but the first Air Board did not convene until 15 May 1916. It is possible, therefore, that the 'A' over arrow just indicates equipment specifically intended for air use. (Simon Lannoy Collection)

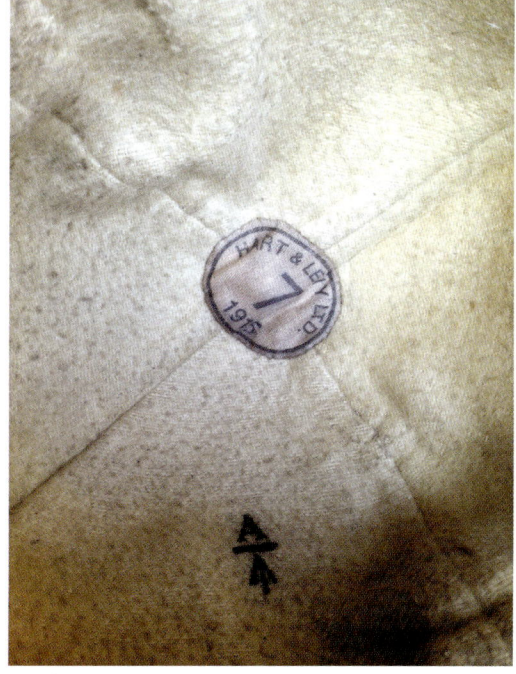

Cowl Helmet

Thought to have been introduced in 1916, the cowl or hood type of flying helmet was a long, shoulder length, leather balaclava with a single-face aperture. The early versions were not adjustable, though the more common subsequent ones had straps with small buckles to adjust and tighten the helmet around the face aperture. Although popular with observers and gunners, these designs were frequently customised in the field to make them easier to wear and so that they could be used by pilots; the modifications included cutting down the length of the helmet and opening them at the lower front.

FLYING CLOTHING

RIGHT AND OPPOSITE: A typical example of a chrome leather cowl helmet. It is fur-lined and fitted with both ear flaps and the sausage-like wind deflectors on the sides in front of the ears. There are adjustable straps across the forehead and protection extends over the neck. Considered to be too restrictive by some pilots, these designs were frequently altered. (Phil Phillips Collection)

BELOW: A cowl helmet laid flat, showing the ear flaps, with pierced leather covers but no wind deflectors, the aperture for the face and adjustment on the forehead. In Appendix III, these are referred to as 'Caps, fur-lined, winter'. (Mick Prodger Collection)

ABOVE: Wearing a cowl helmet and goggle mask, Second Lieutenant W.G. Bodley is standing in front of a D.H.6 at Netheravon, early February 1918. Bodley is also wearing fur gauntlets and a long, leather flying coat. (Historic Military Press)

LEFT: An RFC officer wearing what looks like a modified cowl helmet. Note also the gloves with fold-over mittens to enable more feeling when making small movements, note-taking or fine adjustments. (Mark Hillier Collection)

The cowl or hood type of flying helmets were rabbit-fur or blanket-lined. The pilots were not too keen on them as they restricted their ability to turn their heads and get a view of approaching enemy aircraft. Issued examples can be found with a WD (for War Department) mark within, but private-purchase unmarked versions were also available. These helmets were mostly produced in brown chrome leather.

FLYING CLOTHING

RIGHT: Some pilots and observers are seen in period images wearing just a tunic with a jumper underneath and a scarf tied around the neck and tucked into a Sam Browne belt. This mock-up gives an idea of how this would look. The helmet in this image is dated inside 1914, though the type can be seen being worn into 1915, 1916 and after. The scarf is homemade and has two purpose-made loops to fix it onto the leather coat collar. Pilots and observers can be seen wearing a wide variety of kit and uniform which often makes it difficult to date images. Helmets and goggles were often used until they were broken or worn out, literally falling off as they were often an airman's favourite or considered a lucky talisman. (Simon Lannoy Collection)

LEFT: The cowl helmet worn by Flight Sub Lieutenant Gerrard Fane, RNAS. This flying hat was worn by Gerrard during the shooting down of Zeppelin *L.21* off the Norfolk coast in the early hours of Tuesday, 28 November 1916. Fane was one of three crew members of the RNAS aircraft during the engagement, the others being Flight Lieutenant Egbert Cadbury and Flight Sub Lieutenant Edward L. Pulling. It was announced on 3 December 1916 that Fane and Cadbury were to be awarded the DSC for their actions, and Pulling a DSO. This helmet is on display at the Fleet Air Arm Museum at Yeovilton. Note the attachment of early wireless equipment by the ears; although this is an RNAS helmet, the RFC was using similar equipment on the Western Front for Morse and wireless work. This equipment is quite rare as only 600 sets had been manufactured by the end of the war. (via Historic Military Press)

ABOVE: A pristine cowl helmet with War Department markings for 1918. Part fur-lined, part blanket-lined, it was manufactured by E.S. Parfield. Note the WD mark. (Simon Lannoy Collection)

OPPOSITE: An example of a cut-down RFC cowl helmet which still bears the name of its original owner, W.C. Goudie, this being just discernible under the ear flap. From Moose Jaw, Canada, William Couper Goudie started his flying training with 28 Squadron, before being posted to 74 Squadron flying Royal Aircraft Factory S.E.5s. The ear flaps are secured by press fasteners and the helmet by a wide, leather chinstrap. Inside, there is half-fur lining and a chamois lining in the crown. (Mark Hillier Collection)

FLYING CLOTHING

RIGHT and OPPOSITE: Introduced in 1916, the cowl or hood type flying helmet was almost like a shoulder-length leather balaclava with a single face aperture, adjustable with small buckled straps. Although popular, it was frequently modified in the field to make it easier to wear and use. This example has typical alterations, its length being reduced and the front of the helmet 'split' to enable the wearer to don the helmet more easily. (David Farnsworth Collection)

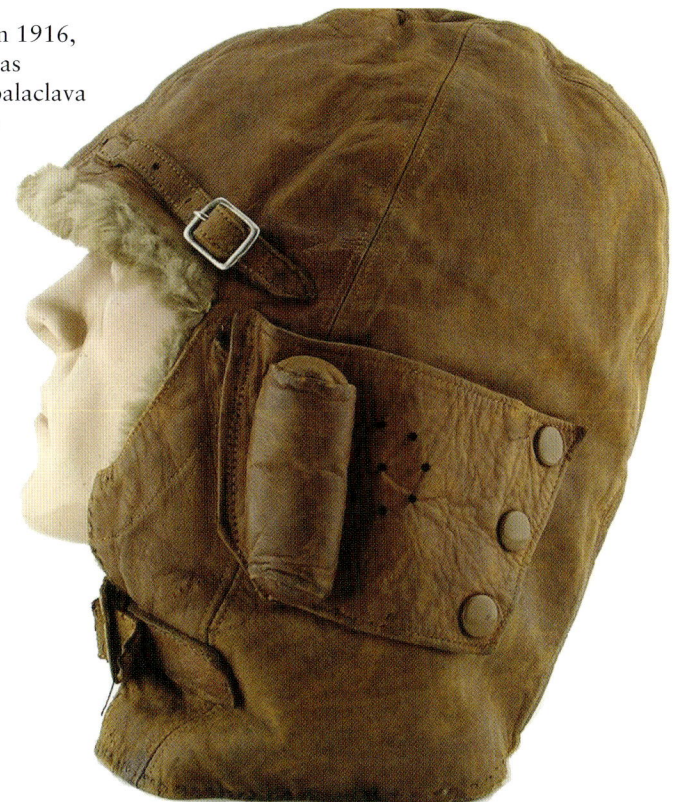

Mk I Flying Helmet

This particular style of flying cap was introduced in about 1916 and later re-designated the 'Flying helmet, Mk I, 22c/12' by the RAF in 1918. It is thought that these are what were known as 'Caps, leather, summer' by the RFC, being sealed as a pattern in December 1916 but available prior to this date. This style can also be found as a private-purchase model.

Usually this helmet was fashioned out of tan chrome leather with fur trimmed fold-back peak, press-studded ear flaps for use with Gosport communication earpieces/tubes and cylindrical wind deflectors. Earlier versions can be found without the wind deflectors. Some examples have an extended rear neck protector. They were mostly blanket-lined in the crown with a fur lining in the lower section.

The use of speaking tubes with this type of flying helmet is mentioned by Alan Bott MC in his book written about his time as an observer on the Western Front.

> He circled over them to let me plot the pin point position on the map and sketch the aerodrome and its surroundings. The Hun pilots, with thoughts of a possible bomb raid, began to take their machines into the air for safety. 'Got em all?' Thus V., shouting through the rubber speaking-tube, one end of which was fixed inside my flying-cap, so that it always rested against my ear.[12]

ROYAL FLYING CORPS KITBAG

LEFT and ABOVE: A 1918 issue Mk I flying helmet and the pilot's original silk scarf. Note the fold-up front peak, wind deflectors and ear flaps with three studs for fastening. It is also War Department marked. (Simon Lannoy Collection)

ABOVE: Another variation of the style of helmet later known as the Mk I. This one has a full woollen lining, a typical fold-down front flap secured by a press stud, wind deflectors made from leather, ear flaps secured by three press studs, wide leather chinstrap and a leather-covered buckle. These are listed in Appendix III as 'Caps, summer'. (Phil Phillips Collection)

ROYAL FLYING CORPS KITBAG

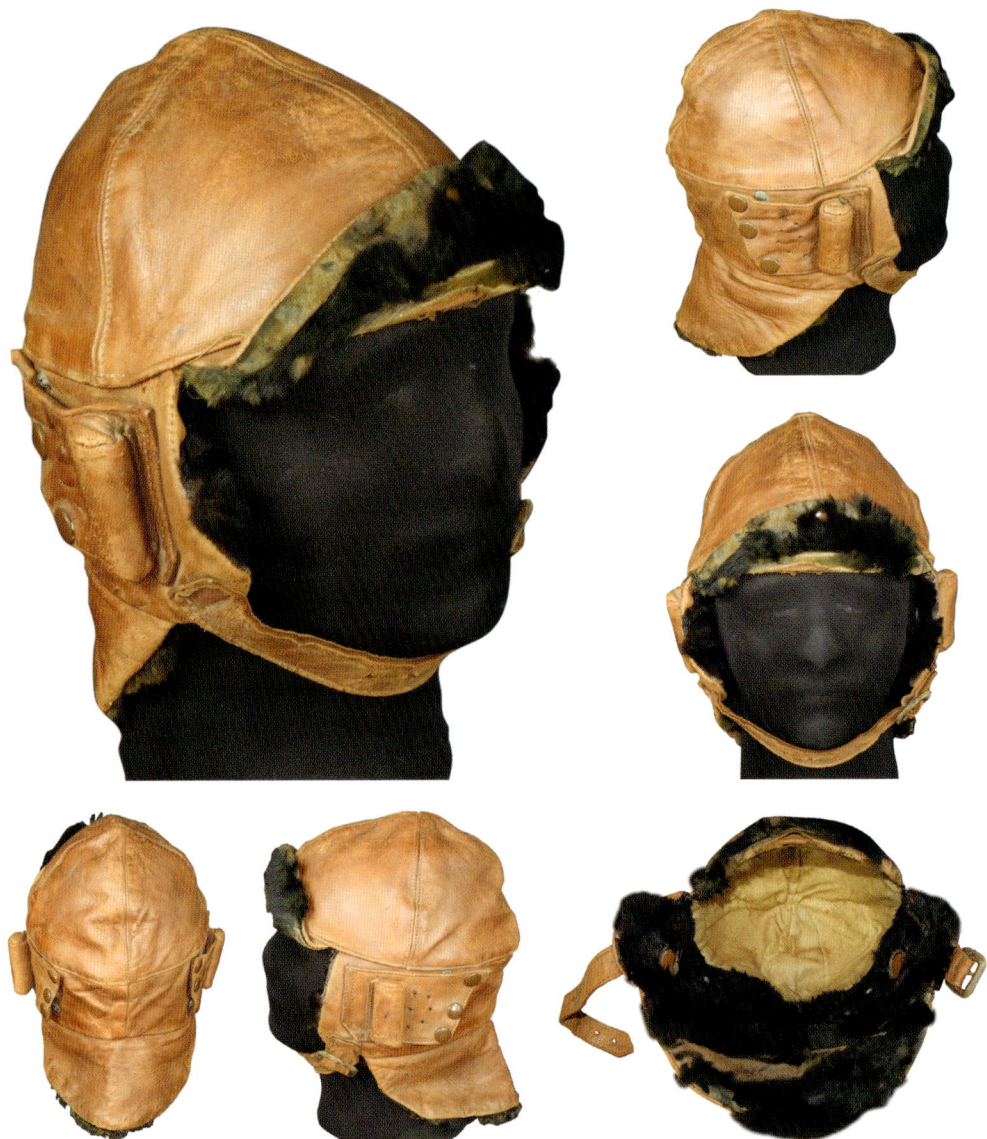

ABOVE: An example of the iconic First World War RFC helmet, later known as the Mk I. It is beautifully made with medium brown leather, which is part lined to the crown in a beige blanket wool, while the side, peak and neck flap are lined with black rabbit fur. On each side a ventilated ear flap with wind deflector is held closed with press studs. First World War period helmets have an open stud, which is quite distinctive, rather than the flatter press stud. (Mark Hillier Collection)

The Gosport tube as we know it was developed by Robert Raymond Smith-Barry, who took over No. 1 (Reserve) Squadron at Grange in Gosport in 1917, and one of his inflight commanders, Sidney Parker. Like all instructors, the problem of the instructor communicating with the trainee pilot, while in the air, was one that baffled Smith-Barry.

FLYING CLOTHING

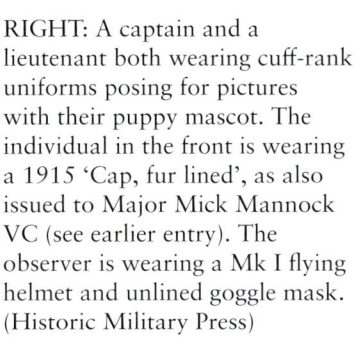

ABOVE and LEFT: An example of a private-purchase helmet which looks similar to a Mk I. However, the rolled-up ear flaps, lack of cylindrical pads and bare metal buckle, plus the addition of goggle-retaining tabs, preclude it from being an issue item. (Scott Rall Collection)

RIGHT: A captain and a lieutenant both wearing cuff-rank uniforms posing for pictures with their puppy mascot. The individual in the front is wearing a 1915 'Cap, fur lined', as also issued to Major Mick Mannock VC (see earlier entry). The observer is wearing a Mk I flying helmet and unlined goggle mask. (Historic Military Press)

LEFT: A typical press-stud fastening found on First World War leather caps. (Mark Hillier Collection)

BELOW: Two RAF pilots at Bissegem (Bisseghem) aerodrome, December 1918. On the left is Major Hugh Vivian Champion de Crespigny, Commanding Officer of 65 Squadron. On the right is Captain James-Williams, one of the Flight Commanders. Bissegem is situated near Courtrai on the River Lys. The Germans built an airfield in the village, and it was used by Allied units after the capture of Bissegem in October 1918. Note that Hugh has personalised his Mk I flying helmet with a pom-pom, while James-Williams, on the right, wears a knitted balaclava over his flying helmet. James-Williams is wearing a leather flying coat with map pocket. De Crespigny joined the Special Reserve of the RFC in 1915. He went on to be Officer Commanding 29 Squadron on the Western Front and then Officer Commanding 65 Squadron. He was awarded the MC and DFC for his bravery in the air. (Historic Military Press)

FLYING CLOTHING

In 1912 a primitive speaking and listening tube known as the 'Audiophone' could be bought for 3½ guineas and some aircraft were fitted with this appliance, but this was less than satisfactory. Many tried to communicate through throttling back the engine and slowing the aircraft down by raising the nose to reduce the wind noise and only then was it just possible to hear. Not an ideal way of imparting the art of flying to a novice.[13]

An electrical system was also experimented with, but this didn't provide a solution. Sidney Parker then trialled a series of speaking tubes connected to the recipient's ear and, known as the Gosport Tube, this was successfully tried over the Solent on 20 June 1917. From then on, this system became the norm and was in use with air forces across the world until after the Second World War. The earphones could be secured under the ear flaps of the Mk I or cowl helmets.

Private-Purchase Headgear

It is often very difficult to tell with extant examples what was issued and what was not unless a label survives with the manufacturer's details. Often the tailors making the private-purchase options were also employed on government contracts to provide the kit. This section shows examples of the types of headgear available for private purchase by airmen and they look very similar and in some cases are identical to the issue variant.

ABOVE: Published in *Flight* magazine in August 1916, this advert by Gamage's contains an example of a private-purchase Mk I-style flying helmet which the company has named 'The Hendon'. The cowl-style helmet below it is called 'The Flanders'. The advert describes the latter as 'the latest government regulation headpiece for flying', confirming that it was an issue type at this time. (Historic Military Press)

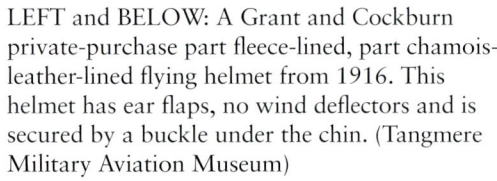

LEFT and BELOW: A Grant and Cockburn private-purchase part fleece-lined, part chamois-leather-lined flying helmet from 1916. This helmet has ear flaps, no wind deflectors and is secured by a buckle under the chin. (Tangmere Military Aviation Museum)

ABOVE and RIGHT: A 1917-dated, private-purchase flying helmet in tan leather, blanket-lined and with single press-stud ear flaps. Belonging to an individual named Hunt, it was made by the Miller Manufacturing Company. While there are no wind deflectors, there is a neck flap and fold-down peak. (Tangmere Military Aviation Museum)

ABOVE: An advert that appeared in the issue of *Flight* published on 6 July 1916. It details various private-purchase items of headgear being sold by Robinson & Cleaver Ltd. Note the fur cap that some pilots and observers wore while flying and the private-purchase goggle mask. (Historic Military Press)

ABOVE and LEFT: A lovely example of a 1917/1918-period Mk I-style, private-purchase, fur-lined flying helmet. It has a chin protector which is secured by buckles at the rear. This could be a combination produced by Bates of 91 Jermyn Street, London, which sold them along with their 'Tempest' leather flying helmet. (Adrian Kilby Collection)

The 1918 Flying Cap and Breathing Mask
Although not in common use and certainly not in single-engine fighters, there are Air Board publications dating back to January and March 1918 that feature specifications and diagrams and descriptions of the Mk I and Mk II masks and the 'Combined breathing mask and helmet'. These masks and helmets were being developed and experimented with during the last few months of the RFC and have therefore been included.

Period photographs of the sets in use are very rare. These combined sets were produced and submitted by A.V. Roe and Handley Page and were adopted for use in their high-altitude bombers – they were different variations of much the same thing. The need for radio communication in night bombing was found to be of paramount importance and the number of radio helmets in service increased in 1918.

FLYING CLOTHING

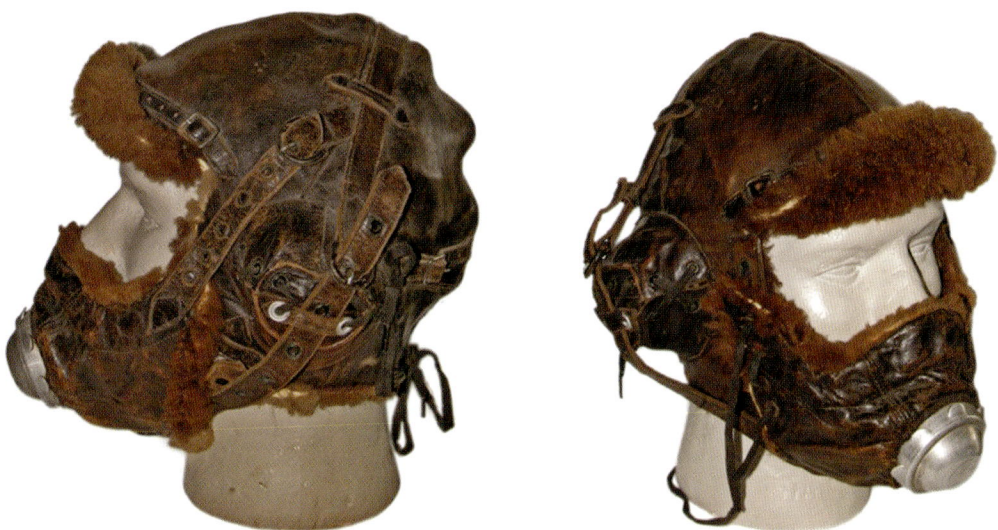

ABOVE: This particular piece of headgear is listed in a set of Air Board specifications dating from 1918 and is an example of a radiotelephony helmet and oxygen mask. The mask, produced by Siebe-Gorman, is correct for the Air Board specification on oxygen delivery. The leather cups for the receivers can be seen at the ear positions. Manufactured from leather and fur-lined, this is a very rare piece of surviving First World War flying clothing. Oxygen equipment was issued to bomber crews from 1917 onwards, with some forty pieces available by the end of the year. (Courtesy of Mick Prodger, now in the Phillips Collection)

BELOW: An extract from the Air Board specification for the flying cap with detachable oxygen mask which was developed in 1918. (Mick Prodger Collection)

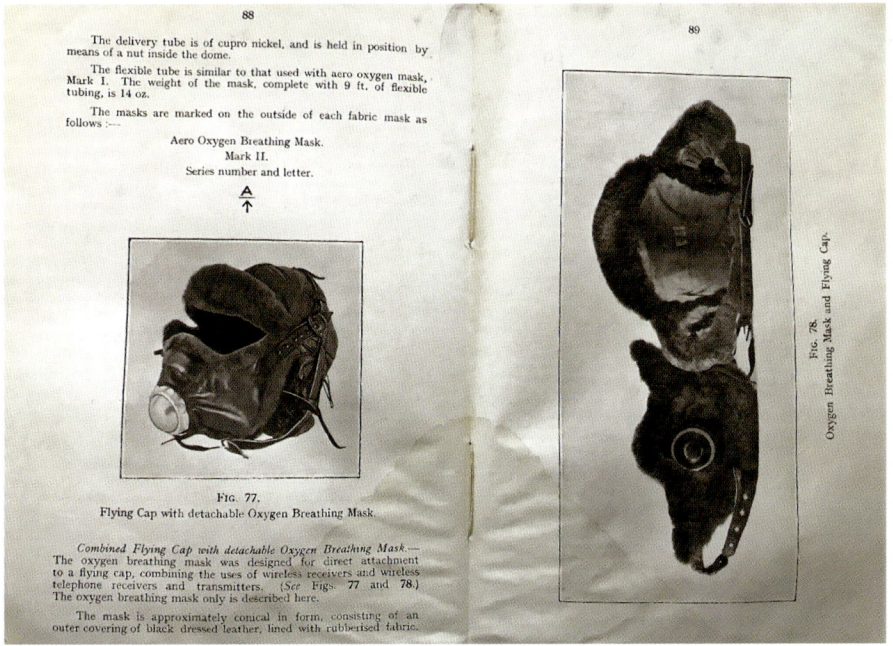

ROYAL FLYING CORPS KITBAG

A publication from October 1917 discusses the use of radio telephony. Some earlier examples of radio helmets have an RFC cowl that was converted to a cut-down radio helmet, with telephone compartments similar to those on the modified Mk I radio helmets shown here. Again, a mostly leather construction and fur-lined, by the end of the war it is thought that around 600 sets of wireless-equipped helmets were in use.

Facial Mask and Chin Protector

Although not many photographs exist of these useful pieces of equipment, they are mentioned in several pilots' diaries and memoirs including the diary of James T.B. McCudden VC, DSO, MC, MM. During December 1915 the weather was particularly

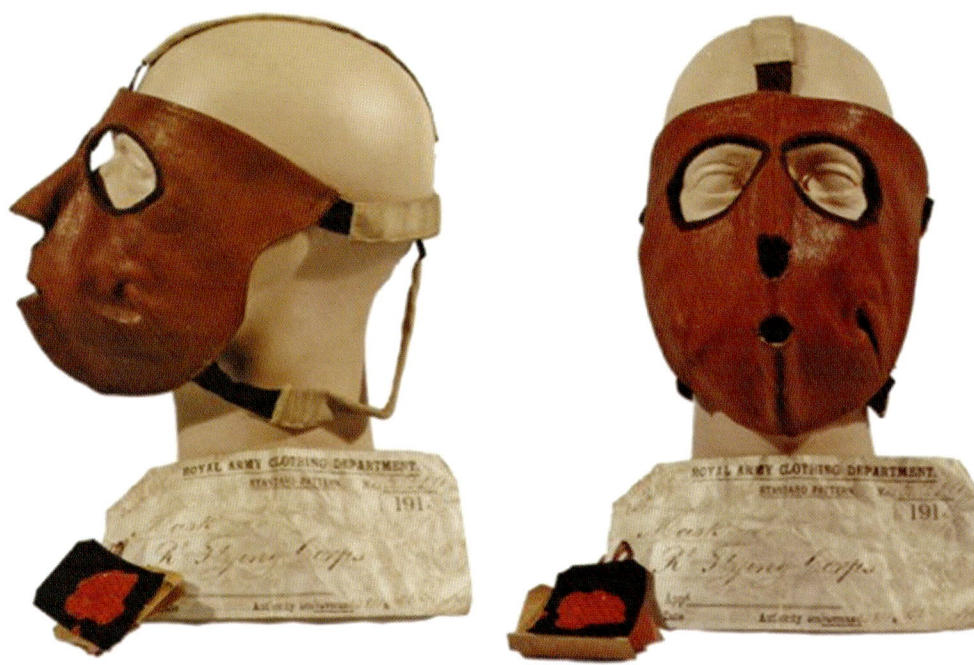

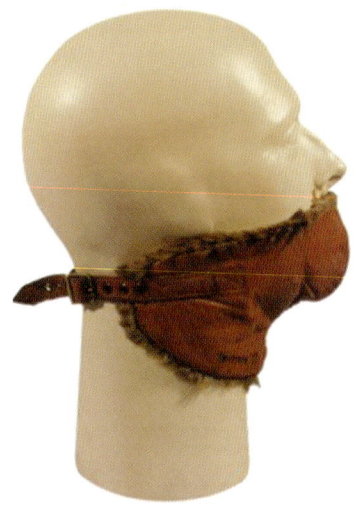

ABOVE: The RFC standard-issue face mask, which helped to prevent frostbite on the face, seen here with its pattern seal. All issue kit was sealed as a pattern and examples retained, many of which survive to this day in the care of the RAF Museum at Hendon. The tag seen here carries the date 2 February 1915, this being when the design was officially adopted. The tables for issue kit in the Army Orders of 1915 indicate these masks were available from that date. (Courtesy of Diane Prodger)

LEFT: An example of the leather chin and neck protector which was fur lined and usually worn with the Mk I flying helmet, although these are most likely private purchase as they do not appear on any issue lists. One tailor that provided such items was Bates of 91 Jermyn Street, London, which sold them along with their 'Tempest' leather flying helmet. (Courtesy of Diane Prodger)

FLYING CLOTHING

fowl, and James McCudden acting as observer, flying with Major Ludlow-Hewitt with 3 Squadron, commented that, 'The weather during this period was very cold indeed, and after having my face frostbitten, I decided to wear the official pattern mask that was issued for use'.[14]

Captain Norman Macmillan MC, AFC flew Sopwith 1½ Strutters with 45 Squadron in 1917. In his memoirs he recalled one particular formation flight, going on to comment on the observers in the other aircraft: 'The formation was perfect. Every machine was in its place, not one blinding the fire of another, and each observer, tight lipped and grim faced beneath his mask, standing or crouching in his favourite attitude for handling his gun to his best advantage.'[15]

FLYING GOGGLES

Flying goggles are a mixed blessing, and you really want goggles with a good field of view and optically as perfect as you can get. Yes, they will if worn protect against dust, oil, insects, cold and flying shrapnel\wood splinters in combat, but some pilots still found them a nuisance, as described by Captain Bogart Rogers of the RAF: 'This afternoon I just fooled around some more, but my wind shield broke and I had a fierce time with oil flying back in my eyes. As goggles are an awful bother and rather obscure your vision most of the fellows depend on the windshield.'[16]

However, some pilots and observers saw the benefits in combat of developments such as tinted lenses. The 1914 Army Orders scale of provision for the RFC states only 'Goggles' in its description. By 1915 the scale of provision lists 'Goggles with triplex lenses', as well as what is described as 'Glasses tinted or clear'. The earlier goggles were mainly the ones seen with the two-part straps and oval lenses, an example of which is seen below.

By 1917 the choice has increased dramatically to: 'Goggle mask, leather with nose piece' and 'Glasses (for winter use)'; 'Goggle mask, leather without nose piece and

ABOVE: An example of the early style, issue, rubber-framed flying goggles with an elastic strap. These were found to be somewhat uncomfortable and prone to fogging up. (Phil Phillips Collection)

glasses (for summer use)'; 'Glasses, triplex, for goggles (light tinted for pilots, dark tinted for observers)'; and 'Glasses, triplex, non-tinted (in case) pairs' (see Appendix III for the 1917 scale of provision).

Written at the end of 1916, Alan Bott's book describes the benefits of having tinted lenses when looking out for enemy aircraft, especially on blue-sky days when the sun was beating down: 'The sun was pleasantly warming, and I look towards it gratefully. A few small marks, which may or may not be sun spots, flicker across its face. To get an easier view I draw down my goggles, the smoke tinted glasses of which allow me to look at the glare without blinking. In a few seconds I am able to recognise the spots as distant aeroplanes moving in our direction.'[17]

As we have just seen, what is thought to be the first true service-issue pair of goggles, which are often seen in early RFC photos, had clear circular glass eyepieces set within a rubber frame. It is thought that these were adopted from those issued to mechanical transport drivers. Unfortunately, they were prone to misting up as moisture was trapped in the eyepiece whereas later goggles vented through gauze mesh sides. They were relegated to issue to despatch riders and mechanical transport drivers again, although some mid-war photographs show that these goggles were still being worn.

These early style goggles began to be replaced by Triplex goggles, of which there were two variants, as described in the army scale of provision of 1915. Both goggles were of similar design in having glass eyepieces set within a leather mask but were available as Set 1 for pilots and Set 2 for observers, pale and dark shade (pale was for use by the pilots, while dark was for observers). These were sealed as a Pattern Nos 8235 and 8236 and there was a variation to this in March of 1916, but the nose of the wearer was still uncovered.

In December 1916 a new goggle mask was introduced, based on the Triplex AB Aero Mask, and featured the protective nose covering that was later designated as the 'Goggle mask, Mk I' and in 1918 the Mk II came into being, although there seems to be little difference between the two styles. The 1917 scale of provision (see Appendix III) gives descriptions of the styles available. Evidence also exists of some limited development of a pair of goggles with drop-down tinted lenses, but these were not mass-produced during the war.

One pilot found out to his cost the problem with not wearing goggles. Cecil Lewis preferred not to use goggles because of issues with them misting up, but this led to medical complications:

> Six months continuous flying low over the trenches had affected my eyes. I had long ago given up goggles because they fogged in the oil and fumes from the engine. Besides leaning out of the cockpit to scan the ground carefully – for you dared not make a mistake as to the identity of men in the trenches when the guns bombarded the place on the strength of your report, was almost impossible with goggles on. Now it was getting colder; acute conjunctivitis was setting in. I had to stop flying, and went home for another fortnight's sick leave.[18]

By 1917 the stock lists show just 'Goggles with nose piece (winter use)' (probably fur-lined) and one without nose piece for summer use, and that there was a choice of tinted or non-tinted lenses available (see Appendix III).

 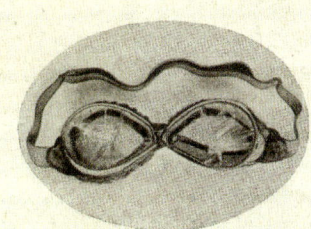  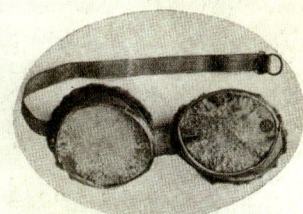  

ABOVE: An advert for the Triplex Safety Glass Co. from January 1916. It illustrates a number of flying goggle designs. (Historic Military Press)

OPPOSITE and ABOVE: These issue goggles are marked with an 'A' over a broad arrow indicating air use. They probably pre-date the goggle mask and, with tinted lenses for observers, are from the 1915/16 period. It is known that they were worn by 859 Air Mechanic Charles Albert Cordeaux, who joined the RFC in 1913. A wireless expert, Cordeaux occasionally flew as an observer and the goggles, helmet (which is dated 1915) and a pair of gloves (not shown) were found together in a house clearance. (Simon Lannoy Collection)

ROYAL FLYING CORPS KITBAG

LEFT: What is believed to be a pair of issue goggles, these belonged to Second Lieutenant Thomas Harry Laing. They are fur-lined and fitted with round Triplex lenses that could be changed. These goggles, which appear in a number of period photographs, predate the Mk I and Mk II goggle masks. They are not marked but could be those referred to as the 'Goggle mask, without nose piece' in Appendix III. Aged 23, Laing was killed in action while flying with 55 Squadron, on 30 August 1918. (Courtesy of Jo Sohn-Rethel; Europeana14-18)

ABOVE: The two pilots on the right of this photograph are wearing examples of the goggles seen above, whereas the officer on the left has a Mk I or Mk II goggle mask with the lenses that met over the nose. Both of the men on the right are wearing the pocketed leather flying coat. The second lieutenant on the left appears to be wearing a cut-down cowl helmet; he also has a wound stripe on his left sleeve above his rank badge. (Tangmere Military Aviation Museum)

FLYING CLOTHING

ABOVE: Pilots and observers posing in front of a Royal Aircraft Factory B.E.2, 1917. All of these airmen are wearing long, issue flying coats and Mk I flying helmets. Note, once again, the goggle masks with round lenses, either private purchase or issue, so prevalent in period photographs such as this. These were either a popular private-purchase option or issue. (Historic Military Press)

ABOVE: This pilot is wearing a Mk I style flying helmet with a similar set of goggles to those seen above, the latter with more rounded lenses and Triplex glass. (Tangmere Military Aviation Museum)

RIGHT: A set of typical flying clothing of an RFC pilot or observer of late 1917 or early 1918. It includes a Sidcot suit, Mk I flying helmet, goggle mask with round Triplex lenses and leather, fur-lined gloves. This mannequin can be seen on display in the RAF Museum at Hendon. (Mark Hillier Collection)

ROYAL FLYING CORPS KITBAG

ABOVE: Another set of early goggles with round Triplex lenses. Unlined, they are also unmarked. They are believed to be the type issued as 'Goggle, mask without nose piece'. For that reason they have been included here to show the progression of RFC goggles; the next to be issued were the Mk I and Mk II goggle masks. The goggles seen here belonged to 269 Air Mechanic William Percy Parker, who enlisted in the RFC on 18 July 1912. He remained in the RFC and the RAF through the war. (Simon Lannoy Collection)

Mk I and Mk II Goggle Masks

The Mk I flying goggles set was the designation of a design introduced in December 1916. It can be distinguished from other goggles by its nose piece with Triplex glass lenses.

Introduced in 1918, the Mk II was generally the same as the Mk I. It is thought that the only difference was the addition of tinted lenses, though both versions seem to exist with tinted and non-tinted lenses, though both versions seem to exist with tinted and non-tinted lenses. From stock listings, it would appear that these goggles were designed to have interchangeable lenses.

ABOVE: A Mk I goggle mask with the box it was issued in. These are fur-lined and secured by an elasticated strap. Note the 'A' over the broad arrow on the left-hand side of the leather face-mask section, indicating that they were an issue item. (Scott Rall Collection)

FLYING CLOTHING

ABOVE and RIGHT: Two views of a 'Goggle, mask, flying', Mk I. Manufactured by Howard Spence of 19 Hanover Square, W1, they comprise pear-shaped, laminated yellow tinted glass lenses set in black-painted metal frames within an extended brown leather face mask. They are also fitted with a simple elastic strap and were often backed with rabbit fur. Once again, note the 'A' over the broad-arrow marking showing they are issue equipment. This mark can be found in use as early as 1915, though the goggle mask seen here dates from between 1916 and 1917. (David Farnsworth Collection)

ABOVE: A pilot and observer in a DH.6 wearing Mk I goggle masks, 1917. These goggles met in the centre of the nose and had Triplex lenses. (Tangmere Military Aviation Museum)

ABOVE and LEFT: The Mk II issue goggle mask, which was made of leather with fur lining and this version with clear lenses. Note the markings on the side with an 'A' over a broad arrow indicating the issue type. Many private-purchase examples were also available with or without Triplex lenses. (David Farnsworth Collection)

FLYING CLOTHING

ABOVE: An example of a private-purchase goggle mask. Once again it is fur-lined and fitted with Triplex glass. (Mark Hillier Collection)

ABOVE: A set of classic private-purchase teardrop-shaped goggles which, with tinted lenses, were manufactured by the Triplex Safety Glass Co. They are fitted with fur trim to the eye piece and are vented around the eyes to prevent fogging up at altitude. Prior to the adoption of the Triplex goggle mask, it is likely that this style of teardrop-shaped goggles with a fur lining against the face was the first type sealed as a pattern for use by the RFC, although no examples exist to prove this theory. They are quite likely to be the style described in the 1915 scale of provision as Triplex goggles. (Mark Hillier Collection)

FLYING CLOTHING

ABOVE: A very early example of a private-purchase aviator goggle mask. This set does not have Triplex safety glass and is secured by a clip-on elastic strap at the back. It is also in black leather, which was favoured by the RNAS. (Phil Phillips Collection)

ABOVE: An advert for Triplex goggles which is typical of those found in issues of *Flight* magazine dating back to 1914. Triplex glass gave much better protection to the eyes and did not shatter into tiny shards. (Historic Military Press)

ROYAL FLYING CORPS KITBAG

LEFT and BELOW: Another popular style of Triplex goggles with tinted lenses in their original box. They were worn by Lieutenant F.J. Bull who flew operationally with 27 and 99 Squadrons. Note the very simple elasticated strap to secure the goggles. (Tangmere Military Aviation Museum)

LEFT: An advert that appeared in *Flight* magazine in July 1916 showing the goggles in the photograph above, available in tinted or clear lenses. (Historic Military Press)

FLYING CLOTHING

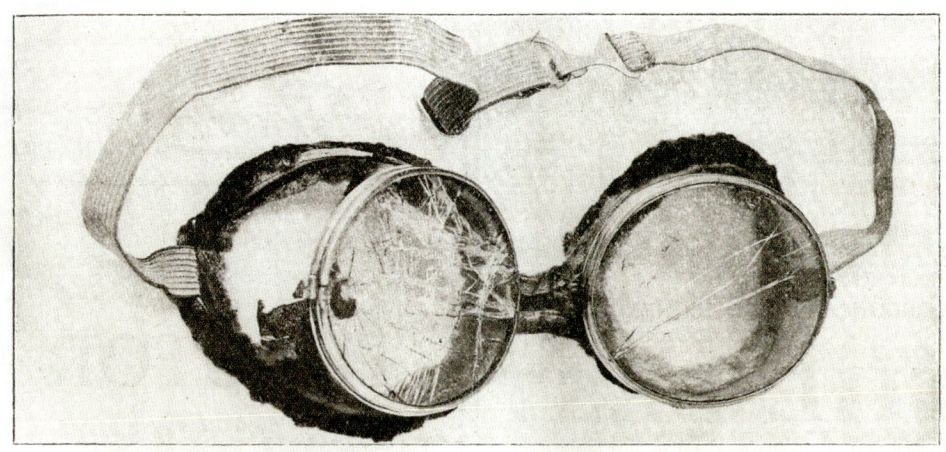

ABOVE: This advert, showing an earlier style of goggles dating to September 1915, also appeared in an issue of *Flight* magazine. (Historic Military Press)

ABOVE and RIGHT: A pair of Triplex goggles which, with tinted lenses, are similar to those that appeared in some of the *Flight* magazine adverts. This set was once the property of Second Lieutenant Thomas Dowsett, an Australian who joined the RFC in 1915 as 2834 AM1 Thomas Dowsett. He was promoted to sergeant on 28 December 1916, then temporary second lieutenant on 25 September 1918. Dowsett was posted to 47 Squadron on 5 October 1918. The goggles are marked on the bridge with a patent date of August 1917 but were available from 1916. (Simon Lannoy Collection)

GLOVES

Period photographs indicate a wide variety of gloves, gauntlets and mittens in use by the RFC, some in just leather but lined, some fur-backed, others made partly of canvas and partly leather. Some had mitten covers for the fingers which could be pulled back to help with the operation of guns or other equipment. These were often tied by string threaded through the sleeves of the jacket linking the gloves so that they were not lost when taken off for any purpose, as anything loose would disappear in the slipstream. In 1914 the scale of provision only talks about leather gauntlets, but by 1915 it is clear that chamois leather liners were available in an attempt to combat the cold.

The temperatures at 10,000ft in an open cockpit biplane could lead to frostbite fairly quickly for an un-gloved hand. Alan Bott writes about the difficulties of flying in 1916, commenting that pilots and observers still struggled to keep the circulation going even with a gloved hand:

> It was cold on the ground, it was bitter at 5,000 feet. It was damnable at 10,000 feet. I lean over the side to look at Arras but draw back quickly as the frozen hand of the atmosphere slaps my face. My gloved hands grow numb, then ache profoundly when the warm blood brings back their power to feel. I test my gun, and the trigger pressure is painful. Life is worse than rotten, it is beastly.[19]

The temperature was one thing but the windchill while flying along at 70–80mph also drastically reduced temperatures to sub-zero and drained heat away from the crew's extremities. This made simple tasks difficult and gloves were essential, although sometimes cumbersome. Some gloves had fingers with mitts over for added protection,

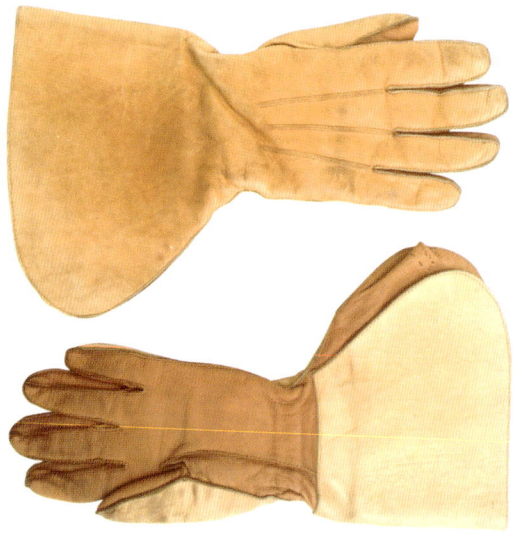

ABOVE: A very early issue pair of gauntlet-style gloves which once belonged to Second Lieutenant James Deardon Smithie. Dating from 1913, they were manufactured by Fownes as the 'Allcar' brand. These gloves are easily identified in period photographs as they make a distinctive triangle shape at the cuff end. (Simon Lannoy Collection)

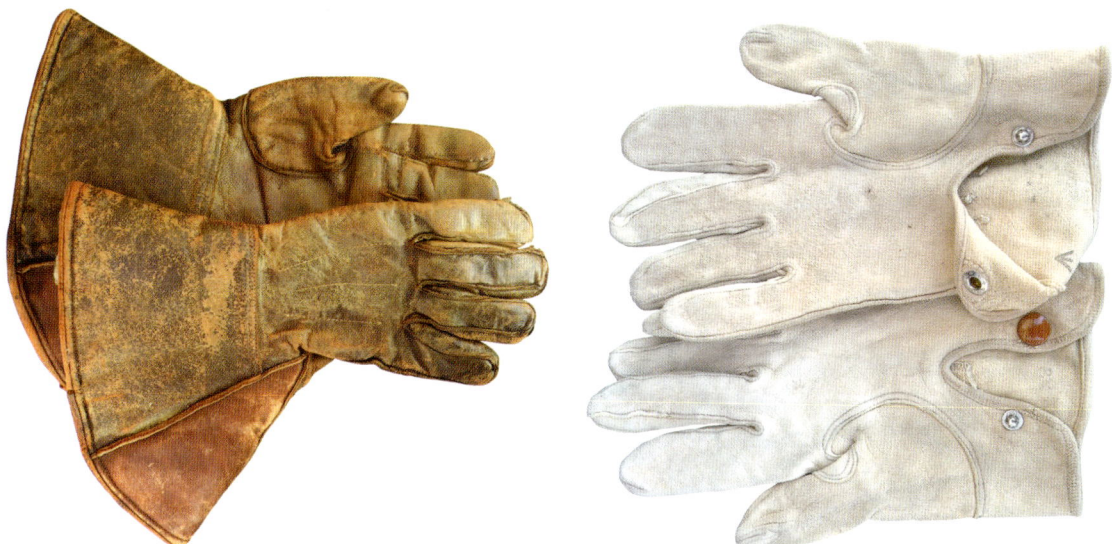

ABOVE: A pair of leather gauntlets and chamois liners that once belonged to 269 Air Mechanic William Percy Parker. The liners are marked with a broad arrow and are mentioned on the 1915 scale of provision as 'Gloves, chamois leather'. (Simon Lannoy Collection)

and gunners could get trigger finger style gauntlets to help them operate the guns, but these could also prove tricky. Gunner/observer A.J. Whitehouse mentions this when taken by surprise by enemy action:

> Whitish pencil lines streaked across the front of our nose. Red spots, hell! They were firing at us! Tracers! My God, Huns! Thousands of em. I stuck my feet out stiff and clutched at the pipe mounting. I would have screamed, only the slip stream choked me. I saw the other gunners pouring fire into the black ships and I tried to get across to my own gun. I went to my knees in an attitude more suggestive of prayer than punch and tried to get the Lewis in action. My fingers tried to find the trigger guard, but I had forgotten to pull the leather mitten covering back from the fingers of my gloves.[20]

This style of gauntlets was manufactured by Fownes, the renowned glove-manufacturer. The pattern of 'double-gauntlet' was created and patented in 1907 by Henry Urwick, the son of one of the company's partners. It was designed as a two-in-one glove. The inner one being an ordinary glove made in light-tan-coloured, soft chrome leather with a wide, mid-forearm-length cuff and unlined five-finger hand section. The outer glove shared the cuff section of the inner and was in the form of a fleece-lined mitten without divided fingers and without any palm. The thumb and backs of the two gloves were sewn together but the fingers not connected to each other so that the airman could turn back the mitten revealing his fingers whilst still wearing the inner glove. This proved popular with many RFC airmen during the First World War. By 1917 the scale of provision described the following types on issue: 'Gauntlets (observers only)'; 'Gauntlets (pilots only)'; and 'Gloves, chamois leather'. The stock listing for the RFC of the same year shows 'Gloves, wool lining for gauntlets and silk inners' (see Appendix III).

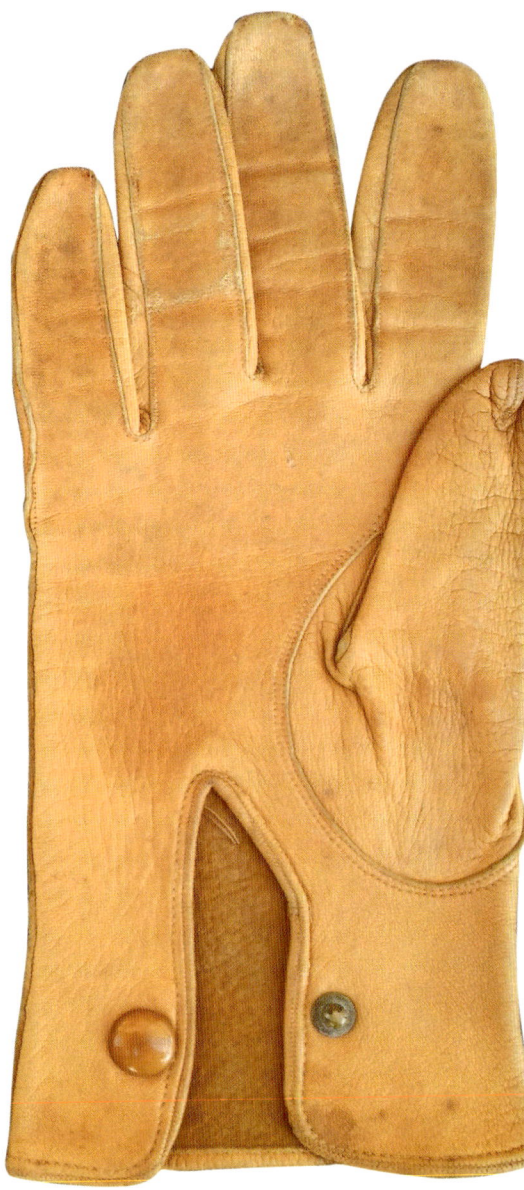

ABOVE: A pair of leather gloves that are marked with the broad-arrow and 'A' above which suggests they were for air use. It is known that Major Mick Mannock often flew with just lightweight leather gloves in the summer, though these could also be worn in the winter as liners to gauntlets. (Simon Lannoy Collection)

FLYING CLOTHING

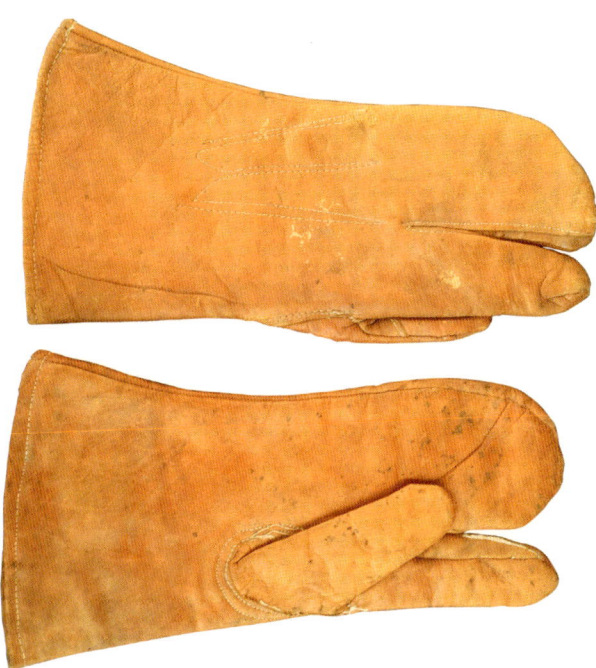

ABOVE and RIGHT: A pair of 1915-dated gauntlets. Broad-arrow marked, this pair was worn by 859 Air Mechanic Charles Albert Cordeaux. (Simon Lannoy Collection)

ABOVE: On the left is a pair of the double-gauntlet-style gloves which were popular with RFC and, in due course, RAF aircrew. This pair was manufactured by Fownes. On the right is a pair of seal-skin gauntlets which were fitted with a leather palm and a trigger finger to aid operation of a machine gun. (Mark Hillier Collection)

ABOVE and LEFT: A pair of War Department-stamped, trigger-finger gauntlets with a canvas and leather structure. These date from around 1917 or 1918, the 'A' and broad-arrow mark indicating air use. (Phil Phillips Collection)

LEFT and ABOVE: An issue pair of mitten-style leather gauntlets, or 'Gloves, aviator', which are fur-lined and have an adjustable strap. The label indicates that the manufacturer was H.G. & Co. They are dated 1918. (Phil Phillips Collection)

FLYING CLOTHING

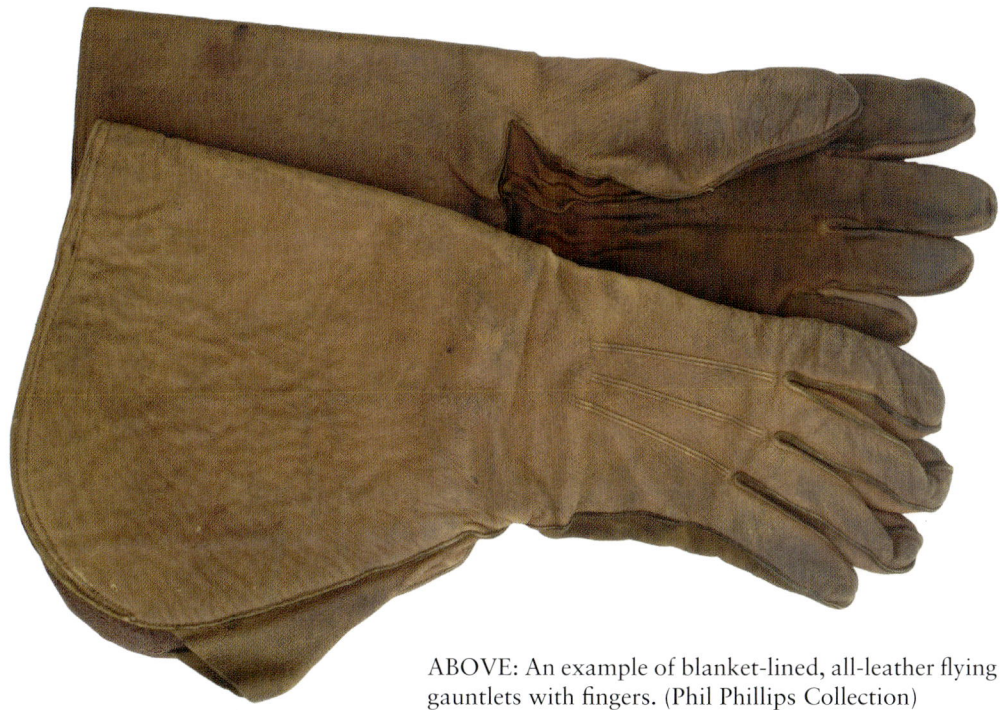

ABOVE: An example of blanket-lined, all-leather flying gauntlets with fingers. (Phil Phillips Collection)

RIGHT: A pair of blanket-lined Fownes' mitten gloves in chrome leather, dated 1917. (Simon Lannoy Collection)

ROYAL FLYING CORPS KITBAG

ABOVE AND LEFT: Two examples of short, fur gauntlets with leather underside. Often seen in period photographs, these are probably private-purchase items. (Phil Phillips Collection)

FLYING CLOTHING

RIGHT: A pilot and an observer pictured wearing Mk I flying helmets and goggle masks, *c.* 1917. The observer is also wearing huge fur gloves, while the pilot has a pair of Fownes-style mittens. Note the RE badges on the observer's lapels. (Mark Hillier Collection)

BELOW: This pair of fur-backed and fur-lined gauntlets with leather palm is quite long in comparison with the other examples included here. (Simon Lannoy Collection)

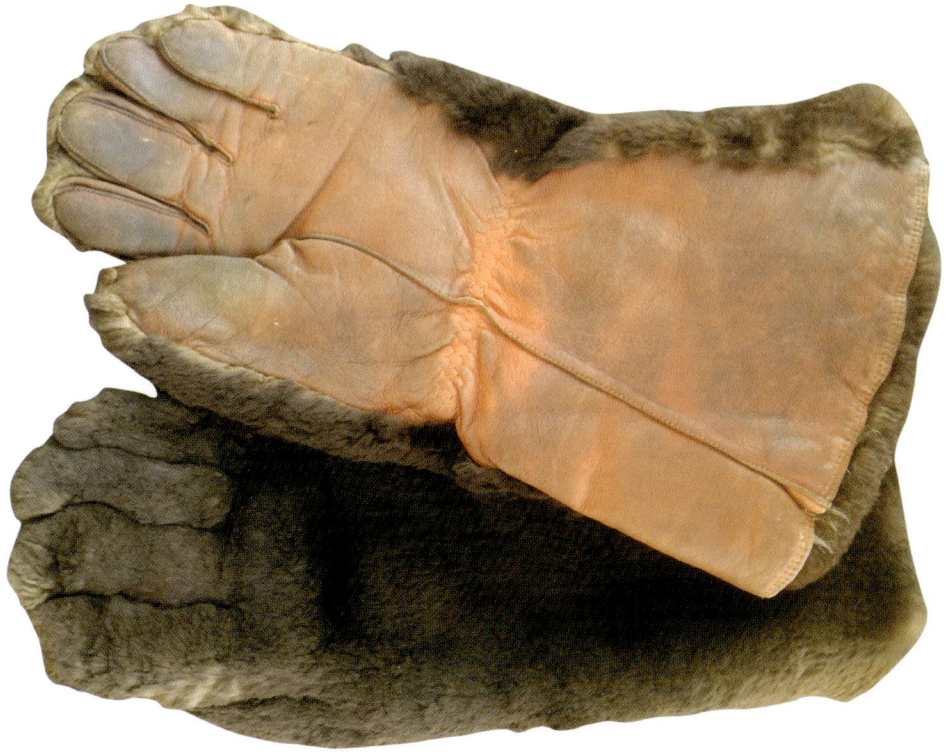

67

ABOVE: Second Lieutenant F.W. Washington standing in front of a D.H.6 at Netheravon, early February 1918. Note the fur gloves, RFC flying coat and what appears to be the earlier goggle mask with round lenses. (Historic Military Press)

ABOVE: A pilot and observer get ready to depart on a sortie. The observer is wearing his leather flying coat with map pocket and leather gauntlets, while the pilot has a pair of the fur-backed gloves. Both have Triplex goggles. (Mark Hillier Collection)

FLYING COATS AND JACKETS

Without doubt the reason for leather being commonly used for flying clothing is that it offers good protection against the elements. The RFC and Army Orders specifically mention brown or chrome leather to be worn, although the RNAS chose black leather flying clothing and equipment to differentiate itself from the RFC. Leather offers a high degree of wind proofing and rain resistance. The private-purchase options could also be lined with a choice of materials which added to the warmth. Some pilots, such as Major Lanoe Hawker VC, DSO, opted for fur coats to keep out the cold, warm but bulky in a small cockpit.

Layering was seen to be advantageous in keeping warm too, although some chose to use just their warm jackets over pyjamas, as mentioned in Alan Bott's book:

> We wrap ourselves in flying kit and cross the road to the aerodrome. There the band of leather coated officers shiver while discussing their respective places in the formation. A bus lands and taxies to the shed. From it descends the Squadron commander, who, with his gum-boots and a warm coat over his pyjamas, has been 'trying the air'.[21]

In December 1914 the RFC adopted 'Sweater, aviators, temporary' to aid pilots and observers with layering and keeping warm. Sadly, although a layer of leather or even a jumper with a thick woollen warm coat added some protection against the elements, they did not stop shrapnel from wounding or even killing pilots and observers. One sortie nearly came to a sticky end, as recalled by Lieutenant Colonel L.A. Strange DSO, MC, DFC, who was flying a B.E.2 with his observer over the Western Front in 1915 when they were targeted by 'archie':

> We struggled painfully back, until we reached Menin, where we were literally smothered in shellfire from the archie there. The black and white burst around were terrific, but we could do nothing but plod steadily onwards as we were now down to 2000 feet and still losing height. Holes began to appear in the fabric of our wings, while the oil pressure gauge went down to nil and the engine started vibrating badly. Then I suddenly saw a tear appear on the shoulder of De Halpert's flying jacket and thought he must have been wounded.[22]

'Coats, leather' and 'Trousers, leather' do appear on the 1914 scale of provision and this continued until 1917 when they were drawn down in favour of the Sidcot suit.

Private-Purchase Flying Coats
Flying coats were developed from leather motoring coats, some with storm cuffs, often double-breasted and long to ensure that when seated the rain would run off below the knee. Mostly leather windproof and waterproof jackets are seen in period photographs as they added a degree of protection to the aviator and many private-purchase examples can be found, as seen from the adverts below.

ABOVE: An interesting example of a private-purchase, full-length leather flying coat. It was taken from a British airman during the Battle of the Somme in 1916 by Gunner George Knibbs, Royal Artillery. Having remained in Knibbs' family since the war, the coat's background was revealed by one of his descendants: 'At the Battle of the Somme, skirmishes in the air above the battlefield resulted in an aircraft crashing to the ground behind allied lines and catching fire. The pilot was dragged from the wreckage with a broken collar bone and taken to a Field Hospital. Private Knibbs picked up the coat which had been taken off the pilot. He then left the scene and the coat has remained in the family for 100 years.' This coat differs in style from the standard-issue version and appears to be a private-purchase piece manufactured for aviators and probably retailed by Gamage's. It is double-breasted, has two flapped pockets and a waist belt. Each sleeve terminates with a storm cuff. It has a very typical camel-coloured blanket lining. (Mark Hillier Collection)

FLYING CLOTHING

ABOVE: An advert for the 'Aerophil' coat that was published in *Flight* magazine in 1916. This private-purchase coat was manufactured in finest chrome leather, black or tan, for members of the RFC or RNAS. (Historic Military Press)

ABOVE AND FOLLOWING PAGES: A selection of adverts from 1916 and 1917 displaying the wide range of styles and manufacturers of flying coats and equipment that was available to those RFC pilots and observers looking to make a private purchase. (Historic Military Press)

ROYAL FLYING CORPS KITBAG

FLYING CLOTHING

AVIATORS! MAKE YOUR PURCHASE AT
GAMAGE'S

LEATHER COAT FOR AVIATORS.
The newest pattern, as approved by Officers in the Navy and Army. Large quantities in daily use at the front. In service has proved to be the most useful and practical of all coats for aviation purposes. The length shown in the illustration is the most popular, but it is also procurable in other lengths.
- In Black Chrome dressed Leather, lined warm tweed ... Price **84/-**
- Do., made with Camel Fleece lining ... " **95/-**
- In Tan Leather, Chrome dressed, lined camel fleece ... " **£5 10 0**

AVIATORS' BREECHES.
- Black Leather Breeches, wool lined ... Price **37/6 & 42/-**
- Tan Leather Breeches, wool lined ... " **42/- & 63/-**

AVIATORS' CAPS.
The "**Brooklands**" (as illustrated). In black or brown leather, lined fleecy wool, with protective rolls for the ears and tapes to tie under chin. Finest quality ... Price **12/6**
The "**Aerocar,**" **the** cap for flying. In black or brown leather, lined with fur. Will keep the wearer warm at the highest altitudes. Wind cannot penetrate ... Price **21/-**

FUR CAPS FOR AVIATORS ... Price **12/6 21/- & 25/-** each

AVIATION HELMETS.
The Gamage Patent **Non-Concussion Flying Helmet.** Fitted with patent flaps for minimising the sound of the engine ... Price **47/6**

AVIATORS' BOOTS.
The "**A.W.G.**" High Legs, Quality "A," made of fine quality Brown Waterproof Hide Fronts and Golosh and Sheepskin legs—Caracul fur lined all through, exceedingly warm and comfortable Waterproof Soles ... Price **45/-**
Also made in Quality "B," uppers are of Brown Waterproof Hide, lined with thick Caracul and have also an inter-lining of warm material, are impervious to WIND, COLD, RAIN, ICE-WATER, SNOW, etc. ... Price **50/-**
Usual height of both these boots is 18½ inches.

THE BURBERRY AIRWARM
A coat to fly in that does for ordinary occupations as well.

ON THE PLANE, The Burberry Airwarm provides greater security and more comfort than any leather, and is really nice to wear anywhen and anywhere.

BURBERRY SUPPLIES the airman's need—warmth and a normally dry skin whatever the weather.

NON-VENTILATING CLOTHS, such as rubber, fail because they set up artificial heat which quickly turns to chill—circulation impeded.

THE BURBERRY SYSTEM :—Densest weaving—to keep out wind. Thickest, light linings—to keep in warmth.

SIR ERNEST SHACKLETON, speaking of protection against the bitter cold of the Antarctic, says :—
"*I would take Burberry if it were double the cost.*"

GABARDINE, exceedingly light-in-weight, preserves a wonderful natural warmth because it is self-ventilating, yet wind cannot penetrate. Lined with very thick fleecy cloth, it maintains a healthy glow of warmth in a hundred-miles-an-hour blizzard.

BURBERRYS Haymarket LONDON
8 & 10 Bd. Malesherbes PARIS ; & Provincial Agents

Every Genuine Burberry Garment is labelled "Burberrys"

Illustrated Catalogue & Patterns of Gabardine Post Free.

Everything the Airman Needs Ready for Use or to measure in 2 to 4 days.

FLYING CLOTHING

War Department Issue

From the formation of the RFC in 1912 it is thought that a leather jacket was available to aviators as an issue item, made in tan-brown, chrome leather. This first jacket was of mid-thigh length construction with a broad skirt, two pockets on the skirt, a cross over chest similar to the maternity tunic, a map pocket on the left breast with flap fastening and then belted with a single-prong buckle and broad leather belt. In 1913 some modifications were made with an unflapped map pocket, and this version was issued with leather trousers. Jackets and trousers were often tagged with a War Department mark. Jackets were lined internally with camel-coloured fabric. The next variation, which is more commonly seen, had a longer knee-length skirt. At first due to the unsuitability of the short jacket, these were altered and pieces of leather added to lengthen the skirt. In the earliest stock lists these are referred to as 'Coats, leather' but later on in 1915 'Jackets, leather', and both terms appear to be correct.

ABOVE: A 1913-Pattern, short, leather flying coat as issued to the RFC. This example does not have a flapped map pocket. The Army Orders scale of provision in 1914 and 1915 mentions 'Jackets, leather RFC'. These were still available in 1917, although of the longer variety. When the Sidcot suit was introduced these coats were recalled and replaced. (Phil Phillips Collection)

ABOVE: Two aircrew standing in front of an Avro 504 at Netheravon, 1914. The individual on the right is wearing the short, leather flying jacket with storm cuffs and unflapped map pocket. (Historic Military Press)

LEFT and BELOW: A pair of leather trousers and close-up of its markings. The latter include the War Department stamp and broad arrow, as well as the date of manufacture, October 1914. Interestingly, there is also a further WD stamp showing that the pair went back into stock, was re-inspected and re-issued or just manufactured and not issued till later. (Phil Phillips Collection)

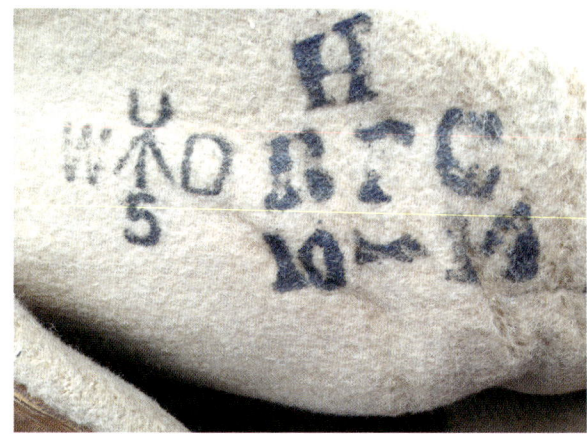

FLYING CLOTHING

ABOVE: Another variation of the leather trousers with a flared/galosh-style bottom. Though not shown here, there is a maker's label that gives a date of manufacture of 1914, as well as a War Department marking with a subsequent inspection stamp. (Phil Phillips Collection)

MIDDLE RIGHT and RIGHT: A very typical long, chrome-leather flying coat in a design that is thought to have started to appear in 1915/16. It has concealed buttons, a single unflapped map pocket and a camel-coloured lining. This style can be seen in period photographs right up to the end of the First World War, despite the fact that the Sidcot suit was designed and introduced to replace such flying coats. (Phil Phillips Collection)

ROYAL FLYING CORPS KITBAG

LEFT: Layering was important for staying warm, and many aviators chose to wear a leather liner under the outer flying jacket. This one was made for the 1913-style coats, and consequently has similar large brown buttons. It follows the cut of the outer jacket, but with no collar. (Phil Phillips Collection)

RIGHT: Another example of a leather liner worn under the long, leather flying coat. This was available after 1915. (Phil Phillips Collection)

FLYING CLOTHING

LEFT: An aviator at Courcelles, France, 1917. He wears a sleeveless leather jerkin, rather than a full jacket, over what appears to be some sort of trench coat. His goggle mask has round lenses. (Mark Hillier Collection)

RIGHT: Probably pictured in France during late 1917, these two airmen are wearing fur-lined thigh-length fug boots and long, leather, issue flying jackets with map pockets on the left breast. The man on the left wears a wide, leather belt with a single-prong fastening. The individual on the right is wearing what appears to be a Mk I style helmet, the man on the left wearing a thin, leather, unlined flying cap. Both styles of goggles are Triplex and probably private purchase. Both men also have heavy, leather gauntlets. (Mark Hillier Collection)

ROYAL FLYING CORPS KITBAG

LEFT: Dated 1917, this picture shows an observer dressed for flight. He is wearing a leather flying coat with angled map pocket, fur mittens with a leather wrist strap for tightening, a cowl helmet and goggles. (Tangmere Military Aviation Museum)

RIGHT: A pilot with his B.E.2, probably photographed in early 1916. As well as a long flying coat, he appears to be wearing galoshes over his boots, though these could be a pair of 'Overshoes, gaitered'. (Mark Hillier Collection)

FLYING CLOTHING

RIGHT and BELOW: Front and rear views of a well-worn RFC long flying coat with map pocket. This jacket has a pair of RFC wings sewn on, which was not a common occurrence. (David Farnsworth Collection)

ABOVE: An interesting and somewhat unique sheepskin undercoat. Although, according to the equipment lists of 1917, 'Coats, fur lining' were available to pilots, this is a fur-lined jacket made from fug boots stitched together. It was worn by Second Lieutenant William Chester who joined the RFC in 1917 and served with 206 and 27 Squadrons on the Western Front until he was wounded in 1918. Chester flew both the DH.4 and DH.9 in action and was awarded the Croix de Guerre. (Simon Lannoy Collection)

FLYING BOOTS

Prior to 1914 there was no specific flying footwear and marching boots and field boots were used. Some aircrew continued to use these during the war, but special footwear was introduced into the RFC in October 1914 with the sealed pattern being known as 'Boots, knee'. These were superseded swiftly by an improved pattern that was longer in the leg.

In November 1914, 'Overshoes, gaitered' were introduced and appear to have been made of waterproofed, black fabric, intended to be worn over shoes. Although conventional army footwear was also often used when on flying duties, cold temperatures at high altitude became a problem, and this was remedied by the thigh-length, sheepskin-lined 'fug boots' introduced in 1917.

FLYING CLOTHING

ABOVE: A pair of 'Boots, knee', which were manufactured under Pattern 8137 of October 1914. They are listed on the army scale of provision dated 1915. This pair is dated 1914. They are knee-length, square-toed boots of light-brown leather which are rubber soled and have a buckled leather band on each boot to close a small expandable pleat. The boots have suede uppers and are sheepskin-lined. (Phil Phillips Collection)

RIGHT: A sergeant pilot wearing a maternity tunic with flying boots, or 'Boots, knee'. This photograph was taken in France in 1917. (Tangmere Military Aviation Museum)

ABOVE: This pair of private-purchase, non-issue boots is interesting in that it was custom-made with a rubber sole by the military outfitters Stallwood & Son. These boots were intended for use by flying personnel after it had become apparent that leather soles were prone to freezing at altitude when they became wet. The rubber sole runs the length of the boot through into the heel, the idea being that they would therefore not slip on the controls. (Mark Hillier Collection)

Fug Boots

Officially termed 'Boots, thigh', this type of footwear was sealed in December 1916. Invented by Major Lanoe Hawker VC, DSO, they replaced earlier attempts at equipping aircrew with footwear that was suitable for their special purpose. Initially Hawker had them made at Harrods, which christened them the 'Charfor' boot. However, they soon became universally known as 'fug boots'.

These boots were a high, thigh-length, fleece-lined, brown suede boot with outer adjustable straps to the tops and with buckles and other straps and buckles to the foot and to the lower calves. Both boots had buff leather toecaps and heels and a rubber sole.

Interestingly, they were very popular with, and much sought after by, German aviators. Worn with a fleece-lined, long coat, they went some way to protecting the long-suffering aviator. For some this was not enough, and they went one stage further with the addition of a pocket warmer such as that used by Captain George McElroy MC and Two Bars, DFC and Two Bars while flying with Lieutenant William MacLanachan of 40 Squadron in S.E.5s. McScotch, as MacLanachan was christened by Major Mick Mannock, described the cold that they encountered and McIrish's (McElroy) cunning plan to keep him warm, which backfired:

> On the few days we were able to carry out official patrols we scoured the whole front from Douai to Armentieres, frequently landing in such a condition that several of us had to be lifted from the machines to restore movement to our stiff and almost frozen legs. Having had less experience of high flying the younger members suffered severely from the cold and McElroy complained most. 'There's no need to go up so high – you keep below 12,000 and we'll be alright,' I heard him telling Mannock.
>
> McIrish was not easily defeated, and he discovered what he thought was a clever idea of avoiding the results of our high-flying propensities. He sent home for a 'pocket warmer', a small cylindrical tin with smouldering charcoal inside, which would at least keep one part warm. When it arrived McIrish demonstrated it to us with great pride, and before our first patrol he 'chafed' us about freezing time that was in store for us. He did not then know what was ahead of him. A pocket warmer may be quite a comfortable gadget in a coat pocket with fairly thin clothing over it but in Mac's trouser pocket [uniform], which was covered by the thick sheepskin of his long flying boots and also by the still heavier skin of his fur lined flying coat, the heat from the charcoal was allowed to accumulate. At first, he felt it becoming 'warm', and as the temperature continued to rise, he frantically attempted to remove it. Unfortunately for him his coat and flying boots prevented him from reaching the pocket and long before the patrol finished, he was in agony. When we landed, the mechanics lifted him from the machine, and on discovering the trouble we found that the 'pocket warmer' had burnt his leg so badly that there was a blister about the size of a hen's egg. Mac's 'patent pocket warmer' was a joke in the flight for a long time, and if anyone complained of the cold, he was advised to try it. We afterwards decided to keep our patrols under fourteen thousand feet, and even then, the cold was intense. We were issued with evil-smelling whale oil with which to lubricate our faces and hands.[23]

In his memoirs, Gunner/observer Arthur Whitehouse described how he attempted to keep out the cold at altitudes of 18–23,000ft:

> I wore two sweaters under my tunic, a pair of long woollen stockings that came up over my thighs, a smaller pair of boot socks and fleece lined flying boots that reached up to my hips [fug boots]. I wore a woollen helmet under my issue leather one and used to wrap a six-foot scarf around my neck. Silk gloves went on under regular woollen ones, and over that we drew our regular leather flying gloves which had a fold over mitten to protect the fingers when we not using the guns. Still I was never so cold in all my life.[24]

ABOVE: A pair of First World War-period British aviator's boots, or fug boots. This pair belonged to Major G.S. Sansom MC, DFC, a balloon officer. Sansom was born on 7 August 1888, the son of Samuel George Claydon Sansom, a solicitor, and his wife Annie, née Freeman. During the First World War, Sansom is believed to have initially served as an ambulance driver for the British Red Cross Society. However, he joined the RFC and had a distinguished career as a balloon officer and was awarded the MC and DFC. His citation for the MC reads: 'Temporary Captain George Samuel Sansom, RFC, Special Reserve. For conspicuous gallantry and devotion to duty. Although attacked three times by hostile aircraft, he remained in the air with his balloon at its maximum height and completed his task. He has on many previous occasions done fine work.' (Phil Phillips Collection)

FLYING CLOTHING

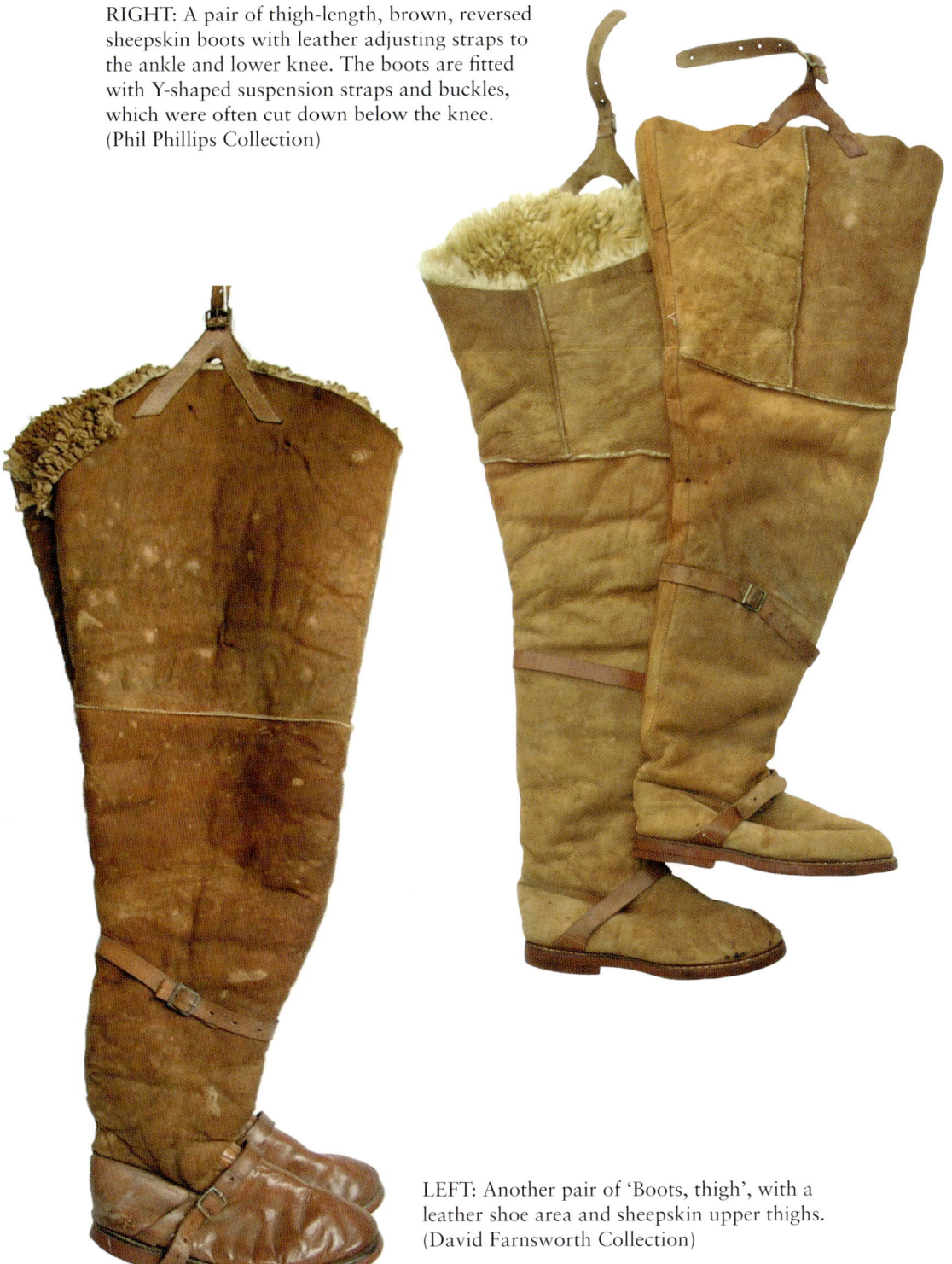

RIGHT: A pair of thigh-length, brown, reversed sheepskin boots with leather adjusting straps to the ankle and lower knee. The boots are fitted with Y-shaped suspension straps and buckles, which were often cut down below the knee. (Phil Phillips Collection)

LEFT: Another pair of 'Boots, thigh', with a leather shoe area and sheepskin upper thighs. (David Farnsworth Collection)

ROYAL FLYING CORPS KITBAG

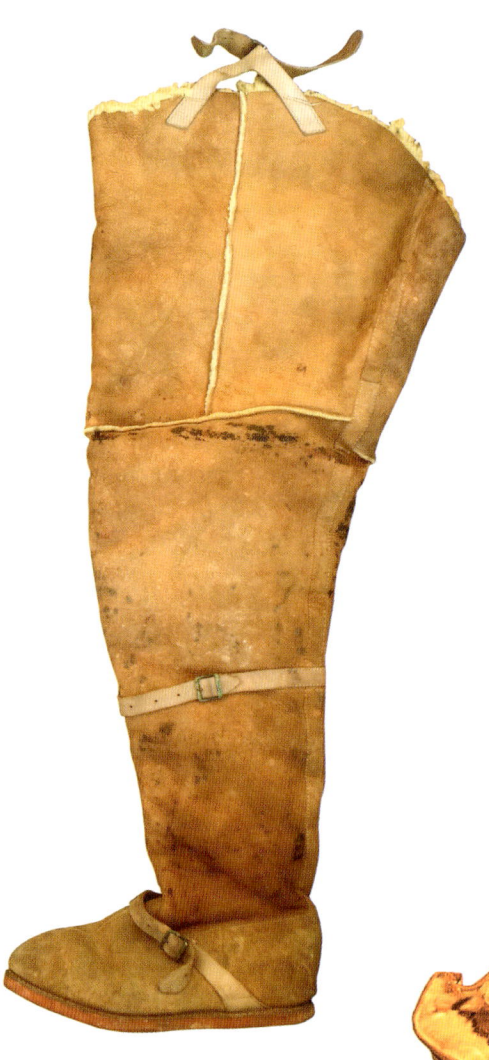

LEFT and ABOVE: A fug boot with a flat heel. The leather straps at the top of the boot are clearly stamped with the War Department and broad arrow marks. (Simon Lannoy Collection)

RIGHT: Pilots and observers were known to cut down fug boots to mid-calf length or just below knee, as can be seen here. The intention was to make a more practical flying boot. (Scott Rall Collection)

FLYING CLOTHING

RIGHT: Another pair of cut-down fug boots. Various different styles/patterns of fug boot were made, but most had a two-tone appearance with a different type of leather or suede used for the shoe section to that of the main body of the boot. In addition, most had stitched leather soles, a buckled strap over the top of the shoe section and a similar strap just below the knee. A small inverted V-shaped strap/buckle was stitched to the top outer edge of the boot – this could be connected to the wearer's other clothing using a separate strap. This pair has a finished (chrome) leather shoe section with chestnut brown suede uppers. The practice of converting to 'knee boots' was not uncommon as the full-length boots could be cumbersome, particularly when worn with the Sidcot suit. (David Farnsworth Collection)

FLYING SUITS AND THE SIDCOT SUIT

The idea of the flying suit, a one-piece practical coverall for the aviator, had been in existence as a private-purchase item since 1912. Companies such as Aeronautical Accessories and Dunhill advertised their products in *Flight*, for example, fleece-lined leather and camel-fleece suits with adjustable belt and wind cuffs. In 1913 the RFC had issued the short, leather flying jacket with map pocket which also had an accompanying pair of leather trousers. It was not a flying suit and most photos of RFC aircrew confirm that they mostly flew with layers over uniform for warmth and leather jackets on top to provide wind, weather and contaminant protection. However, in early 1917 it was beginning to be recognised that the current system of clothing and protection for pilots and observers was not up to the rigours of high-altitude flying in the winter. A letter was sent to the Director of Aircraft Equipment from Brigadier General Robert Brook Popham, Deputy Adjutant and Quartermaster General of the RFC in the field, discussing the issues, dated 21 May 1917:

> It is considered that the question of flying clothing for next winter is one that should be taken in hand at once. In view of the great heights at which fighting and certain reconnaissance machines now do their work, clothing such as has been supplied up to the present is inadequate.
> Electrically heated gloves and socks will no doubt solve part of the difficulty, but the question still remains to be solved as to how to keep the body warm. Adding thick garments and overcoats is not a satisfactory solution. It is not considered that

this is the best method of keeping the body warm, it adds a lot to the weight to be carried, and further greatly impedes any movement of the arms, and thus causes unnecessary fatigue.

It is therefore important that every effort should be made to produce some form of clothing that should be very warm, as light as possible and allow free movement of the upper part of the pilot's body.

Overalls would probably be best, and these might be made of oilskin or some very closely woven fabric suitably lined. It is suggested that firms that have supplied equipment for the North and South Pole expeditions may be able to give useful advice.

It is hoped that the matter will be taken in hand at once in order that a solution may be arrived at before the cold weather arrives.[25]

One contender for the trial of clothing to be conducted was the Sidcot suit, the brainchild of Sidney Cotton, an RNAS pilot with No. 8 Squadron. After flying in oil and grease-soaked overalls on one sortie rather than his normal flying attire, he realised that the soaked material had helped to retain his body heat. Working with Robinson & Cleaver in London, he had a flying suit made for him to his design. The suit had three layers, a thin lining of fur, a layer of airproof silk and an outside layer of light Burberry's material, all made into a one-piece suit, just like his overalls. Robinson & Cleaver were asked to register the design on behalf of Cotton and the flying suit took its name from the inventor and was called the Sidcot suit (SIDney COTton).

LEFT: An example of a Sidcot suit, in this case made by Robinson & Cleaver. Developed during the winter of 1916 by Sidney Cotton of the RNAS, the suit was patented by a friend, J. Evans of Robinson & Cleaver. The Sidcot suit is one of the most well-known items of RFC flying clothing. It consisted of a one-piece, khaki, twill, proofed-cotton outer with a rubberised cotton interlining and 'fur' lining. It had a large buttoned chest flap, open pockets on the knees and buttons at the wrists and ankles. (Phil Phillips Collection)

FLYING CLOTHING

ABOVE: A Sidcot suit with a Robinson & Cleaver label, early 1918. It has a short, fur lining, button front and the remains of a War Department stamp inside. This version has no fur collar; it is not clear which version (i.e. with and without fur) came first. (Simon Lannoy Collection)

In response to Brook Popham, the following reply was received on 24 August 1917:

With reference to your letter C.R.F.C 1718 Q. dated 21st and 23rd of May 1917 and subsequent correspondence on the subject of warm and of fireproof clothing. I am directed to forward for your inspection and trial five sets of clothing which have been specially made up. I am to say that, four of these sets are fireproofed with asbestos, but, as perhaps warmth and ease of movement are more important than fireproof qualities, one suit is claimed to be cold and waterproof only [Sidcot].[26]

In September 1917 Brook Popham returned his comments to the Director of Aircraft Equipment as follows: 'Suit number 5 [Sidcot] is considered to be very satisfactory, the fly should however be lined or made of stronger material, as at present it is too thin. Please push on as quickly as possible with the manufacture of Suit No. 5 and say how soon deliveries may be made.'[27]

In this correspondence it is also apparent that some tests were done on flameproof clothing and helmets by pouring petrol on them and igniting it. Also, this method was used on one hapless airman in a flameproof racobal flying suit, but 30 seconds after ignition the man had to remove his arm from the garment as it was too hot, and he was slightly burnt! None of the flameproof equipment tested in 1917 was adopted but the Sidcot suit was to become an issue item, although there were some protests from certain quarters, as mentioned in a letter signed by Captain Fraser for Brigadier General of the Training Division, RFC to the DAE on 19 October 1917:

> I do not consider that the Sidcot suit No. 5 should supersede the old leather jacket. It is suggested that this suit would prove very useful for scout squadrons and pilots and observers of fighting squadrons for winter use in this country but should not take the place of the leather coat and knee boots at present issued to units at home.[28]

As a result of the trials and communications, an order was placed with Robinson & Cleaver for 2,000 suits. It took a while for all units to receive the new clothing, but a letter

ABOVE: Airmen photographed in France shortly after the formation of the RAF, as evidenced by the officer in the centre whose cap has an RAF badge. The majority of the men are wearing Sidcot suits. The exception is the individual second from the left, who is wearing a leather coat. Two of the suits feature fur collars. The man on the far right is wearing thigh-length fug boots over his Sidcot suit. (Tangmere Military Aviation Museum)

FLYING CLOTHING

of 9 March to all RFC units from the Comptroller General Equipment, Air Board Office required the return of all issue leather coats in lieu of the issue of the Sidcot suit.

One letter from 6th Brigade RFC acknowledging receipt states:

> I am instructed to acknowledge receipt of your letter No.87/Stores/2156 (A.Q.S.5.a) dated the 9th instant and have to inform you that immediate steps have been taken to withdraw all coats, leather, in possession of pilots and observers who have been issued with the new Sidcot Flying Suit. A return will be forwarded to you in the course of the next few days showing the number of leather coats released to date and available for re-issue.[29]

Whitehouse, a gunner/observer working his way to his 50 hours on active flying duty to gain his observer brevet, wrote in his memoirs of the cold and also the introduction in early 1918 of the first electrically heated suits:

> All our work was now carried out at 18,000 feet, and once we did a show at 23,000 feet. It was bitter cold, and we all went around with blue-green splotches on our cheeks as the result of frost bite. We smothered ourselves with whale oil and stunk to high heaven. They brought out the first electrically heated Sidcot flying suit, but the pilots, who sat up close to the engine, were the first to get them.'[30]

It seems that by August 1917 the RFC had started to adopt some electrically heated clothing. This took the form of a gaberdine-lined fleece jacket, which was prone to malfunction and overheating and if next to exposed skin could cause burns.

Research was also carried out on the idea of an electrically heated waistcoat, initially for the RNAS, but this was adopted by the RFC in late 1917. Manufactured by the Radio Clothing Co. Ltd, it was fashioned out of gaberdine material which was lined with fleece. The waistcoat was not that successful and malfunctioned regularly.

RIGHT: These two airmen are wearing Sidcot suits with fur collars. The individual on the right is also wearing a maternity tunic underneath, the collar of which can just be seen, whereas the man on the left is wearing a service tunic. (Tangmere Military Aviation Museum)

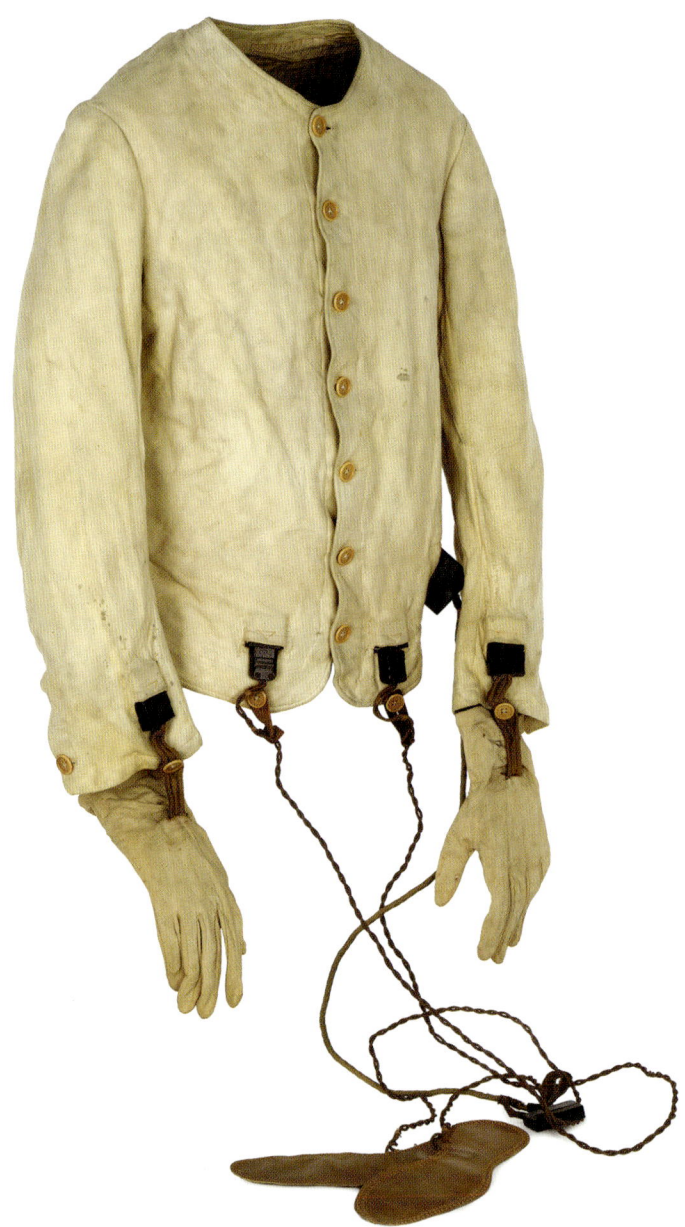

ABOVE: An electrically heated waistcoat. These were worn particularly on night operations by RFC, RNAS and RAF crews in 1917 and 1918. The heating current was generated by a dynamo which was mounted on an undercarriage strut and driven by a small propeller in the slipstream of the main airscrew. The top is a single-breasted, white, fabric, collarless under-jacket with long sleeves, closed with seven buttons to the front, and fitted with electrical terminals. The under-jacket also features two white, heated gloves which are plugged into terminals on the ends of the sleeves, as well as two heated shoe insoles with wires that are plugged into terminals near the bottom of the under-jacket. (Imperial War Museum; EQU 3831)

ABOVE: Two RFC officers of a night-bombing squadron. They are fixing up the connections of the electric foot sole and glove fittings to the electrically heated waistcoat being worn by the man on the left. This officer is also wearing a Mk I flying helmet and goggle mask; the man on the right, meanwhile, is wearing a private-purchase helmet and chin guard which is secured by leather straps at the back of the neck. (Mark Hillier Collection)

ROYAL FLYING CORPS KITBAG

LEFT: A pilot photographed wearing a Sidcot suit over his service-dress uniform, with his maps and notes tucked into his leg pockets. He has a pair of Fownes' mitten-style gloves, a cut-down cowl helmet and either a Mk I or Mk II goggle mask. The image was taken in early 1918. (Mark Hillier Collection)

BELOW: In this squadron photograph taken in 1918, the majority of the men are wearing Mk I flying helmets and leather flying coats. A single individual in the front row is wearing fug boots. At this stage in the war most squadrons were receiving Sidcot suits, and jackets were being withdrawn. (Archives of Alberta)

FLYING CLOTHING

LIFE PRESERVER

At the outset of the First World War, when the RFC sent the aircraft of 2 and 3 Squadrons as part of the expeditionary force to France at 06.25 on 13 August 1914, the thoughts about possible ditching due to engine failure were at the forefront of the aviator's minds. There was a high chance they would be going for a swim.

Each pilot had been instructed to climb to at least 3,000ft in order to have a good chance of gliding from that height to reach the shore in the event of engine failure over the Channel. Some climbed as high as 8,000ft. Each crew member had been issued with an inner tube to provide flotation if they had to ditch, as life jackets had not been provided in time. The navy positioned vessels across the Channel to rescue any downed machines.

ABOVE and RIGHT: A Boddy private-purchase, single-breasted, collarless life-preserver vest. It was made of quilted, khaki, cotton fabric with kapok-filled front and upper rear buoyancy compartments. The vest is closed at the front via four pairs of cotton tying tapes, while the rear can be adjusted by two buckled straps. (Mark Hillier Collection)

RIGHT: The label inside a Boddy life preserver showing the Patent No. 13475/12. This design later became the Boddy No. 5, as adopted by the RFC in 1916, officially with Pattern No. 8652. (Mark Hillier Collection)

ABOVE: Further views of the Boddy private-purchase, single-breasted, collarless life-preserver vest. Note the adjustment buckles on the rear. Only the upper section had buoyancy, the intention being to keep the wearer's head out of the water. (Mark Hillier Collection)

This was to be a regular hazard for those RFC pilots and observers ferrying aircraft back and forth across the English Channel.

Private-purchase life jackets had been available since 1910. One inventor of a life preserver was George Malory Boddy of Boddy Life Saving Appliances who used kapok pads sewn into a jacket to keep the wearer afloat. The RFC formally adopted the Boddy No. 5 Jacket in February 1916, although it was restricted to aircrew below 5ft 9in in height. However, it's clear from correspondence preserved in The National Archives that Boddy life jackets were being considered by the RFC in April 1913 but were rejected at this time. A letter from Headquarters RFC (Military Wing) South Farnborough states: 'I beg to inform you that after careful consideration of the matter it has been decided

FLYING CLOTHING

ABOVE: An example of the 'Belts, life-Saving, self-inflating, Type A, Perrin', also known as the '22c/15, Jacket, life-saving'. Both the inside and outside faces are printed with wearing and operation instructions. (Phil Phillips Collection)

that this jacket is not suitable for adoption in the Military Wing of the Royal Flying Corps. This type of life saving jacket is on the whole too bulky to be quite convenient for wear in the air in military aircraft.'[31]

This type was mentioned as being specifically for aviators but was of a similar style to those used on ships for passengers and crew with some adaptions. However, by August 1914 the Boddy was being purchased by the RFC in limited quantities, with 20 going to Fort Grange at Gosport and a further order for 100 being placed.

The other common type was the Perrin life preserver. Designed by Mr Paul Perrin, a Frenchman, it was patented in Paris in January 1910. His UK agent was Mr Mark Auliff, and he made improvements to the Perrin Life Belt which was then marketed as the

LEFT: The Perrin-Auliff lifebelt. (David Farnsworth Collection)

Perrin-Auliff Life Jacket. This later became the standard issue for many years for the RNAS and RAF. Auliff's modifications meant that an unconscious wearer would float face up in the water. This lifejacket waistcoat was manufactured in airtight/rubberised buff-coloured, thick cotton twill and fitted with adjustable white-cotton webbing shoulder straps. It fastened at the front with two metal hooks engaging with triangular shaped metal 'D' rings. A compressed gas cylinder was fitted internally and deployed for use with a metal lever. In addition, there was a brass oral inflation valve fitted to the upper left front corner enabling the wearer to inflate or top-up manually.

By December 1917 the RFC had two varieties of life preserver in stock, namely 'Jackets, Lifesaving No. 1 (Boddy)' and 'Jackets, Lifesaving No. 2 (Read)', with the Boddy being more numerous. Photographs and references to this version are limited, but the jacket manufactured by Mr H. Read of Falmouth was sealed as a pattern for use by the RFC in February 1916 but could only be used by men of 5ft 9in and over in height.

LEFT: The Savile Row tailors Gieve's were already well known as naval outfitters when, in 1915, they patented their 'lifesaving waistcoat' for use at sea. The patent entry described it as being 'provided with an inflatable tube enclosed in a cover made of the same material as the waistcoat and attached to the waistcoat at its upper edge only. The front parts of the cover fasten together by push-buttons, and the tube is preferably larger over the chest, so that the resultant greater buoyancy in this area maintains the wearer upright in the water.' These were private-purchase items for RFC airmen. (Mick Prodger Collection)

Chapter 2
FLYING EQUIPMENT

The need to observe and make notes on enemy troop locations, annotate maps, navigate and give artillery direction meant pilots and observers required an essential minimum of kit. The observer would have had a notebook and hard pencil with which to make his notes and mark maps but also to pass notes to the pilot.

Any paperwork within an open cockpit environment is a disaster waiting to happen with an 80mph and more slipstream tugging at anything loose waiting to whisk it away. Hence the need for map boards and cases which could hold and secure essential information relevant to the sortie. Maps needed to be clear but made of robust materials as there was a high chance they would get wet or covered in oil from the engine, especially in tractor engine machines with the engine up front rather than pushers.

For observation of ground positions, the observer may have taken field glasses, but these would have been difficult to use on turbulent days and when coming under ground fire or during manoeuvring. Also, the use of binoculars begs the question of where they were to be stowed within the confines of the aircraft or if they were just to be worn with a neck strap. There are accounts of binoculars being used by observers and they are confirmed as being issued for this purpose by Army Form G1098-33-C 'Mobilization Store Table for the Expeditionary Force', 1913 edition, for an RFC Aeroplane Squadron of twelve aircraft they had eighteen pairs of binoculars in leather cases for observers.[1] The same document of 1917 mentions twelve prismatic pairs of binoculars for a squadron.[2]

An absolute essential was the cockpit clock to help with navigation and fuel-burn calculations. Some also opted for a private-purchase wrist compass to aid with navigation in the air and with escape and evasion or making it back to the lines on the ground. The *Training Manual RFC*, Part I of 1914 explained that the aircraft compass was subject to errors and this helps to explain why some opted for a second compass, as illustrated by this manual extract:

2. Errors to which compasses are subject.

The compass is unfortunately affected by errors. The ones chiefly concerning aviation are

(a) variation; (b) deviation; (c) air bubbles in the liquid.

(a) 'Variation'. Suspended magnet, or compass needle, does not point to the 'true' or geographical North, but to a point known as the 'magnetic' North pole. The difference between this direction and the direction of the true North is called the 'variation of the compass', or shortly the 'variation'.[3]

The biggest problem was deviation, as described:

(b) Deviation. – This is due to local attraction of steel and iron fittings in the immediate vicinity of the compass; it varies both in magnitude and direction for different positions of the aeroplane. It will therefore be readily understood that it is necessary to place a compass in an aeroplane in such a position as to be as far as possible free from these influences. This, however, is a difficult matter; but so long as the compass is not affected to a greater extent than about 5° the error can remain uncorrected, as for practical work it will be found difficult to steer an aeroplane accurately enough for this amount of error to seriously matter.[4]

Some then felt that the wrist compass might be of extra benefit as it was not fitted close to lots of metal work and subject to as much deviation.

Navigation was an essential skill that the pilots and observers needed to master hence the importance of maps, timepieces and compasses. The *Training Manual RFC*, Part I of 1914 explained the art of aerial navigation and the importance of the equipment:

NAVIGATION OF THE AIR BY DAY. 1. General remarks.
   – Accurate navigation is obtained by the intelligent use of a compass, combined with a good knowledge of topography to assist in rapidly locating the position. Great difficulty is experienced by pilots in finding their way across country at the first attempt, even if the locality is well known from below. The country presents a very different aspect when viewed from above, and only by constant practice can a pilot become what is known as a good cross-country flier.
   The secret of success in navigating an aeroplane is careful attention to details. The pilot's task is made considerably easier if he has a trained observer as passenger, with suitable means of communicating with the latter.
   Pilots must be well acquainted with map reading. No map on a larger scale than 2 miles to an inch should be used for long flights; it is often impossible to use a larger scale than 4 miles to an inch. It will sometimes be necessary in war to use foreign maps, the scale of which is usually given as a representative fraction.
   Pilots, when supplied with these maps, should immediately construct the corresponding English scale, i.e., so many miles to an inch. This will facilitate rapid calculation of distance in units pilots are accustomed to work with. The pilot, having been directed to proceed to a certain point, or number of points, must closely study his map to ascertain what guides he can best use to assist his navigation.[5]

The Manual goes on to mention the importance of time to the accurate navigation of the aircraft too:

(h) Time. – The taking of times is often very much neglected, but nevertheless, it is an extremely important matter, in an aeroplane it is most difficult to

FLYING EQUIPMENT

estimate time. On calm days it seems to pass quickly, but on a rough journey the minutes pass very slowly; thus, it often happens that a pilot who has not checked the time of passing some object expects to pass the next long before it is really due. From the commencement of a cross-country flight to the journey's end, the times at which the objects selected as guides are passed must therefore be checked.[6]

Early in the war observers were more or less given training on the job but the importance of knowing where one was and passing this on to fledgling observers was noted by Louis Arbon Strange DSO, OBE, MC, DFC and Bar:

> In the first years of the war I took up more than fifty observers, most of whom I had to teach how to find their way about the air. I learnt a lot myself, and so could not grumble if for a time I was called upon to impart my acquired knowledge to others. Many of the things I learnt will apply in the next war, for in some few thousand respects the science of navigating in the air is as immutable as that navigating the sea. As a pilot of a machine you are responsible for that machine all the time, and as always, your fault if you crash it in a forced landing occasioned by engine failure, structural or otherwise, of the machine or its engine. It is your fault if in thick weather you hit the top of any hill that has its correct height shown on your map, for the worst offence you can commit is to lose your way cross country.[7]

These points are just as relevant in today's navigation for light aircraft – up-to-date maps marked with the route, headings worked out and safety altitudes prepared so as to avoid inadvertently hitting high ground in poor visibility. If lost, the principle of fly the aircraft first and navigate second ensures that the aircraft is always under control, which is paramount, and then you can start to worry about checking your position. Today, with GPS and navigation aids, the workload is greatly reduced and error to a degree removed. In the early days of aviation, trying to map-read around a battlefield, often brown featureless mud baths with cities and towns reduced to rubble, could prove difficult. The sun's position would give a clue based on the time of day and the prevailing wind. That said, after an hour of freezing temperatures, aerial combat, anti-aircraft fire and fatigue setting in, navigation would not have been easy.

This section looks at some of the equipment available at the time, used by both pilots and observers, including items for navigation, time-keeping and personal protection in the pursuit of operations over the Western Front.

HOUGHTON MAP BOARD

The Houghton Map Board was used by both RFC personnel and British cavalry officers during the First World War. Designed to be strapped to an arm and used with either a map or plain paper, the rollers on each side could be rolled in either direction for navigation or observation purposes. The front had a compass and two scales while on the reverse an inclinometer sat beneath a Perspex cover. Photographs of this piece of kit in use are difficult to find.

ABOVE: Front and rear views of the Houghton Map Board. It was worn on the forearm and fastened by the leather strap. This example is dated 1914. (Mark Hillier Collection)

LEATHER MAP CASE

This usually comprised a heavy leather folding case with a celluloid window for inserting a folded map, along with compartments for pencils, navigational tools etc. They were carried by pilots and observers while flying in order to navigate but also to search and mark enemy troop movements on the ground which would then be relayed to artillery commanders. The same type of map case was also used by ground forces.

A.G.J. Whitehouse, gunner/observer on 22 Squadron, confirms their use:

> Another aerial gunner who was making himself comfortable in another corner. His name was Mac. He had been in a Jock regiment and had transferred to get out of his kilt. He had been there about a month and had already chalked up about thirty hours over the line. As a matter of fact, he had just returned from a patrol and was contemplating three bullet-holes in his map board.[8]

The *RFC Manual* of 1914 states the importance of the map and case or board as follows:

> A map board or case. For moderate distance flights, the pilot will find that a board placed in a conspicuous position will be quite sufficient to pin his map to; but for longer flights, he may find it necessary to cut his map into strips and use a roller map case. This method has the draw-back that consecutive courses, though perhaps

FLYING EQUIPMENT

ABOVE and BELOW: A leather private-purchase map case with a strap for carrying around the neck. It was used by 859 Air Mechanic Charles Albert Cordeaux. The case is dated 1915 and has a broad-arrow mark with an 'A' above it. Accompanying the case is Cordeaux's compass, complete with its leather case showing an 'A' over a broad arrow, indicating air use. (Simon Lannoy Collection)

differing considerably, will have to be drawn as if in a straight line thus requires a little practice for a pilot to adapt himself to it![9]

Lieutenant Cuthbert Rabagliati, later to become Lieutenant Colonel Cuthbert Euan Charles Rabagliati MC, AFC and who was posted to 5 squadron in 1914 and flew some of the first reconnaissance sorties, wrote about the initial difficulty of dealing with navigation and writing and recording information: 'I took off from Maubeuge and I was told that I should see some advancing German troops. I was very excited as I looked for them. You were very limited in your facilities – you had a map strapped on one knee and a pad with a pencil on the other and it was rather wobbling about.'[10] He did manage to make notes of troop dispositions and got back to the lines to report his intelligence but had great difficulty getting the generals to accept what he had seen and was reporting.

ABOVE: Pilots and observers studying maps in front of an RFC Armstrong-Whitworth F.K.8. at Poperinghe aerodrome, 12 April 1918. A real mixture of clothing is seen here, with the aviators on the right wearing British warm coats, as well as mostly Mk I Helmets and goggle masks. Interestingly, the individual pointing at the map on the right has earphones fixed to his headset for communication by wireless. (Historic Military Press)

FLYING EQUIPMENT

ABOVE: This is a rare RFC/RAF Mk I map board which was manufactured by the General Instrument and Engineering Co. Ltd, London. The back is also stamped with the RFC property mark comprising an arrow with an 'A' above thus confirming its early provenance. It also has an Aeronautical Inspection Directorate stamp; this department took responsibility for the quality control of all manner of aircraft and equipment destined for the RFC from February 1914 onwards.[11] Although on face value it appears too bulky to use in a cockpit, it measures 36cm x 36cm and sits comfortably on a lap. This style continued to be used by the RAF during the 1930s but became bigger and looking at the design it clearly influenced the far more common Second World War map board stores reference 6B/137, but these later variants are all Air Ministry marked with an AM and crown with the stores reference. They would have been used for making sketches and noting observations as well as navigation. It would originally have had a translucent acetate sheet on the face under which the chart would have been retained. It also has a combined protractor and parallel rule, note also a thumb cut-out for holding the board and a brass hook for retaining maps/paperwork. (Mark Hillier Collection)

ROYAL FLYING CORPS KITBAG

ABOVE and RIGHT: Another example of the type but without a map attached, showing clearly the cut out for the thumb to grip the board and the little brass hook for retaining the map or paperwork. If required, the arm could be removed from its little track on the edge and then it simply became a board. (Historic Flying Clothing)

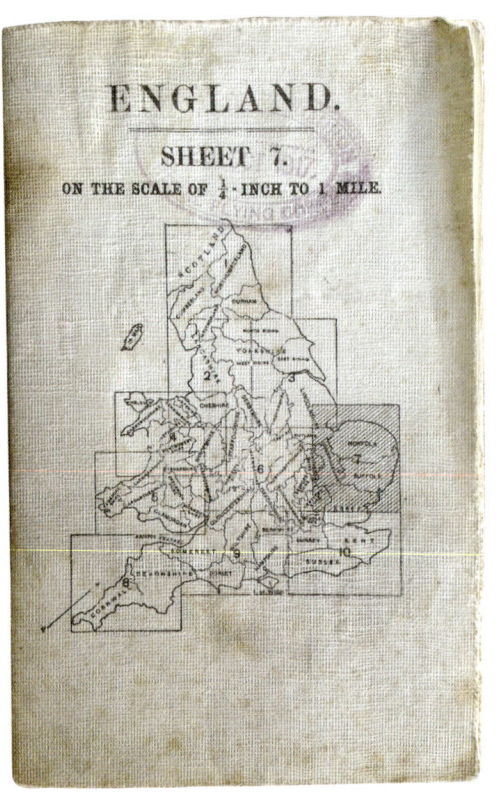

LEFT: A map of Norfolk, once belonging to Lieutenant E.J. Lainchbury, with a reinforced linen type backing, stamped RFC and dated October 1917. Essential for navigation, the pilot and observer could use a map to work out a heading, note critical features on the route to compare the planned route with the actual one and calculate corrections for drift caused by unexpected winds. (Mark Hillier Collection)

ABOVE: A map dated 1916 showing the general area around Ypres and Béthune and the French–Belgian border. This map has a scale of 1:100,000 and is in greater detail than the 2 miles to an inch recommended in the RFC manuals. (Mark Hillier Collection)

OVERLEAF: An example of a trench map, this one being Sheet 66, dated and corrected as of 8 November 1917, which details the front line around Urvillers. The Allied trenches are shown in blue and the German in red. These maps would have been available to the RFC crews for checking on the front line and features for reconnaissance sorties and for artillery direction. At a scale of 1:20,000, these are too small a scale for cross-country flying but ideal for showing detail in a local area. (Mark Hillier Collection)

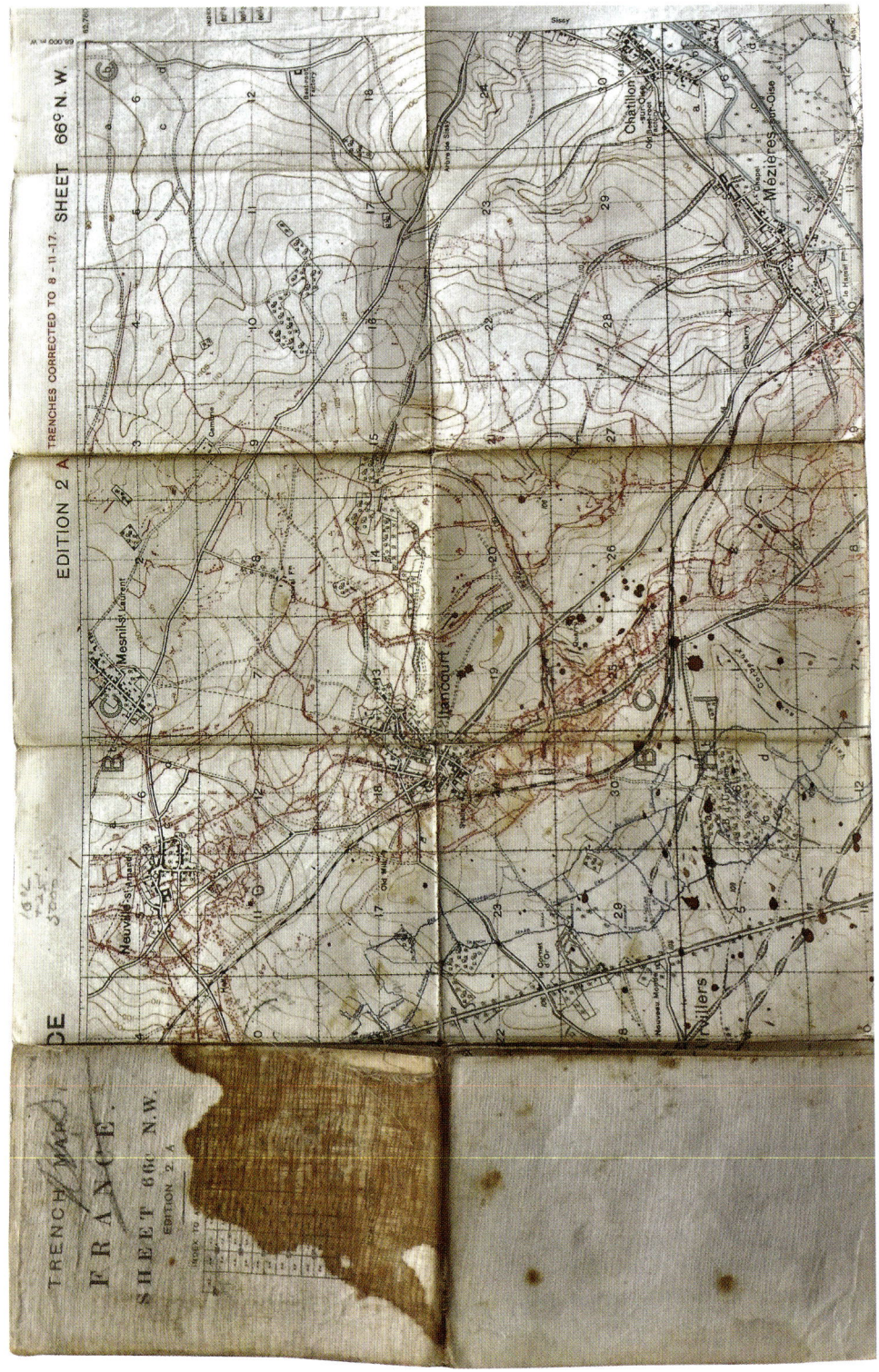

FLYING EQUIPMENT

FIELD GLASSES

These were an essential piece of kit for observers in reconnaissance aircraft trying to pick out enemy movements, strength and strongpoints, as mentioned by Alan Bott and quoting his flight commander on a pre-sortie briefing: 'as regards the observers, don't forget to use your field-glasses on the rolling stock; don't forget the precise direction of trains and motor transport; don't forget the railways and roads on every side; don't forget the canals; and for lords and everybody sake, don't be surprised by Hun aircraft'.[12] The issue and use of field glasses is also covered in the *Training Manual RFC*, Part II (Provisional) of 1915 which contains the following in Chapter III, Observation and Communication: 'Field Glasses – Field glasses are necessary for good observation. Those which have been found best for the purpose are the long "Zeiss N". The glasses should be hung round the neck ready for use.'

ABOVE and RIGHT: These binoculars are by the French manufacturer Lemaire and are focused by a single focusing wheel which moves both lenses simultaneously. While one lens tube carries the War Department and broad arrow mark, the other is stamped S-3 40591. Both barrels are covered in smooth, brown leather which is without loss. The optics are undamaged and remarkably clear. The case is in very good condition and complete with its original carrying strap. To the front is the War Department mark while the lid is stamped H. and J. Cripps 1917. (Mark Hillier Collection)

ABOVE and RIGHT: A pair of No. 3 Mk 3 field glasses dated 1918 with broad arrow mark typical of those available to the RFC, along with the earlier Mk I and Mk II. (Mark Hillier Collection)

COCKPIT WATCHES, WRISTWATCHES AND COMPASSES

Keeping track of time for airmen was particularly important be it for navigation, flying a heading for a period of time or for working out time in the air and how much fuel one had left. Also, it was essential to keep track of time on target to coincide or deconflict with an artillery barrage or meet up with escorting fighters.

Wing Commander Norman Macmillan OBE, MC, AFC, DL mentions the importance of timekeeping in his memoirs: 'As the pilot and observer walked down the cinder track to the aerodrome, the pilot glanced at his wrist watch and spoke to his companions, for service aeroplanes flew to a scheduled time.'[13] It is highly likely he refers to a private-purchase wristwatch worn by aircrew, but for the official purpose of timekeeping and navigation from 1914 the RFC pilot was issued with the Mk IVa or from about 1916 the Mk V watch, and was

FLYING EQUIPMENT

responsible for its safety. The pilot had to sign for the watch and it sat in a mounting in the cockpit. Although not individual kit, it was still issued to the pilot for a sortie and so included. Watches were manufactured by companies such as Zenith, Doxa, Smiths and Omega.

William Urquhart Dykes of 7 and 9 Squadrons, mainly flying RE 8s, utilised his watch and a stopwatch for the purposes of directing artillery shoots and remembers the issuing of watches prior to each flight and the return of them afterwards:

> On completion of a 'shoot' the Squadron Artillery Intelligence Officer always asked me to give back to him the stopwatch he had lent me, before accepting my report. In the eyes of the equipment officer and his staff, the aircraft clock, which was clipped in a holder screwed to the instrument board, was far more important than any other part of the machine. Little did he care if the pilot or the observer were lost so long as his clock was restored to him. Even if you had crash landed on or near to the front and had smashed the entire aircraft to smithereens, he would still have expected you to salvage his precious clock.[14]

Duncan Grinnell-Milne was a pilot who post-crash forgot to recover the cockpit watch from his aircraft and as a result fell foul of his adjutant:

> I got on the phone to the Squadron, spoke to the Newt [Adjutant]. 'I'll send a tender for you' he said. 'Glad you're safe, we thought you were missing. Don't forget to bring back the cockpit watch!' The eight-day luminous watch was the one item on the instrument board which appealed to all men. It was easily detachable, so easily that any machine left unattended for more than a few minutes was invariably looted of its valuable timepiece. The first thing a pilot had to remember, no matter how serious the crash, was to unscrew the watch. But the morning's events must have unsettled me for I left the wretched thing in the machine.[15]

Both issue types were basic pocket watches without a bow for a chain, although surviving examples now often feature the bow which was added later in service as many of these continued from RFC to RAF service into the 1920s and beyond. The face of the watch was either white or black, they were made in luminous and non-luminous and 30-hour or eight-day varieties. It has a long enough stem to allow the pilot to wind and adjust it with a gloved hand while it is mounted on the dash. On the earliest watches on the rear of the watch the case was stamped with a WD stamp and broad arrow; later, after the inception of the Air Board, cases were often marked with an A over a broad arrow signifying air use.

Private-purchase watches consisted of types such as the GAC aero wristwatch with luminous face and clear to read dial, and also an enlarged winder so that again the pilot or observer could manipulate it and alter or wind the watch with a gloved hand. This type of watch was being advertised in *Flight* magazine in 1916.

Other types available included those such as Borgel case watches, the design of which dated back to before the war and had a screw-off face and movement rather than an opening back to prevent the ingress of dirt. Again, these can be found with enlarged winders to assist winding with a gloved hand, but they were private purchase and not issue to aircrew. Known as a trench watch, this style of wristwatch was often sold with a protective metal face or hunter cover, as it is known, and was popular during this period but was not as practical for aviation use due to the small size of the face making it not easy to read in the air.

LEFT and ABOVE: The front and rear of a Mk IVa cockpit watch with an eight-day movement and luminous numbers and hands for night flying. Note the long stem for winding and altering when mounted on the cockpit panel. The rear is marked with an arrow with an A over denoting air use. It is thought that this watch dates from about 1916 as the Mk V started to replace this in 1917. Earlier versions pre-dating this can be found with a War Department marking on the back. (Mark Hillier Collection)

LEFT: An example of the face of a Mk V 30-hour cockpit watch, non-luminous variety. (Mark Hillier Collection)

FLYING EQUIPMENT

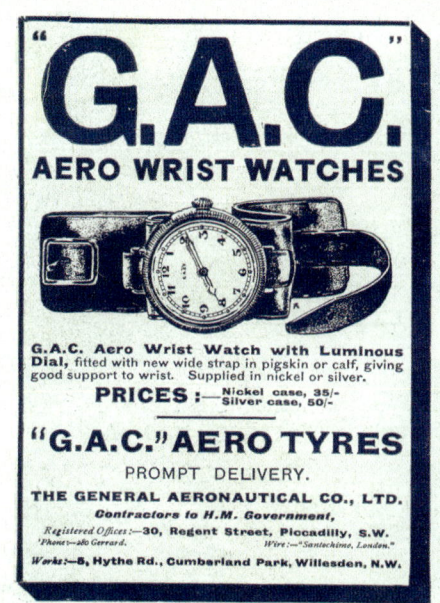

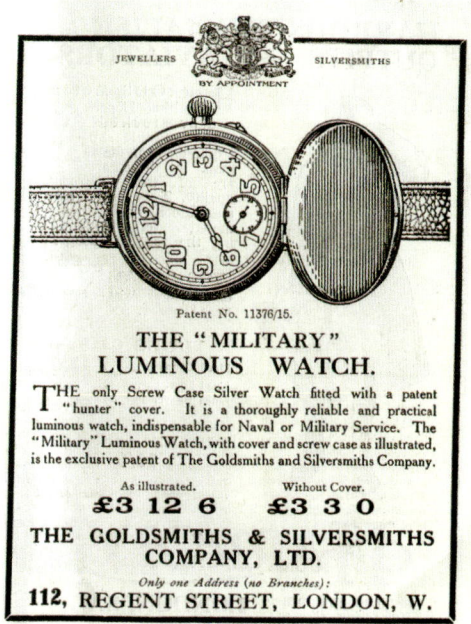

ABOVE LEFT and RIGHT: Two adverts from *Flight* magazine in 1916 showing styles of wristwatch that were common private purchase for aviators. The left is the GAC watch with its broad pig-skin strap and luminous face. The right is 'The Military' luminous watch with a screw case, known as a Borgel case, and a hunter cover. (Mark Hillier Collection)

RIGHT: A 1914 dated example of a Borgel case watch. It is typical of the style with a clear face, making it easy to read, but not luminous or with a hunter cover. (Mark Hillier Collection)

ABOVE LEFT: An RFC second lieutenant posing for a photo wearing his maternity tunic and field-service cap, breeches and short boots with puttees. On his left wrist is a trench watch with a leather strap. (Mark Hillier Collection)

ABOVE RIGHT: An advert from *Flight* magazine dated 2 July 1915 advertising 'Mappin's famed Luminous "Campaign" Watch' which was aimed at aviators. (Mark Hillier Collection)

BELOW: A First World War RFC/RNAS pilot/observer wrist compass. This is a blackened brass body example made by Dent & Co. with a leather strap, often advertised in *Flight* magazine at the time. Although the aircraft often had a fixed compass, error could creep in and often these were not that easy to read. A wrist compass was a useful back-up tool for cross-country flying. (Phil Phillips Collection)

FLYING EQUIPMENT

ABOVE and BELOW: This compass has a much longer strap for mounting around the thigh. It is engraved Lieutenant R.P. Spencer R.N.V., who was presented it or was working for Vickers Ltd, 13 May 1918. (Scott Rall Collection)

LEFT: The GAC aero altimeter wrist model was also available for private purchase but not issue for aircrew. It was more likely to have been used in earlier aircraft that had minimal instrumentation, although altimeters became commonplace in aircraft during the course of the war. (Mark Hillier Collection)

PISTOLS AND SMALL ARMS

On the formation of the RFC, aircraft were not armed but some pilots and observers chose to take weapons with them for self-defence and have a pop at other aircraft. Some took that option to the extreme, such as Kenneth van der Spuy, a pilot who flew with 2 Squadron with the RFC in the early stages of the war. He describes a hair-raising incident:

> I took up a sawn-off shogun, into which I'd rammed bullets on strings, so that they might fall and break up the enemy's propeller. And I had a revolver. I spotted a strange aircraft, which I thought didn't look like any I knew, so I sidled up to him and saw that he was a Hun, so I got my shotgun out, and I fired it all away. Then I got my revolver, and we had a revolver battle up there. We were very close to each other, and I could see him quite well, and he could see me quite well. I finished my six shots and he finished his. We both waved each other goodbye and set off.[16]

Many officers of the RFC chose to purchase their own weapons but at the outbreak of the First World War the standard issue was the Webley Mk V. However, there were considerably more Mk IV revolvers in service in 1914, as the initial order for 20,000 Mk V revolvers had not been completed when hostilities broke out. On 24 May 1915, the Webley Mk VI was adopted as the standard sidearm for British and Commonwealth troops and remained so for the duration of the First World War. One other weapon commonly used by the RFC was the Webley self-loading pistol.

The carrying of small arms fixed to a belt on the outside of flying equipment for defence was impractical. There are some references to pilots using small canvas holders made up for the cockpit. One observer of 1 Squadron who carried his pistol with him prior to use of fixed machine guns and completed over 100 hours' flying over the Western Front in 1915 was Samuel 'Paddy' Saunders, who wrote: 'My role was to keep a sharp lookout and if necessary, you came across another aircraft you would have a go at him. The arms issued to the RFC at the time was the revolver which we took up in the air in our pockets fully loaded but we also had a rifle in the cockpit.'[17]

Employing a pistol for self-defence behind enemy lines was probably of limited value and it is likely that many pilots chose not to fly armed at all, apart from the early duels as mentioned above. However, some took the view that having a revolver might be helpful for other reasons, such as a bullet to the head, which was considered a better way of dying than burning to death as described by Ira Jones (later Wing Commander Ira 'Taffy' Jones DSO, MC, DFC, MM) in his biography of Major 'Mick' Mannock VC, DSO, MC:

> It is strange, but ever since Mannock shot down his first machine in flames in our lines, he has unconsciously from time to time revealed how the ghastly sight affected him mentally. His continual reference to flames, often jokingly, is a positive proof of this. And as time went on it developed into an obsession, and eventually it was obvious that he suffered mental torture from the effects of a premonition of death by being shot down in flames. In his diary he puts this question to Cairns [Captain W.C. Cairns]:
> 'What do you imagine would be your first conscious thought in the event of your aeroplane being set on fire in the air?' The reply was: 'My thoughts would be confused between whether I could put the fire out and what my fate was going to be.' Mannock's reply to Cairns answer was, 'My reply would be – a bullet in my head.' It is believed that Mannock always carried a revolver in his machine in case of such a contingency arising.[18]

FLYING EQUIPMENT

ABOVE and RIGHT: The Webley Mk IV was one of a series of .455in calibre Webley revolvers that were the standard-issue pistols of the British Army from 1887 onwards. They were also available for private purchase. They were robust and powerful weapons that gave excellent service until replaced by the handier Enfield No. 2 revolver in 1932. Until the First World War, officers were expected to purchase their own pistols. The pistol is seen with a holster for the later Mk IV pistol. (Phil Phillips Collection)

LEFT: Another example carried by the RFC was the Webley self-loading pistol which was designed in 1910 by the Webley & Scott company. The Mk I .455in version was adopted by the Royal Navy in 1913 as the first self-loading pistol in British service. The pistol was also adopted by the Royal Horse Artillery and the RFC. Its predecessor was the unsuccessful Mars automatic pistol. The holster for the Webley could be worn on the Sam Browne belt. (Phil Phillips Collection)

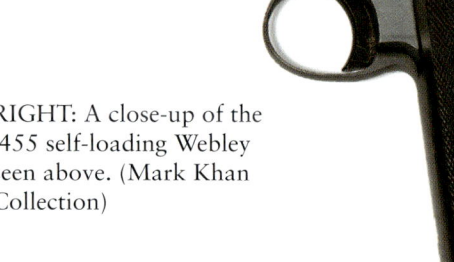

RIGHT: A close-up of the .455 self-loading Webley seen above. (Mark Khan Collection)

ABOVE: Another model of self-loading pistol utilised by the RFC and RAF was the Colt Government model in .455in self-loading calibre (the same round as fired by the Webley self-loading pistol). This pistol and the Model 1911 pistol were supplied as private-purchase items by Colts's London agents, the London Armoury Company. As Webley were well behind on manufacture, it became necessary to purchase pistols from trade sources. As such direct contracts were placed by the Ministry of Munitions from June 1916 for Colt Government model pistols in .445in self-loading calibre, first via the London Armoury Company and then directly with Colt for about 13,000 pistols including the 2 contracts totalling 10,000 pistols placed for the RFC/RAF. As both the M1911 Model and the .455in self-loading pistols are virtually identical, the pistols are marked 'Colt Automatic Calibre .455' on the slide and the magazines are also marked accordingly. (Mark Khan Collection)

FLYING EQUIPMENT

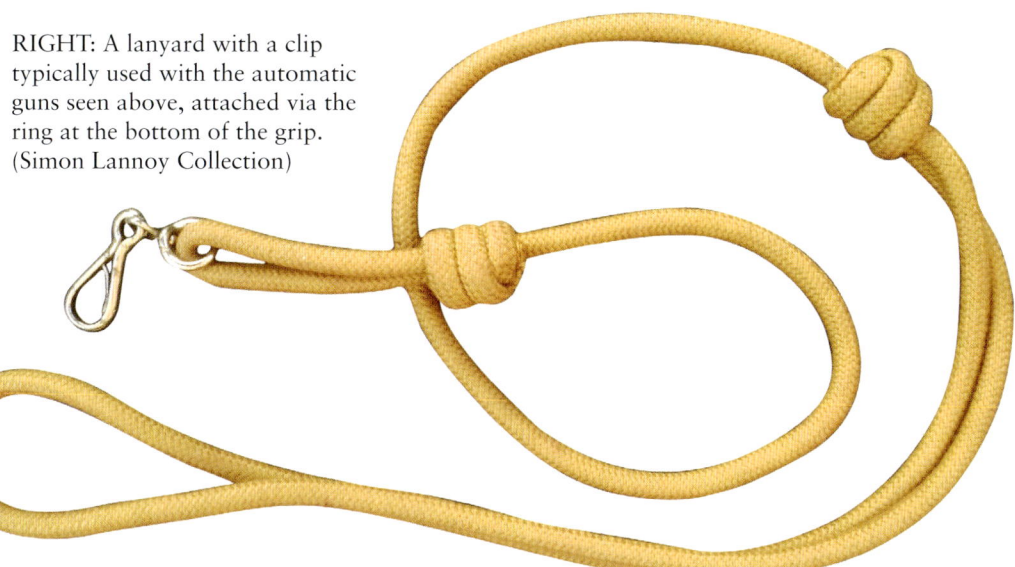

RIGHT: A lanyard with a clip typically used with the automatic guns seen above, attached via the ring at the bottom of the grip. (Simon Lannoy Collection)

FLARE PISTOL OR SIGNAL PISTOL (VERY PISTOL)

A flare pistol was a useful piece of equipment for the RFC for a number of reasons. It could be used to signal to troops and artillery on the ground, for communication between aircraft or setting fire to your aircraft if you landed behind enemy lines. The majority used by the RFC were Webley & Scott No. 2 Mk I single shot, and these were introduced in April 1915. The *Army Artillery Manual* of 1914 discusses the benefits of using Very lights to communicate to artillery units because of the distance at which they can be seen.

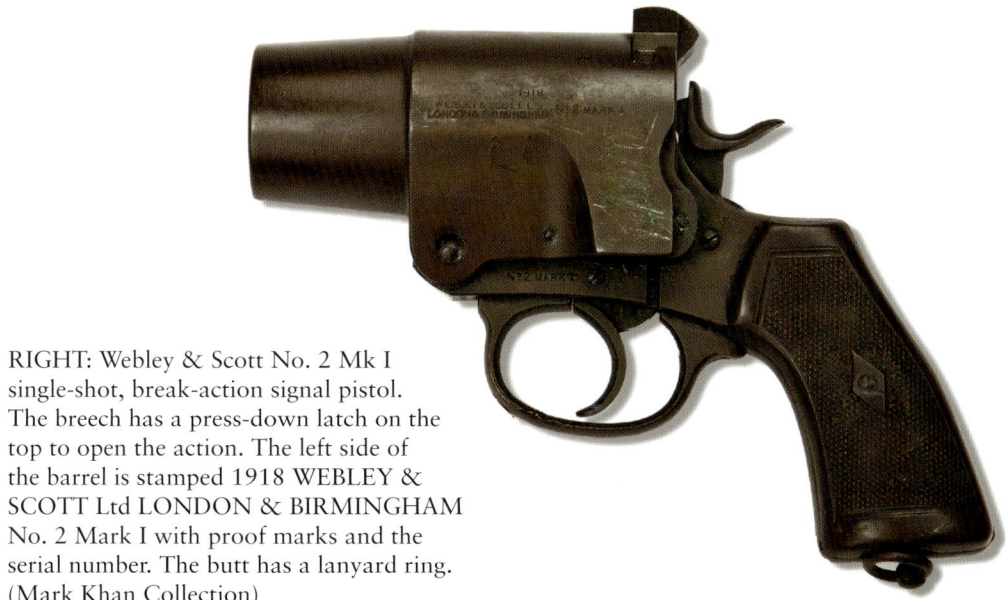

RIGHT: Webley & Scott No. 2 Mk I single-shot, break-action signal pistol. The breech has a press-down latch on the top to open the action. The left side of the barrel is stamped 1918 WEBLEY & SCOTT Ltd LONDON & BIRMINGHAM No. 2 Mark I with proof marks and the serial number. The butt has a lanyard ring. (Mark Khan Collection)

William Urquhart Dykes, in his memoirs, explains the use of the flare pistol to communicate between aircraft when they required a fighter escort for their R.E.8s for a particular reconnaissance in 1917:

> My observer and I made a special point of starting off early for the agreed fighter aerodrome, which was about two miles away, climbing hard at full throttle as we went. We used to look over the side of our machine when we attained an altitude of about 9000 feet, when one saw the fighters were still on the aerodrome. We had misgivings that they were not going to keep their date with us. However, we circled round for quite a short while when low and behold up they came, looking like a swarm of midges as they shot above us to about 12,000 feet, when the leader fired a very pistol as the agreed signal to follow him.[19]

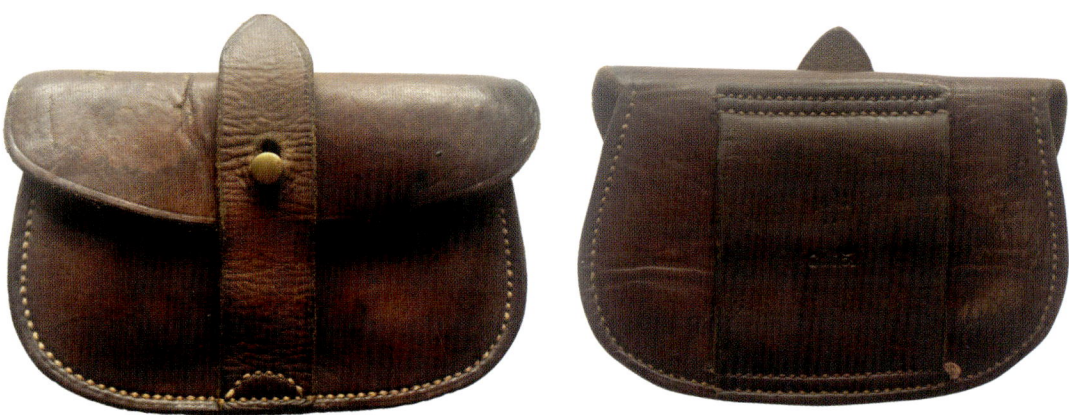

ABOVE: Front and rear views of the small ammunition pouch to be worn on an officer's Sam Browne belt, the rear of which shows it marked with an 'A' over an arrow denoting air use and dated 1915. (Mark Hillier Collection)

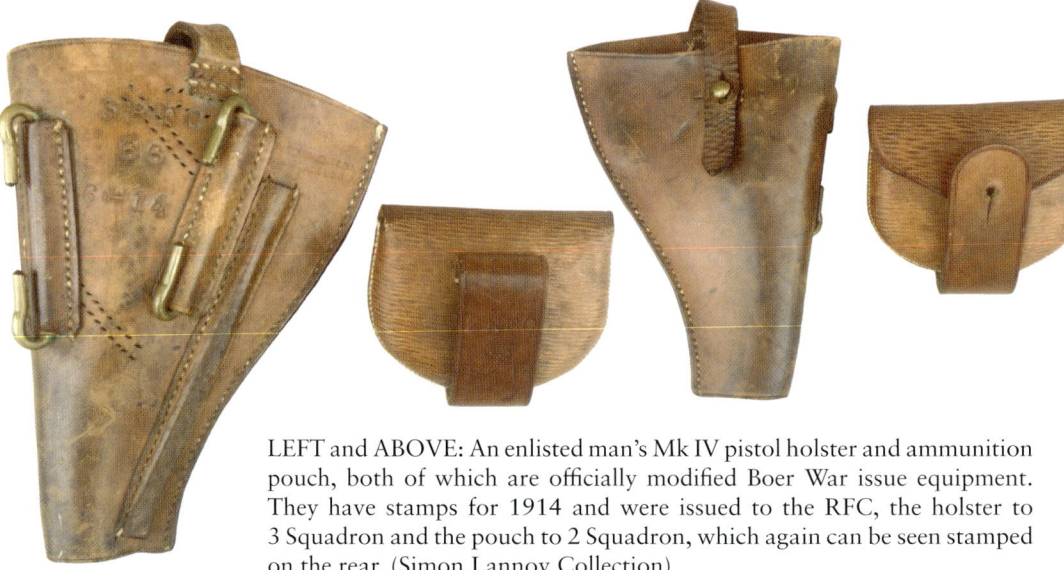

LEFT and ABOVE: An enlisted man's Mk IV pistol holster and ammunition pouch, both of which are officially modified Boer War issue equipment. They have stamps for 1914 and were issued to the RFC, the holster to 3 Squadron and the pouch to 2 Squadron, which again can be seen stamped on the rear. (Simon Lannoy Collection)

FLYING EQUIPMENT

RIGHT and BELOW: Two typical pistol kits. The one above right, although approved for use by other ranks in the RFC in October 1915, is seen in period photos and being worn from 1916 onwards and is the full Pattern 1908 pistol kit with leather holster and pouch. The images below show the pistol kit worn on the belt, again, from about 1914 onwards, the 1908 Pattern belt marked RFC with the ammo pouch and holster seen above which are dated 1914 and modified specifically for the Pattern 1908 belt. (Simon Lannoy Collection)

ROYAL FLYING CORPS KITBAG

RFC/RAF MESSAGE STREAMER

These were used by the RFC and RAF, dropped from aircraft over aerodromes and troops in the trenches in order to supply reconnaissance information to those on the ground, troop movements or artillery direction if the Morse or wireless failed.

The *Army Artillery Manual* of 1914 states that, 'employment of aircraft both during the period of tactical reconnaissance which precedes the battle, and in the battle itself, the aircraft may assist the artillery'. This assistance could only be offered if there was two-way communication between the aircraft and the battery. To this end, the manual covers signalling in some depth, going on to say 'the means of communication from aircraft are, i) Wireless telegraphy, ii) Visual signals, iii) Sound Signals, iv) Dropping written messages'. The section relating to dropping messages confirms, 'Messages may be written on special weighted message blocks and thrown over, or written on an ordinary form and placed in a weighted bag with streamers, or in a parachute.' A place on the ground where the message was to be dropped needed to be identified by the battery and marked with two strips of white cloth, 15ft x 3ft.[20]

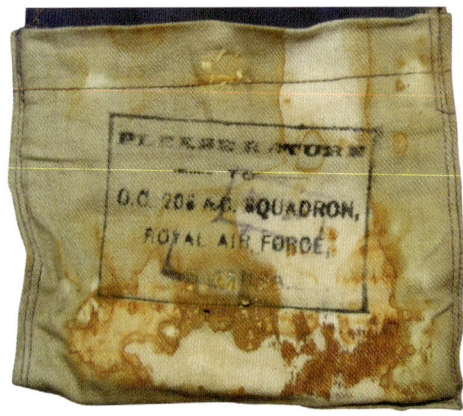

ABOVE and LEFT: A message streamer with a weighted bag at the bottom used to drop important messages to troops, artillery or HQ staff. This one is marked 208 Squadron, which originated from Naval 8 Squadron during the First World War. (Simon Lannoy Collection)

The message streamers were manufactured in panels of different coloured silk or woven cotton with a small pocket at the end designed to house a message and weight. Cecil Lewis writes that early on they also utilised weighted bags to get their reconnaissance reports back to HQ:

> Next morning, we started a practice which was to become a habit during the next few months – going down low enough to see the men in trenches with accuracy and getting our reports this way. We circled above the trenches at a thousand feet, saw the infantry crossing the old no mans land above Fricourt, saw many hun dead round the mine craters, saw the communication trenches running from Mametz to Montauban full of troops, noted it all on scraps of paper, put them in a message bag, and came back swooping low to drop it on the Brigade Headquarters groundsheet, then up again for more information.[21]

William Urqhart Dykes, of 7 and 9 Squadrons, recalled his use of message streamers in the event of the Morse code failing when guiding artillery batteries on shoots:

> Having satisfied myself that the aerial had been let out and there was still no reply to my signals, the usual plan, having wound in the aerial was to write out a message to the effect that I was getting no answer to my signal and that I suspected a fault on their new set, then place the message in a message dropping bag consisting of a weighted fabric pouch to which were sewn a couple of coloured streamers. The whole of this was rolled into a tight bundle and held in my hand. I then flew low over the battery at about 50 feet and threw the bag on top of the ground strip.[22]

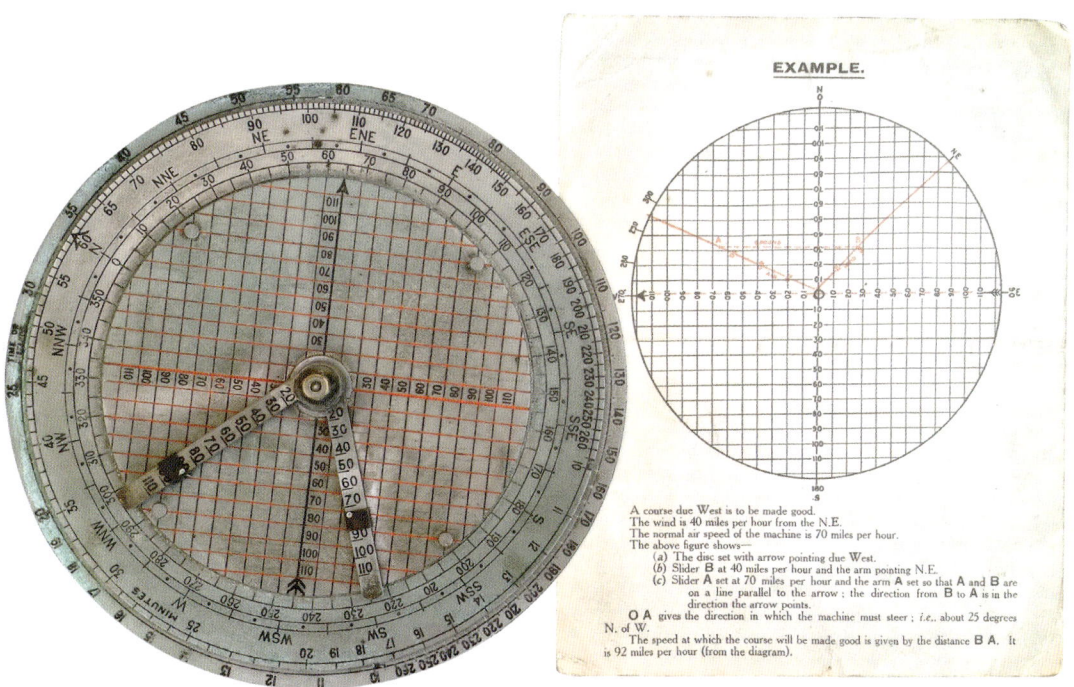

INSTRUCTIONS FOR USING COURSE SETTER.

The points of the compass and also degrees are marked round the rim of the instrument. When the central nut is loosened, the circular plate and both arms may be moved round in this outer rim.

The numbers on arms and disc represent speeds in miles per hour.

The course setter is to be used to find what course must be steered to allow for speed and direction of wind.

The following facts must be known :—

(1) The direction in which it is desired to fly (from the map).
(2) The speed and direction of wind.
(3) The normal air speed of the machine.

Proceed as follows :—

(a) Set movable disc so that the arrow points in the direction of the course to be made good (from (1) above).

(b) Set slider **B** to wind speed and point the arm in the direction *from* which the wind is blowing.

(c) Set slider **A** to air speed of machine and move the arm round until pointer of **A** is on a line parallel to the arrow and under pointer **B**. The direction from **B** to **A** must be that in which the arrow points; if it is opposite to this, move round pointer **A** until it lies on the same straight line under pointer **B** but on the other side of **B**.

The direction of arm **A** now gives the direction in which the machine must steer to allow for the wind, and the distance, parallel to the arrow, between pointers **A** and **B** gives the speed at which the course will be made good; each square representing 10 miles per hour.

N.B.—The direction of the course to be made good and the direction in which the machine must steer are bearings with respect to geographical North ; in flying by compass, allowance must be made for the difference between magnetic and geographical North.

(11837). Wt. 13819—250. 500. 6/17. D & S. **G 2.**

PREVIOUS PAGE and ABOVE: A flight computer available to RFC and RNAS pilots and observers from July 1917. The computer aided planning navigation and was used for calculating wind drift, time distance and speed calculations as well as fuel burn. The instructions for use are dated at the bottom. (Simon Lannoy Collection)

Chapter 3
UNIFORMS

The RFC uniform for day-to-day service use was khaki and followed the army in style, but there were to be some adaptions of standard kit and some interesting variations peculiar to the RFC.

Tucked away in the depths of The National Archives at Kew is a file containing some early minutes which include extracts from the Report of the Standing Sub-Committee of the Committee of Imperial Defence on Aerial Navigation in which the uniform of the potential new air arm of the army and navy is discussed. The minute dated 2 April 1912 pre-dates the official formation of the RFC on 13 April and states:

> The Sub-Committee recommends that officers of the Royal Navy and Army should wear their naval or military uniforms with the addition of the flying badge. Officers not holding commissions in the Royal Navy or Army should wear a uniform of the type of service dress of the Army (khaki) and mess dress. If they so desire, they should provide themselves with a full-dress uniform. These should be quite plain. Light blue colour is suggested. The flying badge should be worn. These officers should receive a grant to meet the cost of providing service uniform.
>
> Warrant officers, petty officers, sergeants and air mechanics should wear the uniform of the Flying Corps. Khaki service dress for working, light blue for walking out. The only distinguishing mark should be the letters 'F.C.' or 'R.F.C.' on collar or shoulder, except in the case of qualified flying men, who should also wear the Flying Corps Badge. Clothing should be an annual issue for all ranks, except officers, as in the Royal Navy and Royal Marines. The flying badge should consist of a brooch or embroidered pattern about 3 inches long, of the design of a pair of wings (or similar design). It should be worn on all occasions in uniform on the left breast, above medals or ribbons, embroidered in the case of service dress, metal brooch in other orders of dress. All fliers of the reserve of the flying corps should wear this badge.[1]

The navy went their own way and continued to use their uniforms throughout the First World War period until the introduction of the RAF.

This more or less meant that initially officers seconded to duties with the RFC usually retained their army cuff-rank, service-dress uniforms. Air mechanics mostly wore the approved maternity tunic. Prior to its introduction and also after that date, some chose to wear the service dress, 1902 Pattern uniform for enlisted men which was sealed for use for the army as Pattern No. 1921 with a 1905 Pattern service-dress cap which was amended in 1908 to have a different chin strap to the officer version.

Interestingly, in 1917 a memo was sent round to the army depots mentioning a shortage of maternity tunics and reducing scale of provision of maternity tunics from two to one per man or issue of the 1902 Pattern tunic with a stand and fall collar instead. Hence why in some period photos from about 1917 airmen can be seen wearing this style of uniform. This also occurs with the draw down in stock around the time of the formation of the RAF when again maternity tunics were not being ordered.

Changes to designs and experimental designs for dress uniform and service uniform were trialled, badges and buttons and flying badges all sent backwards and forwards for approval. However the first real mention of the new style service-dress jacket appears for a design to be used by NCOs and airmen on a memo to the quartermaster general dated 12 April 1912:

> Will you please arrange to have made up the following experimental garments for non-commissioned officers and men of the Royal Flying Corps: -
>
> Service Dress Jacket – Drab serge mixture. Double breasted, fastening at the right side with flat buttons (not metal) in a fly. Collar as in universal service dress jacket. Vertical side pockets fastening with glove fasteners. No shoulder straps. The sleeves to be lined, the lining to the wrist to be closed with elastic as a protection against the wind.[2]

This sets the scene for the design and provision of the jacket commonly referred to as the maternity tunic. First this was issued to NCO rank and below and then later adopted for officers directly joining the RFC. Of course, there are also comments within these memos relating to the RFC full dress uniform which was a high, scarlet collar tunic, the body of blue cloth and the cuffs also matching the collar. This was best uniform, but photographs and examples are rare and as this book is dedicated to day-to-day wear on the Western Front, this has not been included and neither has the officer's mess dress, which was also in an overall blue cloth with scarlet detailing.

Once commissioned into the RFC, officers were given an allowance with which to buy their kit, as described by Ira Jones, who up the time of his commission had been an observer, also previously an air mechanic and was later selected for pilot training:

> I was commissioned on the August 1 [1917] and issued with a cheque for £25 with which to buy my kit. This allowance was nowhere near enough to satisfy the demands of the expensive Oxford tailors, but at least it enabled newly commissioned officers to buy the bare necessities of their rank. That their uniforms were hastily made was damningly proved by the photographers, who were doing a roaring trade at the time.[3]

In the early days of the formation of the RFC a number of the officers were seconded from other regiments and it is clear from the above minutes and memos alongside period photographs that many chose to retain their existing uniforms, and some adopted a mix-and-match approach, as confirmed by Captain William Urquhart Dykes:

> Officers were not transferred from their regiments at that time, they were 'seconded' to the RFC, retaining their rank at the date of seconding. Hence, I started as a 2nd Lieutenant. One could either wear the uniform of one's regiment, in my case khaki tunic and tartan trews, or one could wear the double-breasted khaki coloured tunic, popularly known as a maternity jacket. When we felt like it, we sometimes mixed the two and at times an RFC cap.[4]

Some were not too enthralled with the uniform and boots, as Cecil Lewis described just after completing his primary flight training before moving onto Gosport for his final training:

> Christmas! Three days leave! And the new uniform arrived! How tight the field boots were! Agony, walking to the station! And everyone surely staring at the 'trusty and well beloved' young man in a tunic too small and breeches too big.[5]

There is some doubt that many flew on operational sorties in the RFC maternity jacket as it was thought that its collar and cut made it too restrictive for flying. Indeed, many chose to wear their cuff-rank service-dress jacket for flying with layers over. Why fly in uniform at all?

Aviators had to wear uniform in order that if captured they would be recognised as a prisoner of war. This principle had been established via a declaration relative to prisoners of war, discussed in 1899 and again in 1907 at international conferences held at The Hague. The purpose was to draw up rules of conduct that gained some recognition in international law for the prisoner of war prior to the inception of the Geneva Convention.

Typical examples of the uniform, headgear, trousers and boots or shoes worn by the officers and NCOs who flew over the Western Front are included here, and, as can be seen, there are often quite a variety of combinations.

RFC MATERNITY JACKET AND ASSOCIATED CLOTHING

The maternity jacket was available to enlisted men from later in 1912 and changes were made fairly quickly to its design. The enlisted man's first Pattern front flap did not extend to the shoulder and it had a collar that was made wider than the second Pattern. Soon after the introduction of the first version the second had an extended lapel over to the right shoulder and the collar stood up with less of a gap. Both of these versions had a cuff-tightening tab.

In 1914 the enlisted man's version changed yet again and had shoulder straps and horizontal pockets rather than the slit pockets of the 1912 Pattern and the cuff tab disappeared. These were issue jackets whereas the officer's version was private purchase.

The officer's maternity jacket is seen in period images dating to 1912, although a memo dated 11 September 1913 from the General Officer Commanding in Chief, Aldershot Command to the RFC Quartermaster General states: 'I am commanded by the Army

Council to inform you that His Majesty the King has been pleased to approve of uniform for officers appointed to the Royal Flying Corps other than those who already belong to units of the regular army, special reserve, or territorial force'.[6] This seems to be the official approval of the maternity tunic for the officers as the enlisted man's and NCO's had already been endorsed.

Some of the officers were not so fond of the style, as recalled by Lieutenant Colonel L.A. Strange DSO, OBE, MC, DFC, who had learned to fly at Hendon in 1914 and joined the RFC, and was posted to Central Flying School Upavon later that year:

> My time at Hendon drew to a close and one day, in company with a number of others bent on the same purpose, I left the train at Ludgershall and was conveyed to Upavon in a CFS tender. For the first time I donned the uniform of the RFC, with its forage cap and loose tunic that we ribaldly dubbed the 'maternity jacket'.[7]

The Pattern was very similar to the enlisted man's, but variations were soon introduced, including the adoption of RFC collar badges, although not official use. The material used was much finer as these were mostly private purchase, and the jacket was fastened by flat, concealed buttons under the flap that closed to the right shoulder. The material was secured by hooks and eyes or snap fasteners. The RFC wings were worn on the left breast of the jacket. The shoulder rank tabs or epaulettes were secured mostly without buttons, but examples do exist with RFC brass buttons. Rank was displayed on earlier versions by worsted cloth rank pips or on later versions by the metal type, and both types can be seen in period photographs.

For officers the jacket was worn with a Sam Browne belt and mostly paired with a field-service cap, although this is not a hard-and-fast rule, and any combination can be found in period images. Most commonly a pair of Bedford cord breeches, fastened at the knee with laces rather than buttons, was worn. Sometimes the uniforms were worn with normal khaki trousers and photographs prove many variations. Officers and warrant officers were permitted to wear either brown field boots or brown leather gaiters with their short brown boots, although puttees were often worn instead.

Air mechanics or NCOs wore the maternity jacket unbelted, with a field-service cap and with a broad-cut pantaloon, loose at the thigh but close fitting at the knee, with black ankle boots and puttees worn infantry style wound up the leg. While officers were expected to purchase their kit, the Army Clothing Regulations of 1914 stated that enlisted men would get on issue the following items:

Boots Ankle 2 pairs
Cap Forage 1
Cap Field Service 1
Drawers Woollen 2 pairs
Girdle 1
Jacket, service dress 2
Pantaloons, cord 1 pair
Puttees 2 pairs
Trousers, service dress 1 pair
Tunic 1
Waistcoat, cardigan 1[8]

UNIFORMS

RIGHT: Not all pilots in the First World War were officers and this photograph shows Sergeant Thomas Mottershead VC wearing his maternity tunic.
A brave man, his citation for his Victoria Cross says it all: 'For most conspicuous bravery, endurance and skill, when attacked at an altitude of 9,000 feet; the petrol tank was pierced, and the machine set on fire. Enveloped in flames, which his observer, Lt. Gower was unable to subdue, this very gallant soldier succeeded in bringing his aeroplane back to our lines, and though he made a successful landing, the machine collapsed on touching the ground, pinning him beneath wreckage from which he was subsequently rescued. Though suffering extreme torture from burns, Sgt. Mottershead showed the most conspicuous presence of mind in the careful selection of a landing place, and his wonderful endurance and fortitude undoubtedly saved the life of his observer. He has since succumbed to his injuries.' (Historic Military Press)

ABOVE and OVERLEAF ABOVE: An enlisted man's maternity tunic with buttoned and flapped pockets and epaulettes dating from post-1914. The shoulder flash is typical of the style, although abbreviated versions with just RFC existed. The coarser woollen material is clearly seen here in contrast to the officers' versions fashioned from gaberdine or whipcord. The inside shows the manufacturer's stamp and labels. Note the brown tan lining which appeared in about 1915 during the period when simplified clothing was being introduced as a result of shortages of material. It is probable that this example is of Canadian manufacture. (Scott Rall Collection)

ROYAL FLYING CORPS KITBAG

LEFT: An enlisted man's khaki pantaloons of a pre-war Pattern, again with the flared hip, button fly and button bottoms. Note the coarser material compared with that of an officer's service-dress trousers or breeches. (Phil Phillips Collection)

UNIFORMS

ABOVE and RIGHT: An enlisted man's pair of pantaloons, typical of the 1915 simplified Pattern. These are of 'emergency' manufacture and have been rather roughly and hastily made overall. From the autumn of 1914 until the summer of 1915 British uniform supply was in crisis because of the rapid increase in the size of the army. This state of affairs is fully described in Polendine's Campaign 1914 and 1915 books. Manufacture could not keep up with demand and large numbers of uniform items were made by firms who did not normally contract to the military, and some were even manufactured in the USA. The trousers have a tan lining, tin button fly and WD stamped on the rear of the waistband. The cloth lower sections over the calf areas may indicate American manufacture or conversion in 1918 for RAF use. (Simon Lannoy Collection)

ABOVE: A pair of braces, which are very rarely seen as they were an item that could be used for everyday wear after the war had ended. Note the button connection. (Simon Lannoy Collection)

ABOVE: A group of airmen undergoing machine-gun training, mostly wearing the flapped, pocketed version of the maternity jacket post-1914 and field-service cap. They wear the RFC shoulder title. The man on the far right demonstrates how puttees were worn with the black ankle boot. The man second from right wears a 1902 Pattern jacket. (Historic Military Press)

UNIFORMS

ABOVE: A detail from a squadron photograph taken in France in early 1918. The airmen are wearing the service-dress jacket rather than a maternity one. Stocks of maternity jackets were wound down and in short supply towards April 1918 and therefore there are fewer photographs showing enlisted men wearing this style of uniform. These jackets are being worn with service trousers and black boots. The air mechanic on the left is wearing a service-dress cap rather than a field-service cap. (Tangmere Military Aviation Museum)

RIGHT: An airman wearing a maternity jacket with pantaloons, ankle boots and puttees. On his head he wears a field-service cap. Note he is holding a swagger stick, most of which were made of bamboo or cane with a white metal top, the norm for enlisted men. Note on his maternity jacket he has a wound stripe vertically on his left cuff as well as a good conduct stripe. On his right sleeve he has overseas service chevrons indicating two years' overseas service. (Historic Military Press)

ROYAL FLYING CORPS KITBAG

ABOVE: Airmen, 1917. A flight sergeant observer is sat in the centre of the photo and the others are mostly sergeant rank or in the rear row corporals denoted by the two chevrons on the upper sleeve, the same rank as used by the army. The sergeants have three chevrons and a propeller above and the flight sergeant has a four-bladed propeller with a four-pointed star superimposed on the boss, which was approved for wear in March 1915. All are wearing the maternity tunic and field-service cap with short, black boots and puttees. (Jason Hutton Collection)

LEFT: Although enlisted men wore black boots, this is a pair of brown, leather short boots. Also seen are Fox's private-purchase puttees, often worn by warrant officers who also sometimes followed officers' styling and private-purchase uniforms. (Phil Phillips Collection)

UNIFORMS

RIGHT: A pair of enlisted man's boots in black leather, to be worn with puttees. This is a B5 boot dating to about 1916, its predecessor being the B2 boot. There were other variations known as the tradesman boot. The subject of boots is quite complex and this pair are shown as an example of the type. The most well-known type is the B5 with reverse leather, but this example is in grained leather. (Simon Lannoy Collection)

LEFT: A pair of enlisted man's puttees, to be worn with the short, black boot. The officer variety, private purchase, was made by companies such as Fox. (Simon Lannoy Collection)

ABOVE: Dated 1912, this photograph of the 'officers' first flying course' at the Central Flying School Upavon shows notable figures such as Major Hugh Trenchard (later Marshal of the RAF Hugh Montague Trenchard, 1st Viscount Trenchard, GCB, OM, GCVO, DSO), far right, middle row, and other well-known early RFC pilots who later went on to achieve great things and high rank. Note that several of the RFC officers wear the new maternity tunic with the flap that does not go all the way across the front to the shoulder. In particular the two officers second and third left in the rear row are dressed as such. Some of the officers wear the earlier cuff-ranked, stand and fall collar uniform of their parent unit. This image shows that the maternity tunic was adopted by some as early as mid-1912. (Graham Turner Collection)

ROYAL FLYING CORPS KITBAG

UNIFORMS

OPPOSITE and ABOVE: This is an example of what is thought to be an earlier RFC second lieutenant's maternity tunic showing the flapped pocket and the cuff-tightening tab, which disappeared from later issue variants. The beauty of private purchase was that you could to a degree opt for your own variations. This one is privately tailored by Hall Brothers of Oxford. The rank is denoted by worsted cloth pips on the shoulder and also note the wound stripe on the lower part of the right cuff, which was introduced in 1916. The wing is a very nice eleven-feather RFC version sewn to a fine, black wool. The Sam Browne was mostly worn with one shoulder strap by RFC officers. This belt is dated 1918. (Phil Phillips Collection)

In The National Archives there is a memo dated 1913 which sets out the expectation for officer's uniform and the requirements for full dress uniform and service dress that are to be used. The service-dress section confirms that the cap should be 'Austrian pattern of drab serge with brown leather chin strap. Badge as for the forage cap but in Bronze.' The jacket should be 'Drab serge of special pattern, worn with white strip linen collar [latterly dropped]. Badges of rank in worsted embroidery on the shoulder strap. No Collar badges.' Later variants of the maternity tunic had collar badges and metal rank badges on the shoulder. Again, a variety of styles and patterns was adopted and can be seen in period photographs.

To go with the maternity tunic, the memo mentions breeches, 'Bedford cord, or of special pattern' worn with 'Boots, ankle, paragraph 16 dress regulations' and 'Puttees, drab, paragraph 40, dress regulations'.[9]

ABOVE: Another example of the now extremely rare RFC second lieutenant pilot's maternity tunic. Tailored in a ribbed gaberdine material in the classic style, the much finer material is apparent compared with that of an enlisted man's tunic. On the left breast are the originally applied RFC pilot's wings and show a repair to the left wing where rubbing has removed some of the silk thread. Each shoulder strap is secured by a single brass RFC button with the rank shown by a single bronze pip, and this is not untypical of later RFC tunics in contrast to the cloth worsted variety of rank badge. On each side of the stand-up collar is a bronze RFC collar badge, smaller than the cap badge, and secured by two posts and a sprung pin. There are two flapped pockets and the tunic is closed with the traditional wrap-over front, giving the name. There are seven hidden buttons supported by twelve hooks and eyes to give a smart fitted appearance with three further hooks and one press fastener to the neck and shoulder. (Mark Hillier Collection)

UNIFORMS

BELOW: The same tunic as opposite on a mannequin showing the form of the jacket, the flapped pockets and the shoulder rank. (Mark Hillier Collection)

ROYAL FLYING CORPS KITBAG

LEFT: RFC officers from No. 2 Squadron based in Montrose, Scotland in front of a B.E.2b biplane shortly before they flew to Amiens on 13 August 1914. All are wearing a maternity tunic with a mixture of service-dress caps and the new field-service cap and short boots with puttees. (Archives of Alberta)

LEFT and ABOVE: A rather moth-eaten example of a maternity tunic worn by Lieutenant Reginald Taylor. Note the lovely set of RFC wings with a red backing to the crown. This one has two metal rank pips on the shoulder rather than the worsted variety. (Tangmere Military Aviation Museum)

UNIFORMS

ABOVE and RIGHT: This maternity tunic is thought to have been worn by Major Andrew Edward McKeever DSO, MC and Bar, DFC (21 August 1894–25 December 1919), who was a Canadian First World War two-seater flying ace. Post-training, he was posted to 11 Squadron on 28 May 1917, flying the obsolete F.E.2, although shortly after this the unit was re-equipped with the Bristol F.2.A. He was to score thirty-one victories with his gunners/observers, gaining the distinction of being the highest-scoring two-seater fighter pilot in the RFC or RAF. (Scott Rall Collection)

LEFT: Major Andrew Edward McKeever DSO, MC and Bar, Croix de Guerre wearing a Mk 1 flying helmet and Triplex goggles. (Historic Military Press)

BELOW: Two RFC officers, on the right, pose in front of an Airco DH.4. Both are wearing maternity tunics, whilst one has lace-up field boots and the other has short boots and puttees. (Historic Military Press)

UNIFORMS

ABOVE: Lieutenants Kelly and Warner of 85 Squadron photographed at Hounslow just after the change over to the RAF, which took place on 1 April 1918. On the left, Kelly wears a Mk I issue leather flying helmet with wind deflectors, an RFC maternity jacket with flap pockets, no belt, shoes and trousers rather than breeches or jodhpurs. Warner is wearing a 1917-period shoulder rank uniform and beige breeches with puttees and short boots. Any combination of uniform was possible at this early stage of the changeover. (Mark Hillier Collection)

RIGHT: A pair of officer's breeches worn with uniform, note the button fly, wide hips, laced at the bottom. This pair was made by Anderson and Son of Edinburgh and London. (Phil Phillips Collection)

ROYAL FLYING CORPS KITBAG

LEFT: A pair of officer's Bedford cord breeches with lace-up bottoms finished by two buttons to be worn with long field boots or with short boots and puttees. (Phil Phillips Collection)

BELOW: A pair of lighter brown Bedford cord breeches, with button-up bottoms, which are more frequently seen in period RFC photos than the normal khaki. Many shades and variations of breeches existed. (Simon Lannoy Collection)

UNIFORMS

ABOVE: An RFC officer wearing a maternity tunic with normal service-dress trousers rather than breeches. (Tangmere Military Aviation Museum)

RIGHT: A very typical pair of service-dress trousers, as seen in the previous photograph, worn either with a service-dress tunic or maternity jacket. (Simon Lannoy Collection)

SAM BROWNE

The Sam Browne belt is a wide, brown, leather, waist belt attached to a thinner shoulder cross belt that fastens diagonally across the right shoulder, and although some branches of the army used both cross straps, the RFC only typically wore the right shoulder strap. The Sam Browne belt was originally used for carrying a sword, and more latterly a pistol, although RFC officers can rarely be seen wearing anything on the belt.

The name Sam Browne comes from a British Army officer of the same name, who served with the 2nd Punjab Irregular Cavalry. In 1858 during a battle near Seeporah, Sam Browne charged a cannon as it was being reloaded. He was attacked by one of the cannon crew, suffering two devastating cuts – one to his left knee and a second that

147

severed his left arm at the shoulder. Browne survived the attack but was left seriously disabled by his injuries and lost his arm. He continued to serve in the army, but found it hard to control or draw his sword effectively. Therefore he took it upon himself to modify his existing belt with additional straps to steady the belt when drawing his sword, and by adding the extra connecting rings so he could also carry additional items.

One RFC officer who found it not so easy to use was Cecil Lewis, who describes his first experience of the belt on obtaining his uniform after training: 'and the Sam Browne belt! Let me tell you a Sam Browne belt is full of pitfalls for the ignorant. It is supplied with two shoulder straps; but you only wear one. Which? It has extra links, and hooks for swords, and buckles and clips and it all looks so new!'[10]

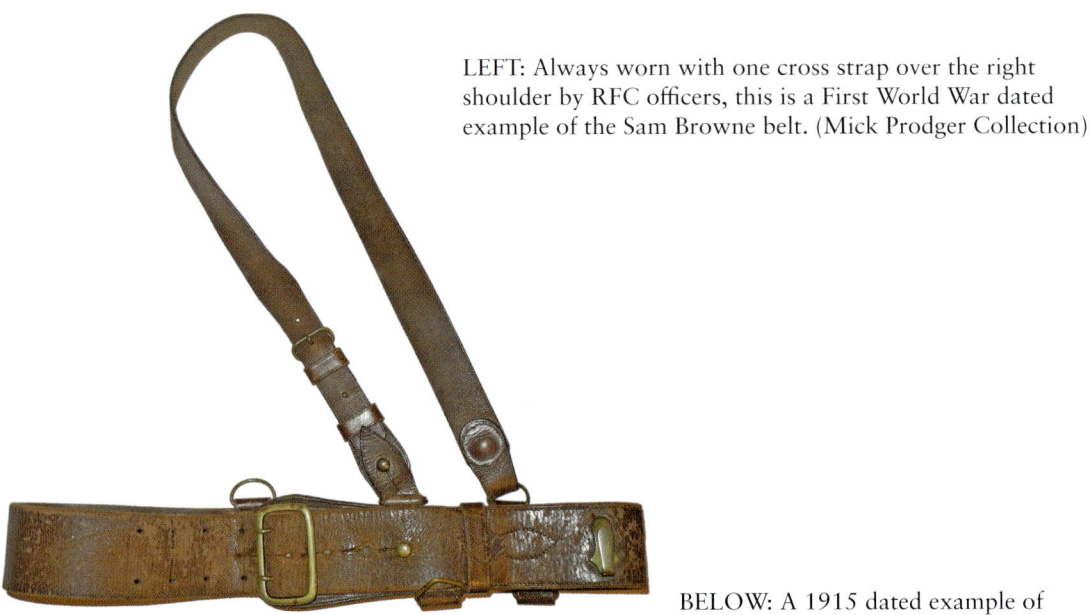

LEFT: Always worn with one cross strap over the right shoulder by RFC officers, this is a First World War dated example of the Sam Browne belt. (Mick Prodger Collection)

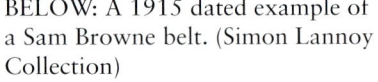

BELOW: A 1915 dated example of a Sam Browne belt. (Simon Lannoy Collection)

LEFT: This second lieutenant pilot wears his maternity tunic with cloth worsted rank badges. Note also the lancer style cuff with the inverted V appearance which was common on earlier jackets. He does not wear any collar badges; some officers chose to wear them even though they were not originally approved for service dress. (Historic Military Press)

RIGHT: This lieutenant pilot wears his maternity tunic with Bedford cord breeches and lace-up brown field boots. Note on his collar he wears the bronzed officer collar RFC badge. (Historic Military Press)

ABOVE and LEFT: Three second lieutenants showing the variety of rank stars or pips worn. The man on the left wears the traditional worsted rank badge, the officer on the right a metal rank pip. The latter also has a gilt RFC collar badge rather than the subdued bronze one usually seen and which can be just made out on the collar of the officer in the middle. The officer on the left has no collar badges, as was original laid down in dress regulations. (Tangmere Military Aviation Museum)

SERVICE-DRESS JACKET, 1912 PATTERN

Officers seconded to the RFC before 1914 initially continued to wear the service dress of their original units with their old unit badges often worn on the collar. The uniforms were khaki with a cuff rank, as approved my Army Orders in 1902. Originally the 1902 Pattern jacket closed at the collar but in 1912 this changed to a lounge-suit style collar and tie. Initially it was worn with a white shirt and black tie but in 1913 this changed to khaki, which is seen throughout the war and commonly appears in photographs. The final style seen was approved for use from 1913 and had four buttons and flat epaulettes and was worn with a khaki shirt. These private-purchase jackets were manufactured from materials such as whipcord, gaberdine or baratheа. Often they are seen with tailored rounded skirts for officers originating from Highland regiments.

The qualification badges for pilot or observer would be stitched above the left breast pocket. Rank on this uniform was found on the cuff, enclosed in a chevron tape forming a false cuff, one star for second lieutenant, two stars for lieutenant. The ring around the cuff also gave a quick indication of rank with a single ring indicating the lowest two ranks as above, two rings around the cuff indicating a captain, three stars within and three rings with a crown for a major, and one crown and one star for a lieutenant colonel.

The worsted rank star is the Order of the Bath and this style of rank badge was also worn on later tunics with shoulder rank. From about 1915 officers of some front-line regiments started removing the cuff rank and replacing the rank with stars or pips on the shoulder to prevent them from being targets for snipers. RFC officers also adopted this approach and although no official designation or recognition exists, it is generally known as the 1917 officers' jacket which was when the change was accepted but not officially recognised till after the First World War. The officers wore the jacket with a Sam Browne belt with a single strap across the right shoulder.

With this uniform the officers would wear plain khaki trousers, breeches or even jodhpurs. Any mix of dress could be found, as shown in contemporary photographs. Most officers would wear field-service boots, of which there are a number of styles all in brown leather, or short boots and puttees. Sometimes this uniform would also be worn with leather gaiters.

RIGHT: Captain Edward Gribben wearing his cuff-rank uniform with his collar badges identifying his previous employment with the 5th Battalion, Royal Irish Rifles, 15 August 1914. He was later seconded to the RFC to train as a pilot, being appointed a flying officer on 24 December 1916 and posted to 70 Squadron early in 1917. He became an ace on the Sopwith Camel. His victories were achieved between 17 July and 13 August, his final tally being two enemy aircraft destroyed and three driven down out of control. On 9 September, he returned to England to serve with No. 44 Squadron as a night-fighter pilot flying the Sopwith Camel. On 26 September he was awarded the Military Cross, the ribbon for which can be seen on his tunic under the wings. (Mark Hillier Collection)

ABOVE: The issued jacket (dated 1918) of Second Lieutenant Thomas Dowsett, an Australian who joined the RFC in 1915 as 2834 AM1 Thomas Dowsett, RFC. He was promoted to sergeant on 28 December 1916 and then temporary second lieutenant on 25 September 1918, being posted to 47 Squadron on 5 October 1918. Although he didn't fly on the Western Front, his tunic is typical of those who did. Note the worsted pip on the shoulder and the RFC collar badges. This jacket could equally have had the cuff rank applied rather than shoulder rank. Note the leather buttons, as opposed to metal examples. This style of jacket can be seen in many pictures from the 1917 period, which is why it is often referred to as the '1917 jacket'. The medal ribbon is that of the Khedive's Sudan Medal. Dowsett was later awarded a DFM for operations in Salonika, the citation for which reads: 'During the operations, August to October, 1918, this pilot was engaged in more than one hundred bombing raids on the 16th Corps front, on several occasions taking part in three flights, and sometimes four, in one day, displaying courage and keenness at all times'. (Simon Lannoy Collection)

UNIFORMS

ABOVE: Two officers standing in front of their DH.9. The observer, on the left, is wearing a maternity tunic with just trousers and short, brown boots while the pilot, on the right, wears his cuff-rank, service-dress jacket and trousers again with short boots. He is also wearing the collar badges of his original regiment. The observer is wearing leather gauntlets for flying and both are holding their goggles and flying helmets. It is thought that many preferred to fly in the cuff-rank jacket rather than the maternity tunic. (Tangmere Military Aviation Museum)

RIGHT: Three RFC officers, two pilots and one observer, posing for a photograph at Courcelles in France, late 1917. The second lieutenant, on the left, wears an RFC floppy style trench cap, cuff-rank uniform with RFC badges and breeches. The observer, a lieutenant, in the middle, wears a 1917-style, shoulder-rank uniform of his original regiment, the RE. The pilot, on the right, wears a cuff-rank uniform of his original regiment. The photo shows the variety commonly seen as well as the maternity tunic. (Mark Hillier Collection)

ABOVE: Lieutenant Horace Fulford, pictured on the right, wears his service-dress jacket with cuff rank. His collar badges are Royal Artillery, the regiment he was with before transferring to the RFC. He wears field boots and khaki breeches, typical of RFC aircrew before 1918. The officer on the left is wearing the 1917-style jacket with shoulder rank, and as this jacket is very light in colour it is probably khaki drill, as sometimes worn in the summer months. He is also wearing jodhpurs and leather gaiters. (Mark Hillier Collection)

LEFT: A second lieutenant pilot in France wearing a service-dress jacket with cuff rank, breeches and a field-service cap. He wears short boots and puttees. (Historic Military Press)

UNIFORMS

ABOVE: This fantastic image of both officers and NCOs features a lovely array of uniforms. In the rear row, second from left, an officer from a Highland regiment now qualified as an observer wears his glengarry hat and modified service dress. The officers are wearing a mix of service-dress jackets with cuff rank and maternity tunics, some of the later having collar badges and some not. A mixture of trousers, jodhpurs and breeches can be seen with short boots and puttees or field-service boots. There is also variety in the hew of the shirts worn ranging from a dark, rich-green khaki to a brownish yellow. The ties could be smooth and sometimes knitted but are nearly always seen with a gold tie bar which was approved for uniform wear. The hats worn are a mix of the 1902 stiff service-dress cap and the field-service cap. Some of the officers are wearing the softer, floppy trench cap. Two of the officers sport the early DFC ribbon on the left breast pocket. (Tangmere Military Aviation Museum)

RIGHT: A collar and tie. The tie could be woollen or made from a variety of cloths, with shirts varying in colour from khaki to a brownish yellow. (Phil Phillips Collection)

ROYAL FLYING CORPS KITBAG

ABOVE: Two shirt and tie combinations. The khaki one, on the left, is seen with a detachable collar and the silk one, on the right, with a collar already attached. Both would be correct for the RFC and many variations in shade were seen. (Simon Lannoy Collection)

RIGHT: A portrait of Lieutenant H.F. Neilsen-Jones, who served with 43 Squadron from March to August 1917. Here he is wearing a knitted tie with gold tie bar and has retained his regimental collar badges, as many did when coming from other regiments rather than direct into the RFC. He was a Squadron Leader Armaments Officer in the Second World War. (Historic Military Press)

ABOVE: Major Keith Park (later to become Air Chief Marshal Sir Keith Rodney Park GCB, KBE, MC and Bar, DFC) in front of his Bristol fighter. He is wearing short, brown boots with Stohwasser leather leggings, a pair of breeches, a 1917 shoulder-rank jacket with Sam Browne belt and under his RFC wings he wears the medal ribbon of the Military Cross and a rosette indicating a bar. With his shirt and tie he wears a gold tie bar. The collar badges indicate his original unit was the RE. On his head he has a Mk I lined flying helmet and goggle mask. The aircraft C814 flew with 48 Squadron when Keith Park was the Commanding Officer. (Tangmere Military Aviation museum)

ROYAL FLYING CORPS KITBAG

ABOVE and RIGHT: A good example of the cuff-rank service-dress tunic for a second lieutenant observer, with bronzed RFC collar badges and lovely gilded RFC buttons. (Phil Phillips Collection)

ABOVE and RIGHT: The cuff-rank uniform of an RFC pilot, the two stars of the lieutenant visible and featuring a nice pair of well-used RFC wings on the left breast. Regimental collar badges of the original unit are seen as well as the original buttons. (Mark Hillier Collection)

LEFT: A second lieutenant pilot of the RFC in 1917 shoulder-rank service-dress uniform. The rank badges moved from cuff rank to the shoulder around this date, although the modification was not officially recognised until much later. He wears a service-dress cap, breeches, puttees and short boots. His observer behind is still wearing his fug boots ready for flying and note he wears a wound stripe on his left cuff. (Mark Hillier Collection)

RFC OFFICERS' SERVICE-DRESS CAP, 1902 PATTERN

The 1902 Pattern officer's service-dress cap was identical to those in use by the army, of which the RFC was a branch. This style of cap remained in use well after the formation of the RAF in April 1918. Tailored in a twill gaberdine, the cap has the classic circular crown of the period with double vents either side. The leather chin strap is again typically thin and was secured at either side with a brass RFC button for an RFC officer but sometimes with general service buttons or even those from previous regiments if seconded to the RFC. The example seen opposite has an originally applied RFC cap badge in bronze and is fixed by two pointed blades. In many photographs officers seconded to the RFC are still wearing collar badges and cap badges from their original regiments just with RFC wings added to the uniform. The underside of the peak here is lined with what appears to be green leather. An interesting feature of this cap is a brass hinged arrangement which enables the brim to be raised or lowered, possibly to allow for a different appearance or for storage. More common from 1915 onwards are the softer style trench cap or floppy style and sometimes the cap known as the 'Gor Blimey'.

UNIFORMS

RIGHT: The RFC officer's stiff service-dress cap with bronzed cap badge and typical thin leather chin strap and a cuff-rank 1912 officer's uniform. This style of cap can be seen in period photographs worn with the maternity tunic and the 1912 Pattern cuff-rank uniform. Often RFC observers and pilots are seen wearing caps with the badge of their original regiments rather than RFC badges. (Mark Hillier Collection)

BELOW: On this particular officer's cap the name H.C. Duxbury is just discernible written in ink on the sweatband. Herbert Cecil Duxbury was a second lieutenant with 54 Squadron flying the Sopwith Pup. He was 18 years old and on an offensive patrol when he fell victim to Fritz Krebs in an Albatross of Royal Prussian Jagdstaffel 6 at 09.35 on 11 May 1917. Duxbury died in the crash and although buried, his grave was lost and he is now commemorated on the Arras Memorial. (Mark Hillier Collection)

ABOVE: An enlisted man's issue service-dress cap with a brass version of the RFC cap badge. The material is much coarser than that used for the officer's service-dress cap. This example is of Canadian manufacture. (Constructive Heritage Collection)

LEFT: This example of another version of a service-dress cap is thought to have belonged to Lieutenant John Sutcliffe. He flew R.E.8s with 6 Squadron and was downed on 9 August 1918 and became a prisoner of war, and was eventually repatriated on 1 January 1919. This cap was made in Toronto, Canada and so he may have acquired it from a fellow officer in the field. It has the typical bronzed officer's cap badge and thin leather chin strap, secured by two small RFC buttons. (Jason Hutton Collection)

LEFT: An RFC air mechanic wearing his service-dress cap and 1902 Pattern tunic. Note the abbreviated RFC shoulder badge and the even rarer badge of the Hampshire Aircraft Parks Battalion, Territorial Force on the epaulettes. (Simon Lannoy Collection)

UNIFORMS

RIGHT: An RFC pilot wearing an issue leather coat with map pocket over his uniform and officer's service-dress cap standing in front of his Bristol F.2.b fighter. (Tangmere Military Aviation Museum)

RFC FIELD-SERVICE CAP

Although used by some regiments of the British Army since 1891, the 'Austrian cap', or field-service cap, became the standard headdress for all ranks of the RFC in 1913. However, some officers retained their distinctive regimental 1902 Pattern dress cap with their service dress. The officer's field-service cap was often of a higher quality, and with bronzed badge and RFC Pattern buttons, although some can be found with general service buttons.

A letter from the Officer Commanding RFC Military Wing addressed to the 'Secretary War Office', which is dated 28 June 1913, confirms the suitability of this type of headgear:

> Sir
> With reference to War Office letter, No 55/Royal Flying Corps/3. (M.T.4) dated 18th inst, I have the honour to report that the drab serge field cap forwarded therewith is satisfactory and meets the requirements of the Royal Flying Corps (Military Wing). It should, however, be supplied with a strong chin strap and I have had one fitted to the sample which is forwarded herewith for inspection.[11]

This adoption was confirmed subsequently by a memo from the director of equipment and ordnance stores on 20 August 1913 to the quartermaster general of the RFC. However, initial comments on the new style were not complimentary and the *Outfitter* magazine was quite outspoken on the new style as can be seen in the clipping below.

ABOVE: A letter slating the field-service cap featured in the *Outfitter* magazine, 15 November 1913. (Mark Hillier Collection)

LEFT: A very nice example of an early RFC enlisted man's field-service cap with leather chin strap. Often surviving examples have hooks for the strap, but the strap has been removed. (Phil Phillips Collection)

ABOVE: An officer's private-purchase field-service cap. The material is of a better quality than the enlisted man's and the majority of officer varieties. Minus the leather chin strap, it has a bronze cap badge rather than the gilded metal one on the enlisted man's cap. (Phil Phillips Collection)

RIGHT: An officer's whipcord field-service cap with a bronze cap badge. (Mark Hillier Collection)

ABOVE: This photograph, taken in early 1918, shows all varieties of hats for both enlisted men and officers. The sergeant in the middle row, third from left, is wearing a trench cap, the officers a mix of service-dress caps and the floppier trench cap. The enlisted men in the rear wear the field-service cap. (Tangmere Military Aviation Museum)

ABOVE and RIGHT: An example of the RFC officer's cap with a white band denoting an officer cadet. The thin leather chin strap is secured by small RFC buttons. (Phil Phillips Collection)

UNIFORMS

ABOVE: An officer's 'Gor Blimey' cap, which was designed for winter wear. It has a floppy appearance and little stiffening to the crown. There is a neck flap with a chin strap in fabric which can be seen above the leather one. This allowed the neck flap to be let down. The hat creates a sort of balaclava for keeping the ears and neck warm. This hat is often seen in period photographs and was popular with the RFC in the field. (Phil Phillips Collection)

RIGHT: A group of officers from 39 (Home Defence) Squadron pictured wearing a wide variety of headgear, including the officer on the right with the black armband and a 'Gor Blimey' cap. (Historic Military Press)

RFC GREATCOATS, WARM COATS AND TRENCH COATS

Greatcoats

RFC officers' greatcoats were in thick khaki cloth with a fly fastening lapel to the right shoulder. The sleeves had cuff tabs and flapped pockets were a feature. Most officers who came from their regiments brought their greatcoats with them. After the war started and from about 1915 onwards officers preferred the British warm coat which was much easier to wear and extended to knee length. Rarely will you see any RFC shoulder titles on officers' greatcoats, but they are usually seen on the other rank's version. The enlisted man's greatcoat was knee length and the fabric was khaki serge. It had a wide falling collar but no shoulder straps for rank.

LEFT: The RFC officer's greatcoat of the pre-war variety. Note the turn-up cuffs, loop for rank boards on the shoulder, a double row of RFC buttons to secure and, typically, it extends below the knee. (Phil Phillips Collection)

BELOW: The RFC enlisted man's greatcoat with shoulder epaulettes. The coat was worn with RFC shoulder titles, either full or abbreviated. (Phil Phillips Collection)

RIGHT: Air Mechanic Harold Thompson wearing an enlisted man's greatcoat worn with RFC cloth shoulder titles, short, black boots and puttees. Note he carries a silver topped walking cane. (Historic Military Press)

BELOW: The wreckage of a Gotha being examined 'somewhere in the UK' by a sergeant of the RFC wearing an enlisted man's RFC greatcoat. (US Library of Congress)

ROYAL FLYING CORPS KITBAG

Warm Coats

The British warm first appeared in about 1914/15 as a military greatcoat for British officers. It was made famous, however, by Winston Churchill. According to Scottish clothmakers Crombie, the term 'British Warm' was coined to describe their version of the coat which was worn by about 10 per cent of officers and men. A British warm was typically designed as a heavy, double-breasted, wool coat made from a 100 per cent wool cloth known as Melton. It was taupe-coloured, had peak lapels and leather buttons, often epaulettes and was slightly shaped. It fell just above the knee and was sometimes belted.

LEFT: Lieutenant H.C. Fulford in front of his aircraft wearing a fleece-lined version of the warm coat. Fulford learnt on the R.E.8 during his pilot training with 15 Training Squadron at Doncaster. This photo was probably taken during the latter part of 1917 before he was posted to 85 Squadron, later becoming the armaments officer. (Mark Hillier Collection)

RIGHT: Known by the RAF as 'Coat, warm', this was an enlisted man's version from 1918. This two-flap pocket, fleece-lined item was worn by RFC and RAF alike, the label showing the date of manufacture as 1918. Note the leather buttons which were not RAF or RFC. (Phil Phillips Collection)

RIGHT: The label inside the enlisted man's warm coat. (Phil Phillips Collection)

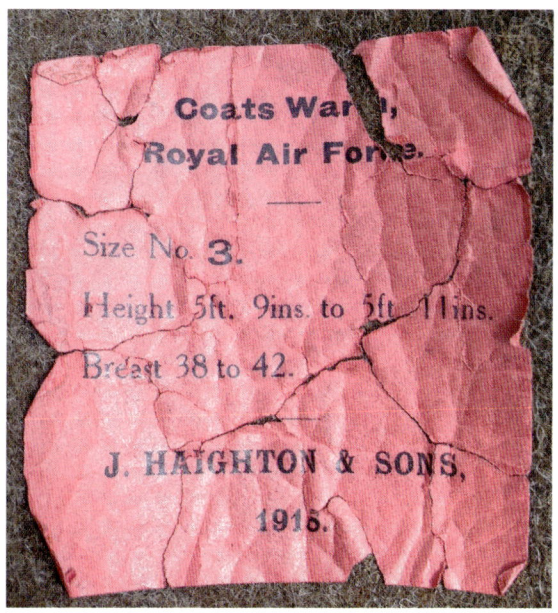

ABOVE: An officer observer wearing a Mk I flying helmet and goggle mask about to fly in his R.E.8 in a British warm coat. (Historic Military Press)

LEFT: This flight sergeant is wearing a warm coat, mounted services Pattern, with his rank on the sleeves but no RFC shoulder titles. The photo dates to the post-March 1915 period when the new flight sergeant badge was approved. He wears what looks like a 1902 service-dress jacket, buttoned down the front rather than a maternity tunic, khaki pantaloons for enlisted men, puttees, short boots and a service-dress cap with the RFC badge. (Mark Hillier Collection)

RIGHT: This officer in France in 1917 is wearing the British warm coat, short, brown boots and puttees. (Tangmere Military Aviation Museum)

Trench Coat

The trench coat was designed to protect from wind and rain. It was not the warmest of coats, but was supplied in a large size so that another coat and layers could be worn underneath it. It was often made from heavy duty cotton gaberdine drill. During the First World War, however, the trench coat was issued only to British officers and warrant officers 1st class and wasn't available for soldiers of lower rank. This helped to establish the trench as a coat of high standards and class and it was also available for private purchase from the likes of Burberry's. The kit list of the deceased Lieutenant Robert Taylor included a Burberry's trench coat.

UNIFORMS

LEFT and ABOVE: An example of the officer's trench coat belted at the waist. This one is classic beige in colour but it was also available in khaki. (Phil Phillips Collection)

RIGHT: A private-purchase trench coat, double-breasted and belted at the waist. (Historic Military Press)

ABOVE: This photograph, taken in April 1918, shows the variety of jackets worn in the field. This includes leather flying coats, the British warm coat and the trench coat, and the men are seen with RAF cap badges and also RFC caps, which was commonplace well into 1919. (Tangmere Military Aviation museum)

BELOW: An advert for a private-purchase Burberry's trench coat published in a 1916 edition of *Flight* magazine. (Mark Hillier Collection)

UNIFORMS

ABOVE LEFT: An officer cadet, denoted by the white band on his field-service cap, wearing a Burberry's trench coat, puttees and short boots. (Mark Hillier Collection)

ABOVE RIGHT: This photograph of three aircrew was taken in 1917, the officer in the front choosing to fly in his trench coat rather than a leather coat. (Tangmere Military Aviation Museum)

RFC OFFICERS' FIELD BOOTS

Many variations of field boots can be seen in contemporary photographs in light brown leather, some with lace-up fronts, some laced just part way, others with straps and buckles to provide easier access, and most were private purchase.

Denys Corbet Wilson, an early RFC pilot, wrote in a letter home on 29 April 1915:

> Will you send me out those old field boots, they are the ones I used to ride in, in Ireland; they lace up the front and are very deep in colour, almost black; not the light brown polo boots; they are probably with them, but the real old pair that lace up much further and are easier to put on.[12]

Often officers would fly in their service boots, as mentioned by Arthur Whitehouse, who had arrived as a gunner on 22 Squadron in 1916. He described the pilot with whom he was about to take his first flight, 'He was tall and handsome! I'd pictured him for months before. Fit and curly-headed with big green scarf around his throat. A short leather coat, field boots, and breeches.'[13]

Some of the field boots were tight-fitting and one would imagine not that comfortable at altitude as the higher you go the less air pressure there is. Air pressure changes cause a build-up of gas in the body, which leads to bloating, constipation and other related gastrointestinal issues. Meanwhile, the lack of movement during a flight could cause the build-up of blood around the legs, heightening the risk of deep-vein thrombosis. Tight boots or puttees would only add to an airman's woes, hence quite a number of photographs show pilots and observers later in the war in knee-length boots, fug boots or similar, for flying. However, some aircrew chose short boots and knee-length socks.

With regards to footwear, the only real stipulation for officer's field boots was that they were practical, suitable and of brown leather, hence why so many variations exist. Officers would sometimes opt for ankle-length boots with leather leggings or gaiters rather than puttees.

LEFT: This officer in cuff-rank uniform is wearing canvas-topped boots of an unusual style. (Mark Hillier Collection)

BELOW: A classic pair of officer's lace-up field boots, as seen in many period photographs. Again of brown leather construction, these were often favoured as they were looser round the top and easier to get on and off than some of the more tightly fitting varieties. (Phil Phillips Collection)

UNIFORMS

ABOVE LEFT: This RFC pilot or observer is wearing his long flying coat, long, leather gauntlets, a cowl helmet and goggle mask but has chosen to fly in his field boots. (Tangmere Military Aviation Museum)

ABOVE RIGHT: This pair of officer's field boots has laces to the ankle and leather straps with a fixed legging style top, again for ease of taking on and off. (Phil Phillips Collection)

RIGHT: This pair was owned by a warrant officer and has wide tops with a leather strap at the top of the leg. Warrant officers adopted similar dress to officers in the RFC. (Phil Phillips Collection)

LEFT and BELOW: A very typical pair of short leather boots of the type worn by warrant officers and officers of the RFC. (Mark Hillier Collection)

ABOVE: A pair of metal boot warmers that could be filled with hot water in cold and wet weather to help dry out field boots. (Phil Phillips Collection)

UNIFORMS

ABOVE: A pair of officer's Fox's private-purchase puttees. Puttee, also spelled puttie, is the name adapted from the Hindi word *paṭṭī*, meaning bandage, to describe the coverings used on the lower part of the leg from the ankle to the knee. They consist of a long, narrow piece of cloth wound tightly and spirally round the leg designed to provide both support and protection. They were worn by both mounted and dismounted soldiers, generally taking the place of the leather or cloth gaiter. (Phil Phillips Collection)

ABOVE: Leather leggings were popular and can be seen worn with short boots by many officers. They came with a variety of fixings and closures from laces to buckles. The pair on the left are secured by laces and the pair on the right are 1914 dated Stohwasser leggings. From the 1911 Dress Regulations it seems that brown Stohwasser leggings were virtually universal wear (with ankle boots) in service dress for officers below the rank of colonel, except for dismounted officers of the RE and infantry. Colonels and above could wear either butcher boots or ankle boots with black Stohwasser leggings. Early correspondence with regards to the choice of kit for aviation specifically mentions these and that it was considered that they were not suitable for aviators as they reduced circulation in the legs. (Mark Hillier Collection)

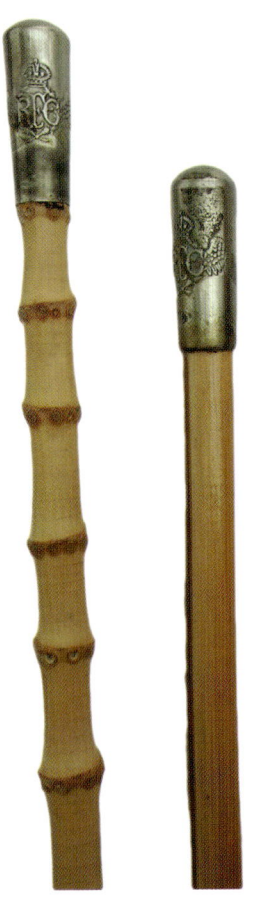

LEFT: A selection of silver topped RFC swagger sticks, bamboo or cane, often carried by NCOs or enlisted men, and again private purchase. The officer would carry a more traditional wooden stick with ball top or carved often from bits of aircraft wing struts or even propellers. However, there were no hard and fast rules on this topic and officers are also seen with canes. (Phil Phillips Collection)

RIGHT: An RFC air mechanic wearing a maternity tunic with field-service cap and carrying a swagger stick. (Historic Military Press)

Chapter 4
RANK, BADGES, INSIGNIA AND BUTTONS

RFC BADGES

Examples of cap badges, collar badges and pilot's wings were all sent for approval by the King in 1912, along with uniform styles and patterns for the new aeronautical branch. The ranks and styles of the badges changed a little after the war started. There was the introduction of new rank structure including flight sergeant and 1st class air mechanic, among others. There was also quite a variety of styles for flying badges as a result of various tailors producing them.

Some badges were commissioned for wear that were not officially approved, such as the combined pilot/observer's wings, although this was soon stamped on by higher authority. Pre-1915 the role of the observer within the aircraft was established but the duty was often taken up by another pilot. As such when the observer flying badge and role was finally formally recognised, some pilot\observers decided that they would instigate a new badge to identify the dual role undertaken by some, and a memo dated 22 March 1917 was sent around the RFC to the effect:

> Attention is drawn to Circular Memorandum 87/9062 (A.O.2) regarding the wearing of badges by all qualified pilots and observers of the Royal Flying Corps. Instances having occurred of pilots wearing wings with an O underneath, it is notified that no badge of this pattern has been sanctioned. Disciplinary action will be taken in the event of any pilot or observer found wearing an unauthorised badge. Lieut. Colonel W Warner[1]

This is not the only anomaly to arise. For many years bronze metal RFC wings with brooch backs or pin were used by officers and men of the RFC from 1912/13 onwards until cloth wings became the norm on service dress. No written record can be found relating to bronze wings, but this does not mean that these were not procured or used. They were private purchase and photographic evidence seems to confirm that bronze wings were used on service dress at the outset, although little written evidence can be found in the official records.

Gilt and gilded wings for mess dress and full dress were the norm and sealed patterns and embroidered versions of both were approved by the King at the same time.

It would seem that all was not well with the discipline of following dress regulations by pilots and observers, as on 15 December 1916 a message was sent out from the War Office to all units of the RFC stating:

> With reference to Army Order 40 of 1913, and 327 and 404 of 1915 (copies attached), I am directed to request that you will issue such instructions as will ensure that the authorised patterns of flying badges (embroidery on blue cloth for service dress) are worn by all qualified pilots and observers of the Royal Flying Corps, and that unauthorised patterns of these badges are not in any circumstances to be worn.

Again, this memo was issued by Lieutenant Colonel W.W. Warner, AAG for Director of Air Organisation.[2]

It is highly likely that variations of badges and dress regulations existed throughout the war and this even extended to how the badges were worn and in what position. Khaki-backed flying badges were also in existence, but they were clearly not authorised for wear and not common so have not been included here. The regulations said flying badges were to be worn on the left breast, but some photos of observers show the badges being worn somewhat in the middle of the chest. There are examples of NCO aircrew wearing officer-style maternity tunics with RFC collar badges which were not officially authorised for airmen. Some officers wore the RFC collar badges, others chose not to.

The role of observer was recognised in 1915 with the issue of the observer flying badge, and there is also evidence that some wanted to see the role of the gunner in two-seat aircraft similarly approved, and a design of badge was put forward for approval. A memo dated 10 June 1917 from the officer in charge of aerial gunners addressed to the Director of Air Organisation, Air Board states:

> I have the honour to forward the following proposal for your approval and authority. I have carefully considered ways and means to encourage my men to the greatest possible efficiency and to induce others to become aerial gunners. I respectfully beg to point out that although each point proposed appears on the surface perhaps a small matter, my conviction is that each will considerably increase the keen-ness of the men, and their general efficiency and bearing.
>
> That: - (1) each man, when he completes the Hythe Course of Aerial Gunnery and renders himself fit for posting overseas, be promoted to 1st A.M.
>
> (2) Men of good conduct, and at my discretion be granted four days leave with free warrants each six months service, providing the leave will not in any way interfere with their efficiency and duty; such warrants and passes to be signed by the officer I/C Aerial gunners.

RANK, BADGES, INSIGNIA AND BUTTONS

(3) a distinctive badge be worn on the right arm above the elbow, denoting that the wearer is a trained (H.S.A.G.) [Hythe School of Aerial Gunnery] Aerial Gunner. I beg to point out that in other Corps and regiments, a gunner's efficiency badge is worn.[3]

This was not to be, and no specific badge was given to those who flew as aerial gunners. However, permission was granted in 1917 for air gunners to wear the 'O' wing. At this stage of the war it must be noted that a significant number of gunners were non-commissioned rank. Below are examples of RFC badges worn by airmen, NCO and officers employed on flying duties, and this includes ranks down to air mechanic level. It was not just the NCOs and officers that flew on operational sorties, as evidenced by the three photographs of Sergeant S.

PILOT'S FLYING BADGE

The original RFC pilot's flying badge, or pilot's wings, was designed by senior officers General Sir Frederick Sykes and General Sir David Henderson. It consisted of the wings of a swift in white silk embroidery with the monogram of RFC encircled by a laurel wreath of brown silk. The monogram was surmounted by a crown.

The earliest known memo relating to the pilot's wings is dated 2 April 1912 and states:

> The flying badge should consist of a brooch or embroidered pattern about 3 inches long, of the design of a pair of wings (or similar design). It should be worn on all occasions in uniform on the left breast, above medals or ribbons, embroidered in the case of service dress, metal brooch in other orders of dress. All fliers of the reserve of the flying corps should wear this badge.[4]

No mention is made of the gilded or gilt badge, although it clearly says a cloth wing for service dress.

A letter relating to officers' uniform dated simply 1913 states: 'Special Badge – A flying badge is authorised for officers possessing certain qualifications. It is worn on the left breast above medals and decorations, in gilt for full dress, undress and mess dress; in silk embroidery on blue cloth for service dress. For mess dress the badge is smaller.'[5]

This was also borne out by subsequent Army Order No. 40 which communicated that cloth wings would be worn on service dress. However, photographs do exist of officers wearing gilt wings on the maternity tunic, although this practice soon stopped due to the impracticality of snagging and rubbing of the material. The gilt wings were later to be replaced on the full-dress uniform with the appearance of bullion wire examples on a cloth backing. The wings were given royal approval by King George V in February 1913 under Army Order No. 40/13.

A letter dated 17 January 1913 from the Director of Military Training to the Officer Commanding the RFC (Military Wing) laid out the circumstances in which the pilot's badge could continue to be worn:

> I am to inform you that the flying badge which has been approved for the Royal Flying Corps will be worn by: -
>
> (a) All military officers of the Royal Flying Corps as long as they remain efficient aeroplane pilots or, and in the case of airship pilots, provided they have once qualified as aeroplane pilots and remain efficient as airship pilots.

(b) All non-commissioned officers and men of the Military Wing or the Military establishment of the Central Flying School as long as they remain efficient as 1st or 2nd class pilots.[6]

Technically this meant that pilots returning to their military units and who were no longer flying could not keep their wings upon their uniform.

Army Order No. 20 of 1912 laid out the expectations of candidates who wished to obtain entry to the new aeronautical service and gain their wings:

> A gentleman not holding a commission who desires to join the Royal Flying Corps as an officer will forward his application to the commandant Central Flying School, quoting the number of his Royal Aero Club Certificate and stating which wing of the corps he wishes to join. If selected for the Military Wing, he will be granted a commission as 2nd Lieutenant on probation in the Special Reserve of Officers. The training of these officers will normally be the same as that prescribed for officers of the Regular Army, and they will receive under the same conditions the sum of £75, if they have obtained the Royal Aero Clubs Certificate at their own expense.

It was expected that pilots would qualify for an Royal Aero Club (RAeC) Certificate privately by their own means, although they could claim back some of that money expended through public funds and then go on to complete a Central Flying School course. To gain one's ticket in 1914 the pilot could, with good weather, complete the training within a week. The requirements included two 5km flights flown around two posts 500m apart with the direction of flight being reversed at each turn, so five figures of eight, an altitude-gain flight of 100m and the ability to spot land engine-off within 50m of a designated point (1914 rules).

This system was inadequate for the supply of pilots in 1914 as war broke out. The RFC opened flying schools at Farnborough and Netheravon and latterly at Brooklands for ab-initio pilot training to increase supply, and these were known as Reserve Aeroplane Squadrons.

The standard of training for those heading to the front line was not particularly great and essentially comprised only rudimentary flying skills, enough to climb, fly straight and level and land. Little thought was initially given to navigation, tactical skills, meteorology, principles of flight or even an understanding of the aircraft engine and systems. If the pilot picked up any information, it would enhance his survival chances.

Moving on to the CFS, more flying hours on a service type initially were delivered and, more importantly, solo flying hours which helped a pilot gain in confidence. Accidents were common but fatalities not as numerous as one would think to start with, with the first accident and fatality occurring in July 1912. By 1916 a pilot had to be able to demonstrate 15 hours flying solo, have flown a service type satisfactorily, done a 60-mile cross-country flight with two landings at an RFC aerodrome, climbed to 6,000ft and carried out night landings to achieve a flying certificate, but again no tactical training, formation flying or aerobatics or any sort but at least some basic navigation.

During 1916 three qualification certificates were introduced. The A Certificate consisted of a theory exam covering theory of flight, RFC organisation and artillery co-operation procedures. The B Certificate comprised tests of practical skills on aero engines, rigging, Morse and machine guns. The C Certificate was the flying test broadly, as outlined above. Once a pilot had completed all three, he could be awarded his RFC Flying Certificate.

RANK, BADGES, INSIGNIA AND BUTTONS

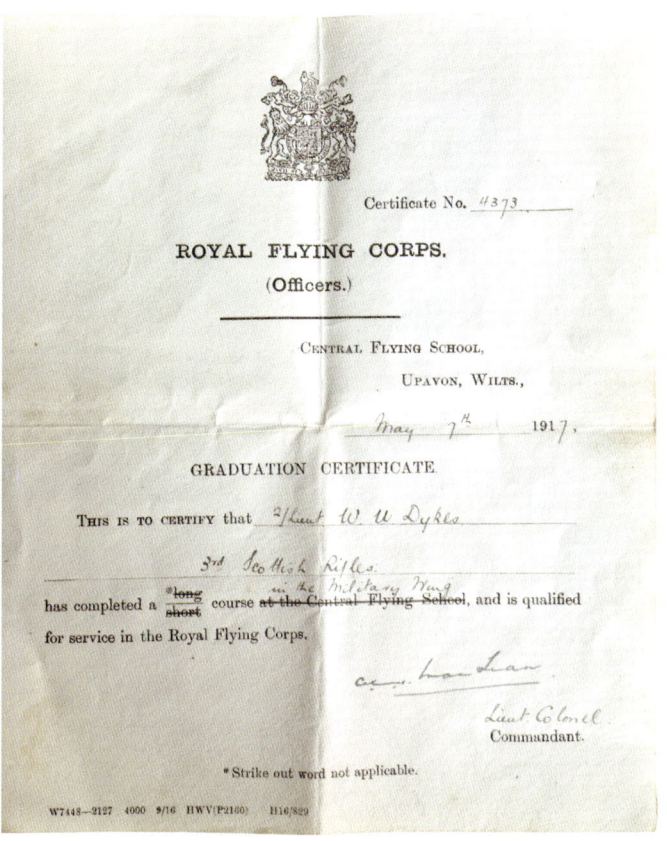

ABOVE LEFT and RIGHT: The RFC Flying Certificate, later known as the graduation certificate, awarded to Second Lieutenant William Urquhart Dykes. He was born on 4 September 1897 in Hamilton, Lanarkshire and was in 7 Squadron RFC up to 23 December 1917, when he was made a flight commander 'and to be temporary captain while so employed'. He then transferred to 9 Squadron. Both of these squadrons were at that time based at Proven aerodrome in Belgium, No. 7 at Proven East, and No. 9 at Proven West. Urquhart Dykes was injured in March 1918 and prevented from flying for a month. According to records, he was transferred from 106 Squadron to 105 Squadron on 25 March 1918. Dykes was appointed as a captain in November 1918 and survived the war. The photograph above right shows Dykes wearing his maternity tunic and Sam Browne with the rank of second lieutenant, shortly after the award of his pilot's badge. (Mark Hillier Collection)

In 1916 the system of training was rethought and included a degree of operational training, gunnery and formation flying etc., alongside more air experience and flying hours as well as recognition of the need to master the aircraft not just to be able to fly it in the most basic manner. This led to the birth of dedicated flying training units rather than utilisation of service squadrons for this purpose.

It is important to note that being a pilot was not merely open to those of commissioned ranks, and in fact NCO pilots had been written in to the RFC plan for its squadrons with

A. To graduate, a pilot must have:—

1. Received certificate A at Oxford or Reading.

2. Had ~~20~~ *25* hours ~~solo~~ in the air. *dual & solo combined.*

3. Flown a service aeroplane satisfactorily.

4. Carried out a cross-country flight of at least 60 miles successfully,—during which he must have landed at two outside landing places under supervision of a R.F.C. officer.

5. Climbed to 8,000 ft. and remained there for at least 15 mins., after which he will land with his engine stopped, the aeroplane first touching the ground within a circular mark of 50 ft. in diam.

6. Made two landings in the dark, assisted by flares (only applicable to B.E. and F.E. 2 pilots; pilots of other machines may do this at discretion of Wing Commanders and Commandant C.F.S.).

ABOVE: Part of the Training Brigade Transfer Card issued to Second Lieutenant James Barclay in 1917. By this time the requirements for graduation as a pilot had changed and the number of hours solo had risen from 15 to 20 and the height gain had increased. (Phil Phillips Collection)

RANK, BADGES, INSIGNIA AND BUTTONS

Size of Gas Mask — 1

TRAINING BRIGADE TRANSFER CARD.

Name J.O. BARCLAY   12892

Rank 2/Lieut.

Regiment R.F.C. (G.L.)

Date posted or attd. to R.F.C. 24·5·17

HISTORY OF TRAINING.
(To be filled in by Squadron Adjutants.)

	From	To	Date
1	Sgt. J. Glenton	40. T.S. ?	28·7·17
2	40. T.S.	66. T.S.	17·9·17
3	66. T.S.	72. Sq.	30·11·17
4	72. Sq.	3. T.D.S.	11-12-17
5	3. T.D.S.	103. Sq.	26·12·17
6			

*Insert School or Squadron—last entry to show date proceeding overseas.

W1849—H4197 8000 5/17 HWV(M767) H17/1189

ABOVE: Training Brigade Transfer Card belonging to Second Lieutenant James Oriel Barclay showing the units he attended for flying training in 1917. A change in pace and delivery of training to RFC pilots is evident from this. (Phil Phillips Collection)

Higher Training Squadron.

FLYING.

	Machine	No. of Hrs.	Signature of Officer Commanding	
Dual Control	AVRO	2.45	Jackson	Major
,, ,,	BE2E	1.35	Jackson	Major
,, ,,	RE8	.25		Major
,, ,,	D.H.q.	.40	F. Corray	MAJOR Major
	avro	.45		
Solo	AVRO	3.0	Jackson	Major
,,	BE2E	32.40	Jackson	Major
,,	RE8	4.0		Major
,,	A.W.	14.10	E N Fuller	Major
,,	D.H.q.	11.30	E N Fuller	Major
Fighting in the Air				Major
Contact Patrol				Major
Formation Flying	BE2E	4.0	Jackson	Major
*Aerobatics				Major
*All Tests for Category C.				Major
Firing from D.H.q. 100 rounds E N Fuller				

* Special Training as may be ordered.

	Date	Type of Machine	No. of Hrs.
GRADUATED.	23-11-17	RE8	41.50
Hours Flown Solo since Graduation		Types of Machines	
38ʰ-25′		BE2E, RE8, A.W., DHq. AVRO, CAUDRON	

Inoculation.
Vaccination.

5

ABOVE: Entries on Barclay's training card record his dual and solo flying time. Other sections include fighting in the air, contact patrols, formation flying and aerobatics, signs of role-specific training that only occurred on the job in the early days of the RFC. Note in particular the C Certificate, or the flying test, line, and although it is not filled in here, the graduation date entry would indicate completion of the A, B and C Certificates. (Phil Phillips Collection)

RANK, BADGES, INSIGNIA AND BUTTONS

only half of the established twenty-six pilots being officers. One of the earliest NCO pilots was Corporal Frank Ridd, who gained his RAeC certificate on 4 June 1912. However, by 1916 only 3 NCO pilots were flying in front-line squadrons and by August 1917 only 28 of 995 pilots were NCO rank, and this was the peak number for the entire war serving with the British Expeditionary Force.[7]

ABOVE and BELOW: A pair of gilt wings for dress uniform by J.R. Gaunt of London. The gilt or gilded wings style was introduced in 1913 and continued in use on mess dress and undress until 1916. This style was commonly replaced in 1916 by the bullion type wings, though some continued to wear the gilded wings on dress uniform until the unification of the RFC and the RNAS into the RAF on 1 April 1918. This example has a very typical brooch pin back, with the ends of the wings that the brooch pin is sat on forming a solid back, as is correct for the type. Some had a full solid back, some with just the ends for the pin mount. (Phil Phillips Collection)

ABOVE: An example of an RFC pilot's flying badge, as it was then known, with the feathers individually picked out by brown thread, all on a black, wool background. (Phil Phillips Collection)

ROYAL FLYING CORPS KITBAG

ABOVE and LEFT: Another variant with close-up view of the monogram in the centre. This is in a similar style to the above pilot's badge, with the feather detail being highlighted by a golden-brown thread. (Simon Lannoy Collection)

RIGHT: A second lieutenant wearing his maternity tunic and RFC collar badges with a very distinctive and attractive RFC pilot's badge. (Tangmere Military Aviation Museum)

RANK, BADGES, INSIGNIA AND BUTTONS

ABOVE: A very worn and tired looking RFC pilot's badge but typical of the style approved by the King in contrast to some of the more stylised versions. There are eleven feathers on each wing in this style. (Mark Hillier Collection)

ABOVE: A pair of wings sewn onto a maternity tunic which have suffered wear over the years and been re-stitched. There are many variations to the RFC cloth pilot's badge including red backing to the crown, wreath colour, droop on the wings etc. (Mark Hillier Collection)

ABOVE: A very nice classic variant of the pilot's badge with a red backing to the crown worn on a maternity tunic held in the collection of the Tangmere Military Aviation Museum. (Tangmere Military Aviation Museum)

ROYAL FLYING CORPS KITBAG

ABOVE LEFT and RIGHT: Two photographs of sergeant pilots that appeared in *Flight* magazine, 13 December 1913, the men having 'recently secured their pilot's flying badge, later known as pilot's brevet, at the Central Flying School, Upavon'. On the left is Sergeant David Patterson who passed on a Short biplane, Certificate No. 677 and went on to fly with 5 Squadron in France; he survived the war. On the right is Sergeant Fred Farrer who passed on a Maurice Farman, Certificate No. 685. He was posted to the aircraft park in France in 1914, gained a commission but was killed on 28 November 1917 while flying an R.E.8, no. A4474 at the Artillery and Infantry Co-operation School in Britain. (Mark Hillier Collection)

ABOVE: Two pairs of well-worn and faded RFC pilots' badges. The top is a flat pair while the bottom a padded example. They were worn by F.J. Bull, an RFC pilot who remained in the RAF until July 1919. On one occasion he was shot down and made a prisoner of war. (Tangmere Military Aviation Museum)

RANK, BADGES, INSIGNIA AND BUTTONS

RIGHT: A photo of Lieutenant F.J. Bull wearing his pilot's badge on a shoulder rank, khaki service-dress uniform with RFC collar badges. He started flying in 1917, becoming operational in France with 27 and then 99 Squadrons. He was shot down in April 1918 and went missing but returned to the UK in July 1918. (Tangmere Military Aviation Museum)

BELOW: An unusual and rare variation of the RFC pilot's badge with an O underneath denoting that the wearer was in their view dual qualified as a pilot and observer. Although never formally recognised or approved, it is clear that these wings were worn, also evidenced by the memo from Lieutenant Colonel W. Warner to all of the RFC quoted above. However, many observers went on to train as pilots and it may be that these wings originated with these airmen. The issue of khaki wings is also not easy to prove or disprove and while there is evidence of their existence, they were not approved by the King. They most likely existed in small numbers as an unauthorised private-purchase option. (Mark Hillier Collection)

RIGHT: Included for completeness and to show how the monogram changed from 1 April 1918, this is a nice example of the first Pattern RAF pilot's brevet. The design is slightly thinner at the roots than that of the RFC wings and obviously the monogram has changed to RAF. (Mark Hillier Collection)

ROYAL FLYING CORPS KITBAG

ABOVE: This fantastic photograph of NCOs with a mixture of pilots and observers is thought to have been taken in 1917. Most are wearing maternity tunics, but some are in the standard service-dress jacket which was issued when the supply of maternity tunics failed to keep up with demand in 1917. Note that some have collar badges on their maternity tunics, which was not sanctioned for NCOs. Interestingly, some wear the cloth 'Royal Flying Corps' shoulder title while others do not. There is also a good variety of styles of pilot's badges seen here. The individual standing fourth from left in the third row is interesting as he is wearing a 1902 Pattern tunic with RFC pilot's badge. This is probably due to war economy measures as the tunics were being issued in lieu of maternity tunics. (Mark Hillier Collection)

OBSERVER'S FLYING BADGE

Before the introduction of armed aircraft, the army identified the main role of aircraft reconnaissance. The need for an observer was established in 1912 and again in air exercises in 1913. They would take notes and help identify troop positions, trenches, supplies and encampments. However, these tasks were often carried out by pilots taking the rear seat, and sometimes other officers were borrowed to fulfil these duties. There follows a brief overview of the development of the role, but the excellent book by Wing Commander C.G. Jefford, *Observers and Navigators and Other Non-pilot Aircrew in the RFC and RNAS*, provides a great deal more detail.

The role of the observer was defined as aiding flight planning to help complete a given task, to aid reconnaissance by taking notes, use field glasses etc. and to report back findings on the destination on arrival back at the airfield. Who this 'observer' would be was not specified for some time.

Captain G.S. Shepard had flown in early exercises and put pen to paper to record his thoughts, mainly that an ideal observer would be an experienced ground-based officer with some technical skill which might be of value in the event of mechanical failure, and who had previously flown with the same pilot or group of pilots. Shortly after this an infantry officer, Captain H.H. Shott DSO, was attached to the RFC to fulfil the role of observer and appears to have been the first specifically non-pilot-trained officer to do so.

The first course for observers didn't commence until 13 July 1914 when ten officers arrived at Netheravon for training. Even when war broke out the RFC didn't have enough observers, and to start with the rear seat was often occupied by another pilot to carry out these duties. In 1914 men were specifically identified to be sent overseas as observers, but again these officers had very little in the way of aerial training and often learnt on the job and qualified while at the front. At this time the role was mainly being filled by commissioned ranks but some of the first airmen to be killed during the First World War were non-commissioned ranks.[8]

The observer was to play a key role in the future of air warfare, from operating a gun on a mounting for defence on the aircraft to being responsible for photographic reconnaissance, artillery spotting or assisting with navigation. It was clear that two-seaters needed a trained man and a recruitment campaign was started in 1915. Officers were seconded from artillery units to develop an understanding of the role of aviation but it was hoped that they might volunteer for observer duties.

The practice of using other non-commissioned volunteers to fly seemed to become a regular occurrence, with many of these men later qualifying in the field as observers. There was also a book available, published in June 1915 and called *RFC notes for observers*, which along with lectures on the squadron went some way to helping define what was expected and to give some advice. However, this was clearly no substitute for a formal training course, and by mid-1915 some observers attached to Reserve Aeroplane Squadrons, or service squadrons acting as training units, were receiving training in map reading and other key tasks.

One such ab-initio observer/gunner was Arthur Whitehouse, who referred to himself as a 'PBO', or 'poor bloody observer'. On arrival at 22 Squadron in 1916 he was issued his flying kit and happened to question his sergeant on when he might be promoted or given a flying badge. The response was:

'Of course, lad. Of course. When you've done yer fifty hours over the line and pass all yer tests on the ground, you gets yer wing. An "O" wiv one wing. We 'ere calls it' – he leaned over and whispered in my ear – 'we calls it the flyin' 'ole!'

I was stunned by the profane explanation, and the orderly-sergeant roared.

'But of course, matey,' he reminded, 'you'd better make out yer will on that blank page on yer pay and mess book. Fifty hours is a long time . . . up there'. I was young and the blood of youth ran in my veins. I never made out that will! But I had joined the Flying Corps – as an aerial Gunner![9]

On 11 June 1915, proof copies of the revised *Flying Training Manual*, Part II were circulated. The role of observer was described in Chapter 3:

Observation from aeroplanes can be carried out by the pilot single handed, but as undivided attention is necessary for observing, it is usually advantageous to carry a passenger who is free to devote his whole attention to the task.

The observer requires air experience and special training. He should have good eyesight, and possess sufficient Military knowledge to enable him to recognise units of all arms in their various formations and to be able to discern the most probable places in which to search for them.

He should be able to read Morse code.[10]

By the summer of 1915 the role had been even more defined by experience in the field and the fact that as most flights were now being engaged by the enemy, the pilots had their hands full with evasive action. Observers needed to know how to use a Lewis gun, an RFC camera, understand and utilise Morse code and carry out artillery co-operation.

Eventually the role was recognised by a flying badge, put forward by Major General Sir David Henderson, and the final version was approved by Colonel Branker on 23 July 1915. The badge was formally introduced in August 1915 by Army Order No. 327 which stated:

> IX – Badges for Observers, Royal Flying Corps.
> A badge consisting of the letter 'O' and an outspread wing, has been approved for wear by officers who are on the list of qualified observers of the Royal Flying Corps. The badge will be worn on the left breast, above medal ribands, in the same manner as the flying badge in worn by qualified pilots.[11]

This was followed shortly after by Army Order No. 404 of 1915 allowing the wearing of the badge by warrant officers and other NCOs who were qualified as observers. This was still, of course, a qualification that was only awarded after experience at the front. It was not until 1916 that the RFC started to offer formal training courses for its observers at Reading, Oxford and Hythe.

It is important to note that the numbers of NCO observers the RFC had on strength was recorded as 230 in January 1918.

LEFT: An observer flying badge on service dress with a Queen's South Africa Medal ribbon, worn on the left breast above the pocket. (Phil Phillips Collection)

RANK, BADGES, INSIGNIA AND BUTTONS

LEFT: Another example of the observer badge, this one with the O outlined with a separate thread. Sometimes the outline can be in gold bullion, and there are several variations of the type, most with beige silk for the wing but this one has a white thread. Most often the early ones are unpadded. The full-dress version was a silver bullion O and gold bullion wire wing. (Phil Phillips Collection)

RIGHT: A second lieutenant observer with what is commonly referred to as the 1917-style jacket showing shoulder rank, RFC collar badges and gold tie bar on his shirt securing the tie. A typical observer badge of the period is seen on his left breast. (Mark Hillier Collection)

BELOW: A well-worn example removed from a uniform showing the beige thread and classic shape of the RFC observer badge. (Mark Hillier Collection)

RIGHT: Two designs of observer badge put forward as samples for adoption but rejected. These were found in records at The National Archives at Kew. (Mark Hillier Collection)

LEFT: Observers were the only other recognised aircrew trade in the RFC and RAF for over twenty-five years, with the relevant half-wing originally authorised for the RFC under Army Order No. AO327/15 of September 1915. On uniforms worn day to day it was usually in a light brown or 'oatmeal' colour silk thread, but it was made in gold and/or silver bullion for the RFC full dress, or 'patrol jacket'. The RFC full dress was predominantly dark blue with scarlet detail, gilt buttons and collar badges, gilt cord epaulettes and, where appropriate, pilot or observer flying badge in bullion, either gilt too, silver or a mixture of both. This sergeant is seen wearing a cowl helmet and goggle mask. (Historic Military Press)

ABOVE: Three images showing one man's progression from air mechanic to pilot in the RFC. Samuel 'Paddy' Shepard Saunders joined the RFC in 1914 as an air mechanic, Service No. 1810, was posted to 1 Squadron and the volunteered for duties as an observer on the Western Front. After 50 hours of flying on active service he was awarded his observer flying badge at the rank of 2nd class air mechanic. He was then sent for flying training and awarded his flying badge as a pilot on 11 May 1917, gaining Aviator Certificate No. 4175. He then went on to become a sergeant flying instructor at Netheravon in 1917 and 1918. (Courtesy of Mrs Roberta 'Bobbie' Webb, née Saunders)

RANK, BADGES, INSIGNIA AND BUTTONS

RIGHT: This photograph of No. 6304 1st Class Air Mechanic Albert Horace Bayes, who served as an observer with 23 Squadron on the Western Front in 1916 and 1917, shows another variety of the flying badge. Bayes joined the RFC as an air mechanic on 14 June 1915 and was posted to France with effect from March 1916. He served on the Western Front and is credited with one claim of a German aircraft whilst flying in a F.E.2b. It appears at some point he was the observer of Lieutenant Wilfred Ferguson Macdonald, who later while on 18 Squadron was shot down by Werner Voss, a German ace eventually credited with forty-eight aerial victories. Macdonald was the twenty-ninth victim of Voss. Bayes posted a memorial to him in a number of papers in which it says he was the former observer of Macdonald. Bayes eventually re-trained as a pilot and gained his aviator's certificate, No. 6226, in 1918 and was commissioned, posted to 4 Training School and remained in the RAF until the end of hostilities. (Mark Hillier Collection)

CAP BADGES AND BUTTONS

The officer's cap badge is usually bronze, and die struck with the RFC monogram inside a laurel wreath. The cap badge should have the correct deep-patinated bronze finish with dished reverse and normally fitted with two flat-blade fastenings at the rear. The badge itself was developed along the lines of the RE badge with the laurel wreath and crown over but with the letters RFC in the centre.

LEFT and ABOVE: On the left a lovely officer's cap badge with blades on the reverse for fixing. On the right, for scale, is the same cap badge with a collar badge under to show the difference in size. These can be found with lugs for attachment. (Mark Hillier Collection)

ROYAL FLYING CORPS KITBAG

ABOVE: Nicely deep-bronzed officer collar badges as seen on a maternity tunic. (Mark Hillier Collection)

BELOW LEFT: A typical enlisted man's brass cap badge. These can be found with lugs for attachment or sometimes a slider. (Mark Hillier Collection)

BELOW RIGHT: An RFC so-called 'economy' manufacture cap badge from the 1915 period of simplified uniform. The cap badge is not fretted out but remains with a solid background to the 'RFC' letters. The reverse is of solid construction, with two fixing loops. This was a variant of the RFC badge and thought to have been produced as a war economy measure. Although the badge appears correct, there is much debate about its authenticity but it has been included here for completeness. So far it has not been possible to establish the provenance of the badge in any records. (Phil Phillips Collection)

RANK, BADGES, INSIGNIA AND BUTTONS

ABOVE: Tucked away in The National Archives at Kew are samples and sketches for uniforms, buttons and badges for the RFC. Some went on to be approved, others did not. This sketch shows the two proposals for the design of RFC buttons, the one on the right eventually being approved. (Mark Hillier Collection)

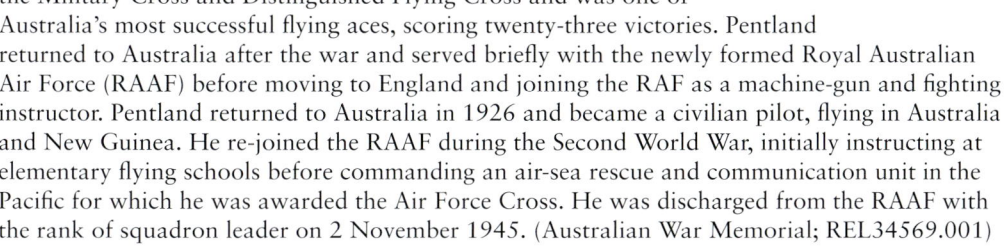

RIGHT: An RFC button to the approved pattern once worn on the uniform of Alexander Augustus Norman Dudley Pentland, known as Jerry. Born on 5 August 1894, at the age of 20 he enlisted in the Australian Imperial Force as a trooper with the 12th Light Horse Regiment in March 1915 and was assigned service No. 674. In August he was deployed to Gallipoli where he served with the 1st Light Horse Regiment as a machine-gunner. After contracting enteric fever in September, he was evacuated to England for treatment. Upon recovering, Pentland was appointed to a commission in the RFC in February 1916. He served with 16, 19, 29 and 87 Squadrons flying SPADs and Sopwith Dolphins. His service included both operational tours and instructor duties. By the end of the war Pentland had been awarded the Military Cross and Distinguished Flying Cross and was one of Australia's most successful flying aces, scoring twenty-three victories. Pentland returned to Australia after the war and served briefly with the newly formed Royal Australian Air Force (RAAF) before moving to England and joining the RAF as a machine-gun and fighting instructor. Pentland returned to Australia in 1926 and became a civilian pilot, flying in Australia and New Guinea. He re-joined the RAAF during the Second World War, initially instructing at elementary flying schools before commanding an air-sea rescue and communication unit in the Pacific for which he was awarded the Air Force Cross. He was discharged from the RAAF with the rank of squadron leader on 2 November 1945. (Australian War Memorial; REL34569.001)

ROYAL FLYING CORPS KITBAG

OVERSEAS SERVICE CHEVRONS

The overseas service chevron was created by the British Army in December 1917 and was awarded for each year of overseas service. Overseas service was calculated from the day the soldier disembarked from the United Kingdom. A blue chevron was awarded for each twelve months of overseas service after 31 December 1914 with a maximum of four blue chevrons. A single red chevron could be awarded for at least a year or more of overseas service before 31 December. The overseas chevrons were worn on the lower right sleeve of the uniform jacket and are often seen in portrait photographs from later in the war.

LEFT: Overseas service chevrons worn on the sleeve of the tunic, these ones denoting four years of service. The fabric beneath the chevrons shows it is an enlisted man/NCO's uniform, and therefore that the chevrons were often worn on the right lower sleeve. These indicate a year's service before 31 December 1914 (in red) and three subsequent years' service. (Mark Hillier Collection)

RIGHT: These three aircrew are posing in France, 1917. The second lieutenant on the left is wearing just his 1912 Pattern cuff-rank jacket, field boots, scarf and flying helmet but note the three years of overseas service denoted by the chevrons on his right sleeve. The other two are wearing leather flying coats with map pockets on the left breast and fur-lined flying helmets of the Mk I design with goggle masks which would have been all chrome tan leather. (Tangmere Military Aviation Museum)

RANK, BADGES, INSIGNIA AND BUTTONS

RIGHT: An RFC second lieutenant pilot who retains his previous regiment's service-dress, cuff-rank uniform. He was originally with the RE. The photo was taken in early 1918 as there is no red stripe for 1914, so this means he has served three years overseas, 1915, 1916 and 1917. (Mark Hillier Collection)

WOUND STRIPE

The British Army began awarding a brass wound stripe in 1916 after the promulgation of Army Order No. 249 on 6 July 1916, with approval by King George V. The badge was worn vertically on the left forearm and inset between the good conduct stripes, initially approved as a strip of gold Russian braid sewn to the lower sleeve of the right forearm. Later it was changed to brass and fixed through the uniform cloth as the cloth version soon tarnished. Additional badges were granted for subsequent wounds.[12]

ABOVE: An example of a brass wound stripe and its backing which was fixed through the uniform on the left cuff. (Mark Hillier Collection)

ROYAL FLYING CORPS KITBAG

LEFT: Taken in late 1917, this photograph of an observer shows him wearing a 1917-style shoulder-rank service-dress uniform with regimental buttons rather than RFC ones and two wound stripes. Although not named, the photograph was annotated as 'at Courcelles'. (Mark Hillier Collection)

BELOW: Two examples of the RFC shoulder title. These were approved for use in the early days of the RFC for wear on the left and right shoulder of the NCO's and enlisted man's uniforms. (Phil Phillips Collection)

RANK, BADGES, INSIGNIA AND BUTTONS

ABOVE LEFT: RFC shoulder titles in gilded metal or brass were for use on the full dress, although sometimes seen on the greatcoat. They were secured by lugs on the rear. (Phil Phillips Collection)

ABOVE RIGHT: As an economy saving, the full RFC shoulder title was abbreviated to just RFC. This would have been worn on the left and right shoulders of the greatcoat or uniform of the enlisted man and NCO. It was approved for use from August 1915. (Mark Hillier Collection)

RANK BADGES

Initially, at the outset of the RFC the rank structure for officers followed that of the parent organisation, in this case the army. The enlisted man's structure was more complicated, most starting as an air mechanic or 'ack emma', as they were known. The first NCO ranks in the RFC were warrant officer and sergeant. The first had a large crown worn on the sleeve of the uniform and the latter just three chevrons on the upper arm. The lowest rank to start was as the army, a private, but this was changed to air mechanic.

The rank of corporal was approved by Army Order No. 174/14 along with that of flight sergeant. The corporal rank adopted two chevrons on the sleeve while sergeants had three chevrons with a four-bladed propeller above. Flight sergeants initially had the same badges as sergeant rank with a crown over but in March 1915 a new badge was approved, a four-bladed propeller badge with a star boss.[13] In 1915 warrant officer 2nd class was approved by Army Order No. 70/15 with a crown worn on the sleeve, and the rank of warrant officer 1st class had an embroidered royal arms cuff badge approved. The rank of technical quartermaster sergeant was used by the RFC from 1915, identified by four chevrons pointing upwards but on the cuff with a star-bossed propeller above.

RIGHT: The cuff of a 1912 Pattern service tunic showing the two stars of a lieutenant. Rank on this style of uniform on the cuff was enclosed in a chevron tape forming a false cuff, one star for second lieutenant, two stars for lieutenant. The ring around the cuff also gave a quick indication of rank with a single ring indicating the lowest two ranks, as above, and two rings around the cuff indicating a captain with three stars within, and three rings for major with a crown, and one crown and one star for a lieutenant colonel. (Mark Hillier Collection)

In 1916 the rank of air mechanic 3rd class was introduced which meant there were three levels. Therefore a badge was approved for air mechanic 1st class, a two-bladed propeller with a circular central boss embroidered in cream and brown worsted onto a khaki ground cut closely to shape. This was approved from October 1916 under the authority of Army Order No. 322.[14]

As a result of problems identifying sergeant and flight sergeants due to the similarity of the four-bladed propeller badges, the RAF chose just a small crown over the three chevrons of sergeant rank which was adopted after 1 April 1918.

LEFT: A metal star/pip used on the shoulder of an RFC maternity tunic indicating a second lieutenant. Note the brass button securing the tab, and although horn buttons were more typical, all sorts of variations existed. (Mark Hillier Collection)

ABOVE: This photograph was taken at Netheravon and appeared in *Flight* magazine, dated 10 July 1914. The description states these are warrant officers and flight sergeants of the RFC. Crowns can clearly be seen on the sleeves of the maternity jackets denoting the rank of warrant officer. In the rear row, there are flight sergeants with crowns shown over the four-bladed propellers, although after March 1915 this was changed to the new flight sergeant badge with no crown over. (Mark Hillier Collection)

RANK, BADGES, INSIGNIA AND BUTTONS

ABOVE: An example of the simple crown badge to be found on the lower sleeve of warrant officers, as seen in the previous photo of staff at Netheravon, 1914. The warrant officer 1st class rank had a royal coat of arms badge on the sleeve and warrant officer 2nd class continued with this. Warrant officer 1st class grade is often given as sergeant major often in personnel records. Flight sergeants wore a small version of this crown over the three chevrons and four-bladed propeller until 1915. The RAF went back to three chevrons and a crown, as seen in later photos. (Mark Hillier Collection)

ABOVE RIGHT: This photograph of an RFC flight sergeant observer taken in 1917 shows the new badge approved in 1915 for use. The crown previously worn by a flight sergeant over the four-bladed propeller has been removed. This man has also seen action as he has a wound stripe on his left sleeve. (Mark Hillier Collection)

RIGHT: The four-bladed propeller badge with a star on the hub was worn above three chevrons for flight sergeants, and was approved on 4 March 1915. Prior to this date a crown over the four-bladed propeller denoted flight sergeant rank, although it took time for the NCO rank structure and airmen's rank structure to be fully defined. It is thought that these were manufactured in theatre, this conclusion being based on the poor quality of workmanship. (Mark Hillier Collection)

ROYAL FLYING CORPS KITBAG

ABOVE: However hard and fast the rules, you will always find photographs of First World War RFC airmen or officers that seem to break with convention or are difficult to date. Here is a DH.9, introduced into squadron service in 1917. The two NCOs standing next to the aircraft are a flight sergeant with a crown over his sergeant chevrons and a sergeant with a four-bladed propeller over his chevrons. However, on closer examination of the photo and dates, it is clear this is early 1918 but because the flight sergeant is wearing a crown over three chevrons it would indicate this is after April 1918, when the RAF changed the system of rank identification and adopted this style. This was mainly as a result of the difficulty of differentiating between sergeants under the previous scheme unless at close quarters, as both had propellers over chevrons. (Tangmere Military Aviation Museum)

LEFT: A group of squadron personnel in France, possibly 1918. The flight sergeant in the rear has just three stripes and a crown over. There is no date on the photo and as RFC uniform was worn and badges used after the introduction of the RAF on 1 April, it was probably taken just after that date. Note the NCO and air mechanic do not wear the RFC shoulder title, which also suggests post-April 1918. The officer wears captain rank on his shoulder and a wound stripe on his left sleeve with RFC cap badge. (Tangmere Aviation Museum)

RANK, BADGES, INSIGNIA AND BUTTONS

ABOVE LEFT: Squadron staff, pilots and observers, early 1918. In the middle is an RFC flight sergeant with just crowns over his sergeant chevrons as well as overseas service chevrons denoting three years' service. The RAF adopted this for their uniform. (Tangmere Military Aviation Museum)

ABOVE RIGHT: A set of sergeant stripes shown under an RFC shoulder title as the rank would have appeared before the approval of the four-bladed propellers in late 1913. This was also prior to the introduction of the flight sergeant rank in 1914 which had a crown over the four-bladed propeller. (Phil Phillips Collection)

RIGHT: A typical set of badges seen on the sleeve of an RFC sergeant, three chevrons with a four-bladed propeller above and the RFC shoulder title at the top of the sleeve at shoulder level used from about May 1914 onwards. When the rank of flight sergeant was added, initially the sergeant layout seen here with a crown over the propeller was used, but in March 1915 flight sergeants were given their own badge with a star-bossed propeller. Corporal rank was the same as the army with two chevrons worn on the sleeve above the elbow. At the outset of the RFC there were just sergeant majors (warrant officers) with a crown and sergeants with three chevrons. Warrant officer rank was worn on the lower sleeve and either a crown for warrant officer 2nd class or royal arms for warrant officer 1st class from 1915 onwards. (Phil Phillips Collection)

ROYAL FLYING CORPS KITBAG

ABOVE LEFT: A close-up of the four-bladed propeller used by sergeants. (Phil Phillips Collection)

ABOVE RIGHT: Badge of the technical quartermaster sergeant rank, approved in 1915 and worn with the point of the chevrons uppermost on the sleeve of the tunic. (Simon Lannoy Collection)

LEFT: A photograph of an RFC corporal, dated 1917. He wears a buttoned pocket maternity jacket, the rank chevrons on the right sleeve (worn both sides) and the RFC shoulder title clearly seen. He also carries a swagger stick. (Mark Hillier Collection)

BELOW: Simplified Pattern corporal stripes worn on the sleeve of the tunic, which were introduced in 1915. The corporal rank was approved in 1914. (Simon Lannoy Collection)

RANK, BADGES, INSIGNIA AND BUTTONS

ABOVE LEFT: An RFC corporal wearing his maternity tunic and field-service cap, photographed at Courcelles, France, late 1917. (Mark Hillier Collection)

ABOVE RIGHT: Air mechanic 1st class badge on a maternity tunic showing the position of the badge on the sleeve. It was approved in 1916 and is seen here worn under the RFC shoulder title. (Mark Hillier Collection)

IDENTITY DISKS AND DOG TAGS

All of the officers and enlisted men in the RFC and RAF would have carried an identity disk, or ID, tag. Some simply used the issued variety, whereas others had personalised silver tags, bracelets etc. They were used so that in the event of death or injury an individual could be easily identified and next of kin informed. The British Army started using aluminium discs in 1907. Army Order No. 9 of 1907 laid down that all soldiers should wear a single metal tag, with name, rank, number, regiment and religion stamped onto it. On 21 August 1914 a single compressed, vulcanised rubber, red-coloured disc replaced the metal tag, and two of these tags were to be carried.

An extract from the coroner's report on Lieutenant Cyril Wynyard Battye:

Battye, Cyril 1916 March 17th Netheravon
   Airman's Fatal Accident
   A young officer in the Royal Flying Corps, Lieutenant C W Battye, was killed at Netheravon on Monday, apparently as the result of trouble with the engine of the aeroplane in which he was flying.

ROYAL FLYING CORPS KITBAG

LEFT: A very early metal identity disk belonging to RFC No. 859, Air Mechanic Charles Albert Cordeaux. Before entry to the RFC he was a professional soldier who joined the West Kent Regiment in 1901 (aged 18), and served in Malta, India and Africa working with radiotelegraphy. He was discharged in May 1913 and joined the RFC in London on 4 September 1913 when he entered the Wireless Section of No. 6 Squadron. He went on to serve in Belgium (Abeale). In March 1917 he was transferred to No. 3 Stores Depot, Milton, as sergeant Major. In May 1917 he became a warrant officer and in April 1918 an officer in the RAF. In January 1919 he joined the Wireless Section, No. 19 Training Squadron, Curragh. (Simon Lannoy Collection)

RIGHT: The identity disk or dog tag of Lieutenant Cyril Wynyard Battye, showing his regiment, rank, name and religion. He was the son of Lieutenant Colonel Montague Battye and Charlotte Battye. Cyril was originally with the Royal Berkshire Regiment and went to France as part of the BEF in 1914. He was subsequently injured by a gunshot wound to the jaw and cheek, and found medically unfit for duty. Having returned to the UK, he applied for a transfer to the RFC and commenced flying training in October 1915, gaining his certificate on the 3 November 1915. He attended the CFS at the start of 1916, and having gained his wings was posted to 32 Squadron. He subsequently died of wounds sustained in a flying accident while piloting a Vickers F.B.5 Gunbus. (Mark Hillier Collection)

An inquest was held on Tuesday at the Military Hospital, Fargo Camp, on Tuesday, by the Coroner for South Wilts, Mr F H Trethowan.
Lieut John Wesley Honey, of the RAMC, stationed at Fargo Military Hospital, said he had superficially examined the body of the officer, and he detailed the principal injuries, which consisted of a number of broken bones. He said it was impossible to say what was the extent of the internal injuries, but those he had described were sufficient to cause death from shock, with the corresponding internal injuries which there must be.
Captain Hellyer, of the Royal Flying Corps, stationed at Netheravon Flying School, said that Lieut Cyril Wynyard Battye was 21 years of age, and his home address was 19, Castle Yard, Windsor. On Monday he was flying by himself at the School a Vickers

RANK, BADGES, INSIGNIA AND BUTTONS

fighter biplane. He was an experienced flyer and had done nearly 60 hours flying. Witness saw him go up. He had flown the same machine before and was taking it up at his own request. He was in good health. Before going up he ran the engine, and when he switched off witness did not think he turned the petrol off, because when he eventually rose the engine mis-fired, and witness formed the opinion that it was choked. He rose about 60 feet and then turned downward. The engine went worse and Mr Battye turned sharp into the wind, intending to land. He did not have sufficient height, and the machine side-slipped, nose-dived, and hit the ground, the nose falling vertically. Witness was about 400 yards away from the place, and he asked Lieut Seagrave to go for an ambulance, while he went to the machine. He found it smashed and Mr Battye in a dying condition. His examination of the machine showed no further cause for the accident, and witness was satisfied that it was in proper order when it went up.

Lieut Seagrave, of the Royal Flying Corps, corroborated Captain Hellyer's evidence and said he was with Mr Battye when he died at 3.30pm, about seven minutes after the accident.

The jury returned a verdict of Accidental Death.

The coroner requested the military authorities, in the event of any death occurring which necessitated an inquest, to let the police officer have all the information they can respecting the death, in order that it may be reported to him at once.[15]

LEFT: The dog tag belonging to RFC officer C. Rayner. His religion is shown as Church of England, but no rank or number are inscribed. Although there are a number of C. Rayners in the RFC records which makes it difficult to research this tag accurately, it is highly likely it was that of Clifford Rayner, appointed as an equipment officer in the RFC in 1916. All other candidates have a second name and the initial would have been included on the tag. (Mark Hillier Collection)

BELOW: A sample RFC armlet in The National Archives at Kew. It was approved for wear by RFC staff officers in the field or officers of the day to aid identification when working with other regiments. (Mark Hillier Collection)

Chapter 5
PAPERWORK AND DOCUMENTS

All branches of the armed forces have created many forms, memos, records and training manuals that give great insight into the relevant doctrines and methodologies. The RFC is no different, but the forms and paperwork are mostly identified by army numbers as this was the parent arm. As well as personal records such as flying logbooks, pay books etc., there were also RFC manuals and technical publications on aircraft rigging, engines and navigation, among others. Initially information relating to the RFC was published in two parts known as the *Training Manual RFC*, Parts I and II. These were dated 1914 and contained a fair amount of useful information on aircraft operations but in the grand scheme of things were still quite limited. The *Army Artillery Manual* of 1914 contains a couple of paragraphs on the use and benefits of aircraft and communication. As the war went on further technical publications became available as well as rigging information, aircraft engine details and a technical notes manual in 1916.

In this chapter examples of the paperwork that was important to the fledgling aviator, including the all-important 'ticket' or aviator's certificate and precious logbook, are featured. There are examples of the types of manuals used, training records and certificates of qualification. There was no doubt much more but paperwork from this early period rarely survives.

AVIATOR'S CERTIFICATE

Initially concerned more with ballooning, as opposed to heavier-than-air flight, the Aero Club was founded in 1901. By the time the club was granted its royal prefix on 15 February 1910, it had developed more of a regulatory role. Indeed, from that year the RAeC was responsible for issuing aviators' certificates, these being internationally recognised by the Fédération Aéronautique Internationale, of which the RAeC was the UK representative.

The importance of the RAeC following the outbreak of war in 1914 cannot be over-emphasised. Its members included – and trained – most of Britain's military pilots up

PAPERWORK AND DOCUMENTS

RIGHT and BELOW: This Aviator's Certificate, No. 5491, was granted to Ronald Albert Kingston on 15 December 1917, which was, in fact, the same day that he completed his test flights, in a Caudron Biplane at Bournemouth Aviation School. Born on 9 August 1900, Kingston's service records reveal that he did not enlist until July 1918, and it can therefore be assumed that he had acquired his pilot training through private means. It is known that he was posted to No. 2 School of Aeronautics at Oxford on 5 October 1918, transferring to No. 8 the next day. Following the Armistice, Kingston was demobilised on 21 January 1919, at his own request. Although RAF, this certificate has been included as an example used by the RFC prior to the transition. (Historic Military Press)

to 1915, when military schools became established. Indeed, by the Armistice in 1918 more than 6,300 military pilots had obtained the RAeC aviator's certificate. Such was the significance attached to these certificates that until as late as 1917 it remained a requirement that a pilot had to hold a RAeC aviator's certificate prior to being granted a commission in the RFC or RNAS.

To obtain an aviator's certificate, or 'ticket' as it was widely known, a prospective pilot was required to complete three separate, solo, test flights, all of which had to 'be vouched for in writing by observers appointed by the Royal Aero Club'. The first two 'distance flights' needed to be of at least 5km, 'each in a closed circuit without touching the ground or water'. The third test was the 'altitude flight', during which 'a height of at least 100 metres [328ft] above the point of departure must be attained; the descent to be made from that height with the motor cut off. The landing must be made in view of the observers.'

By passing this examination the pilot showed that he or she had gained control of an aeroplane efficiently and so could, in theory, take part in all aerial contests and displays run by the club. It is worth noting that the date listed on an aviator's certificate is, generally speaking, not the date on which the pilot actually made the necessary qualifying flights, but the date of the meeting at which the RAeC Committee granted the certificate.

ABOVE: Ronald Albert Kingston in RAF uniform, complete with his pilot's brevet. Having joined the RAF directly, he would have completed several phases of training before qualifying for his pilot's wings. First, he would have gone to a Cadet Training Wing where he would have received basic military training during a two-month course, including drill, physical training, military law, map reading and signalling using Morse code. Once completed, he would have been posted to a School of Military Aeronautics to begin a two-month course of military training and ground instruction. The topics covered included aviation theory, navigation, map reading, wireless signalling using Morse code, photography and artillery and infantry co-operation. He would also have learnt the working of aero engines and instruments and basic rigging. Finally, he would have started flying at a Training Depot Station (TDS). Ronald was expected to complete a minimum of 25 hours elementary flying training – both dual and solo – on Avro 504 aircraft logged over three months. Thorough ground instruction was also provided. This achieved, student pilots received the grade 'A'. Cadets remained at the same TDS for the second phase of their instruction. This two-month course included a further 35 hours flying time with a minimum of 5 hours on a modern 'front-line' type of aircraft. Student pilots also had to demonstrate proficiency in cross-country and formation flying, reconnaissance work and gunnery. Successful cadets were graded 'B' and commissioned. (Historic Military Press)

PAPERWORK AND DOCUMENTS

RIGHT and BELOW: The RAeC Aviator's Certificate No. 7409 which was awarded to James Terrance O'Brien Saint on 15 April 1918. From this photograph, it would seem he enlisted in the RFC prior to the change over to the RAF. (Scott Rall Collection)

ROYAL FLYING CORPS KITBAG

LOGBOOK AND ASSOCIATED DOCUMENTS

A pilot's logbook is his most treasured possession, where he can keep a record of his training, aircraft types, total times and combat sorties. Often, they are so much more and the comments in the log tell the story of that man's life, his adventures, toils and troubles, near disasters and for some the end of their lives.

At the outset of the RFC it was essential that pilots kept a running log of their flights. The pages in the books were divided into rows and columns, the format borrowed from ships' logs, and on one page a pilot penned the date of a flight, aeroplane used, passenger's name, time in the air and course flown. On the opposite page, he recorded height achieved, distance, weather and remarks. Early on flights were often limited by the aeroplane's performance and affected badly by weather and serviceability. The aeroplanes were slow, unreliable and often capable of carrying just an observer and flying for short lengths of time. In 1913, there were no stamps or endorsements indicating that such logs were mandated by authority. The purpose of the logs was to document the capability of the aircraft as much as that of the pilot. The army designated the logbook Army Book 425.

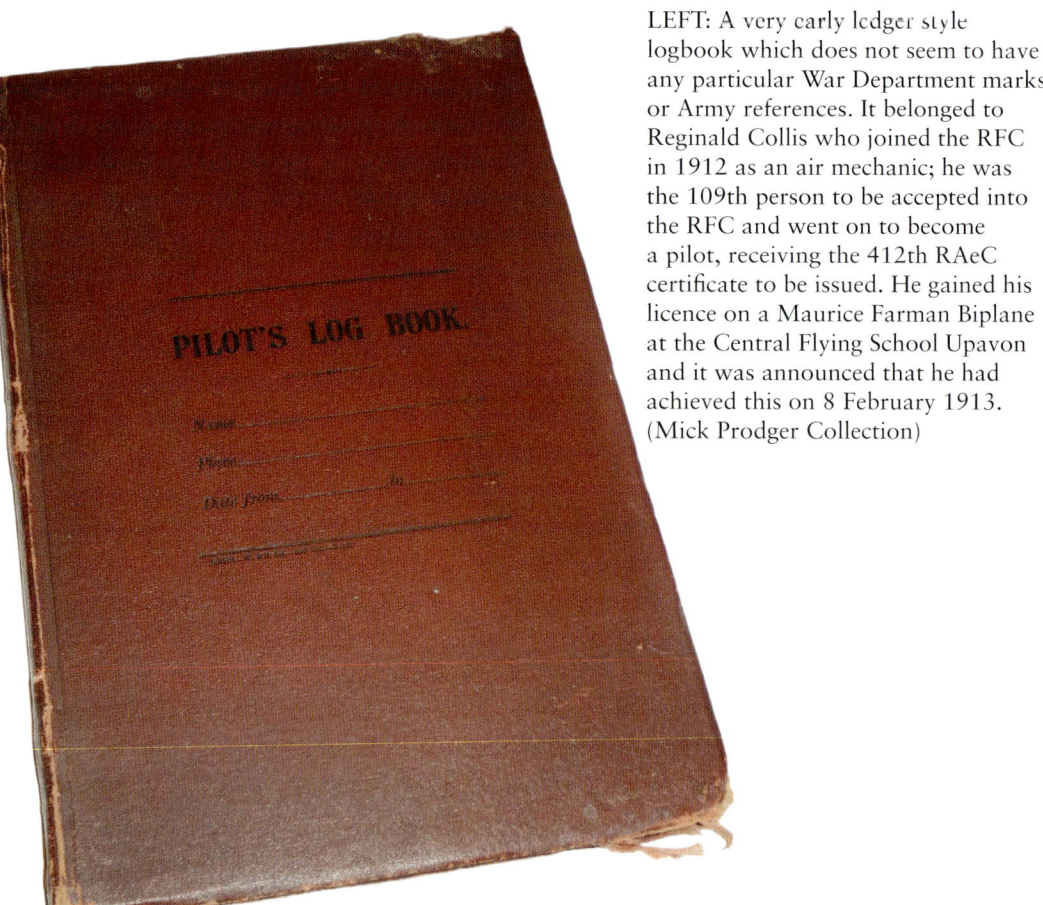

LEFT: A very early ledger style logbook which does not seem to have any particular War Department marks or Army references. It belonged to Reginald Collis who joined the RFC in 1912 as an air mechanic; he was the 109th person to be accepted into the RFC and went on to become a pilot, receiving the 412th RAeC certificate to be issued. He gained his licence on a Maurice Farman Biplane at the Central Flying School Upavon and it was announced that he had achieved this on 8 February 1913. (Mick Prodger Collection)

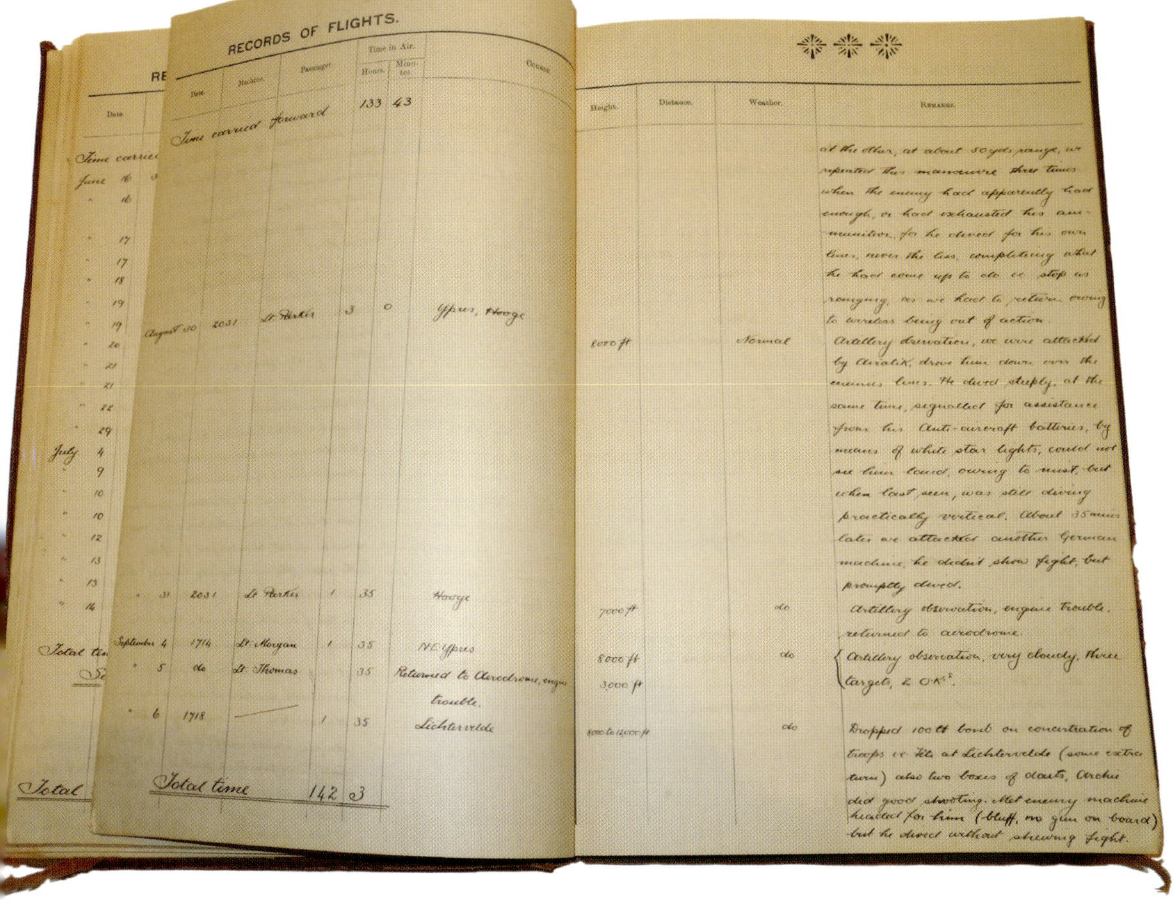

RECORDS OF FLIGHTS.

Date	Machine	Passenger	Time in Air. Hours	Minutes	Course	Height	Distance	Weather	Remarks
Time carried forward			133	43					at the other, at about 50 yds range, we repeated this manoeuvre three times when the enemy had apparently had enough, or had exhausted his ammunition, for he dived for his own lines, nevertheless, completing what he had come up to do ie stop us ranging, as we had to return owing to wireless being out of action.
August 30	2031	Lt Parker	3	0	Ypres, Hooge	8000 ft		Normal	Artillery observation, we were attacked by Aviatik, drove him down over the enemies lines. He dived steeply, at the same time, signalled for assistance from his Anti-aircraft batteries, by means of white star lights, could not see him land, owing to mist, but when last seen, was still diving practically vertical. About 35 mins later we attacked another German machine, he didn't show fight, but promptly dived.
31	2031	Lt Parker	1	35	Hooge	7000 ft		do	Artillery observation, engine trouble, returned to aerodrome.
September 4	1714	Lt Morgan	1	35	NE Ypres	8000 ft		do	Artillery observation, very cloudy, three targets, 2 OK's.
5	do	Lt Thomas		35	Returned to Aerodrome, engine trouble.	3000 ft			
6	1718	——	1	35	Lichtervelde	8000 to 12000 ft		do	Dropped 100 lb bomb on concentration of troops at Lichtervelde (some extra turn) also two boxes of darts, Archie did good shooting. Met enemy machine headed for him (bluff, no gun on board) but he dived without shewing fight.
Total time			142	3					

ABOVE: A sample of the neatly filled pages of the logbook of Second Lieutenant Collis who was announced as a 2nd class flyer with effect from 22 October 1913. He then went to France on 26 May 1915 serving operationally over Ypres in August of that year. The log shows entries from that period, during which he flew a B.E.2c. The 30 August entry shows that during an artillery observation patrol he was attacked by an Aviatik. (Mick Prodger Collection)

RIGHT: Included in Second Lieutenant Collis' logbook is this photograph of the wreck of one of his aircraft hanging precariously from the top section of a gasometer. The accident occurred on Collis' return to the UK in 1916. (Mick Prodger Collection)

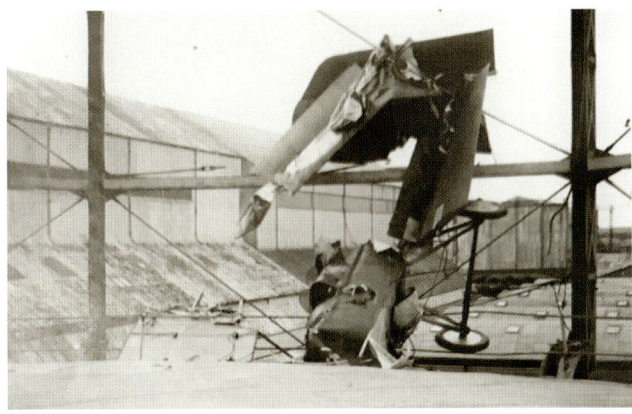

ROYAL FLYING CORPS KITBAG

ABOVE: Also from within his logbook, this picture shows Second Lieutenant Collis having been retrieved from the wreckage and awaiting medical attention. (Mick Prodger Collection)

LEFT: Some pilots opted for privately bound ledgers to keep their flying record in, such as this version belonging to Lieutenant M.D.G. Drummond. Generally containing information such as the dates, times and types of aircraft flown during a sortie, as well as any pertinent remarks, in the hands of the more descriptive aviator the logbook can offer a graphic insight into the life of a RFC airman. A veteran of both Gallipoli and Salonika, as he noted in the opening pages of his logbook, Drummond reported for the start of his pilot training on 14 April 1917, transferring from 206 (Horse Transport) Company, Army Service Corps. With this training duly completed, he was posted to 45 Squadron on 24 November the same year. He left for Italy, where the squadron was based while operating Sopwith Camels, on 12 December. (Simon Lannoy Collection)

PAPERWORK AND DOCUMENTS

Course	Remarks
Military School of Aeronautics READING.	Reported from 206 Coy H.T. ASC. Portsmouth. <u>14/4/17.</u> Did not finish course only there 3 weeks. Passed Vickers gun elementary test. Left <u>5th May 1917.</u>
Elementary Flying. 47 R.S. WADDINGTON Lincoln	Arrived <u>7th May '17</u> (unable to travel 5th + 6th on a/c malarial fever) Taken on strength 5th. Posted to 'B' Flight 47 RS. Transferred to 'A' Flight <u>17/5/17</u> Completed Solo flying on Shorthorn on 19 May 17. Passed Lewis Vickers & Wireless "Elementary". Left 47 R.S. <u>22 May 1917.</u>
Higher Training 54. R.S. HARLAXTON GRANTHAM.	Arrived 22 May 1917. Went to Oxford (S. of M.A.) to take exam (Cert. 'A'.) 4/6/17 and returned 8/6/17. Passed exam. Went to Spittlegate. 24th Wing course of fighting Inst. 21/6/17 Left for Turnberry 22/6/17 28 June

ABOVE: A summary page at the front of Drummond's logbook giving detail of his training prior to posting to an operational squadron. (Simon Lannoy Collection)

ROYAL FLYING CORPS KITBAG

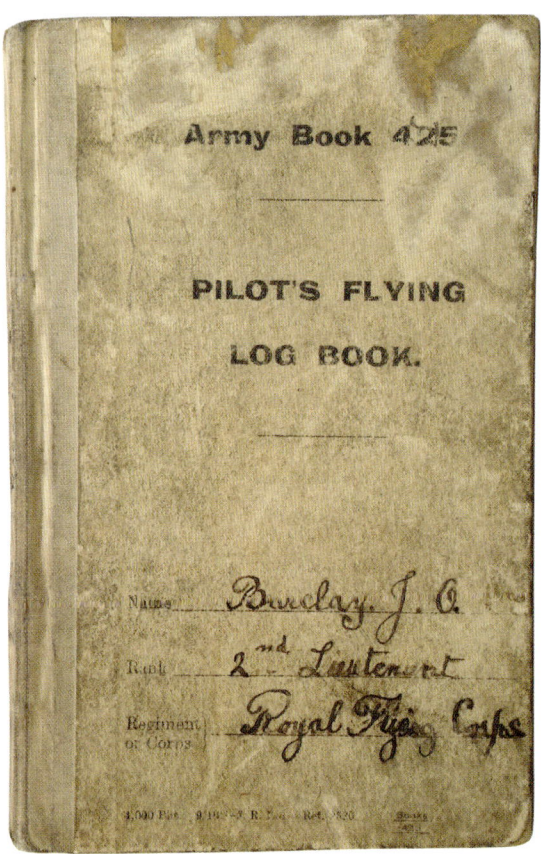

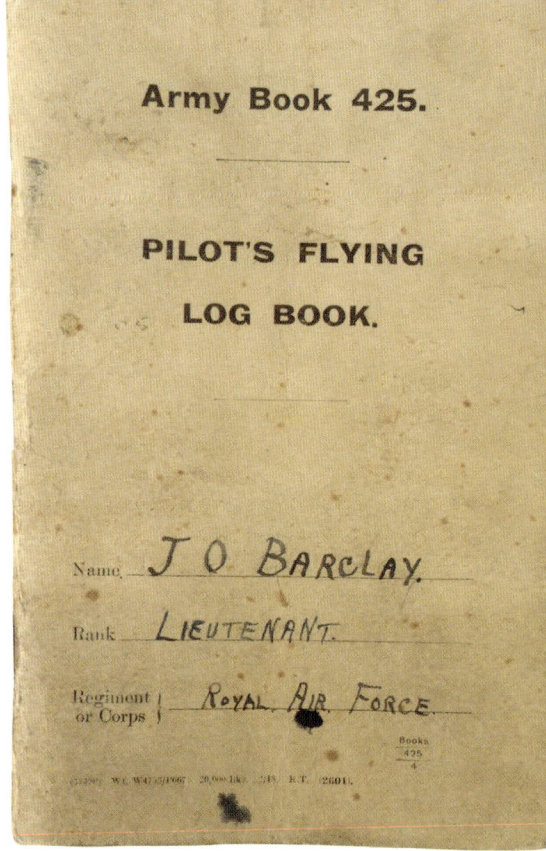

LEFT: Much more common is the Army Book 425. Having been issued to Second Lieutenant James Oriel Barclay RFC, this is a hard-back version with a canvas-strengthened spine dating to 1917. (Phil Phillips Collection)

RIGHT: Second Lieutenant James Oriel Barclay's later logbook which, dating to 1918, shows his transfer to the RAF. It is made of brown card and is stapled. (Phil Phillips Collection)

OPPOSITE ABOVE: The inside of Barclay's RFC logbook showing some of his training entries at 65 Training Squadron. Note the headings have not changed much since the earlier style log but the pilot has altered the wind direction and velocity column to 'Pilot' and the distance is now not recorded. (Phil Phillips Collection)

OPPOSITE BELOW: Contained within Barclay's logbook was a card showing he had undertaken an elementary and higher course in gunnery. This type of course did not exist much before 1916. (Phil Phillips Collection)

Pilot's Logbook

Date and Hour.	Pilot / Wind Direction and Velocity	Machine Type and No.	Passenger	Time	Height	Course	Remarks
19/10/17	Self	BE2E 4009	Solo	1-26	4000 ft	Sedgeford, Docking & District	Vertical Banks. (R+L.)
20/10/17	"	2980	"	1-25	2000 ft	1 Aerodrome.	Ground Strips.
"	"	"	"	1-10	2000 ft		Panneau.
22/10/17	"	4524	"	1-40	10,500 ft	Sandringham, Hunstanton & North Norfolk. No Good for Bombs.	Height Test. at 2500.
23/10/17	"	7214	"	1-35	3000 ft	Aerodrome. Bombs.	V. Gusty & Bumpy with Clouds.

Week 17/10/17 to 23/10/17.
Time for Week   Dual.   Nil.
  "   "   Solo. 7-15

Total - Since Commencement   Dual.   Solo.
  50 H.P. Gnome Caudrons   6-1   2-5
  80 H.P.   "   Avros   4-40   3 hrs
  90 H.P. R.A.F. BE2Es   2-20   7-35
                      Total   13-1   12-40

Total Time In Air Solo & Passenger = 28-21

Signed: O.C. No. 60 Training Squadron R.F.C.

GUNNERY CARD.

WING. .... **SQUADRON.** ....

NAME BARCLAY J.O.   **RANK** 2nd LT   **REGT** RFC GL

	TESTS.	LEWIS. DATE PASSED.	INSTRUCTOR.	REMARKS.	TESTS.	VICKERS. DATE PASSED.	INSTRUCTOR.	REMARKS.
ELEMENTARY	1.	✓			a	✓		
	2.	✓			b	✓		
	3.	✓			c	✓		
	5.	✓						
HIGHER	4.	20.8.17		70%	d	4-9-17		80%
	6.	20.8.17		85%	e	4-9-17		85%
	7.	22.8.17		75%	f	15.8.17		80%
	8.	22.8.17		70%	g	11-9-17		80%
	9.							
TOTAL TIME TO DATE		6 Days 12 hrs				½ hrs		

I certify that this Officer has passed all the above Tests initialled by me, or my Assistant.

WING INSTRUCTOR IN GUNNERY.

Certificate No. 6289

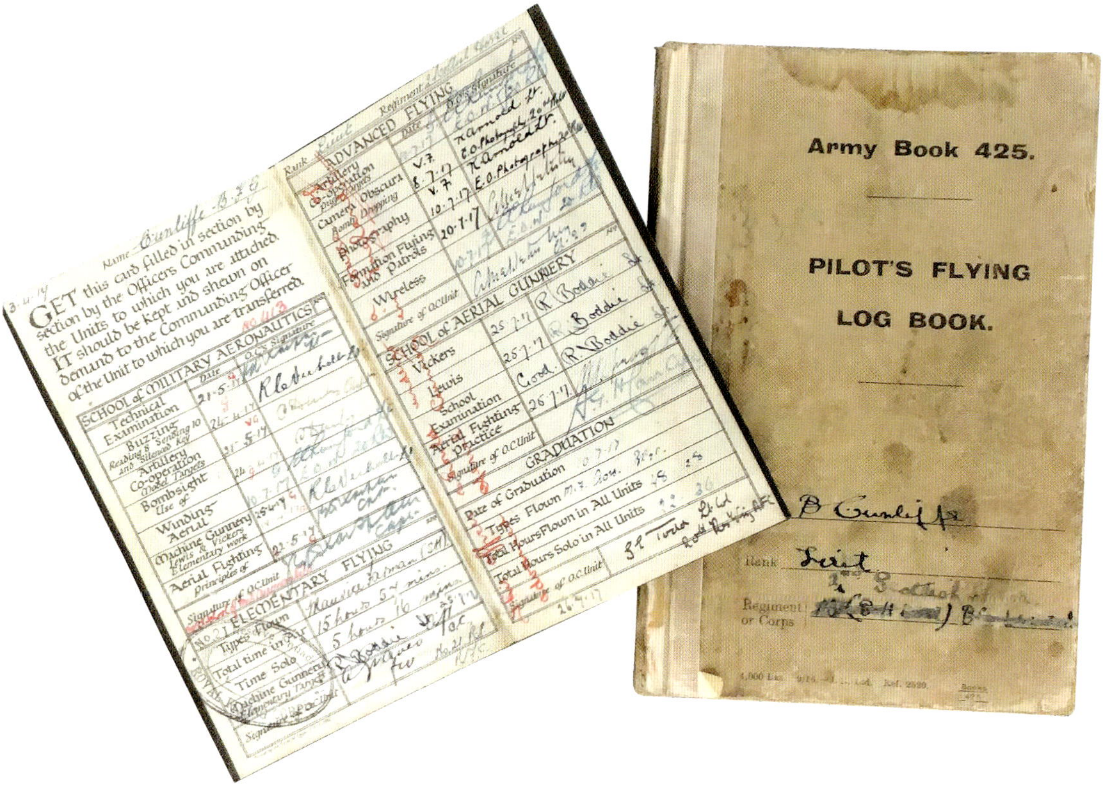

ROYAL FLYING CORPS.

(Officers.)

Central Flying School,

Upavon, Wilts.,

10th July 1917.

GRADUATION CERTIFICATE.

This is to certify that Lieut. B F G Cunliffe 2nd Scotth Horse, has completed a *long ~~short~~ course ~~at the Central Flying School~~ on the Military Wing and is qualified for service in the Royal Flying Corps.

Lieut. Colonel
Commandant.

* Strike out word not applicable.

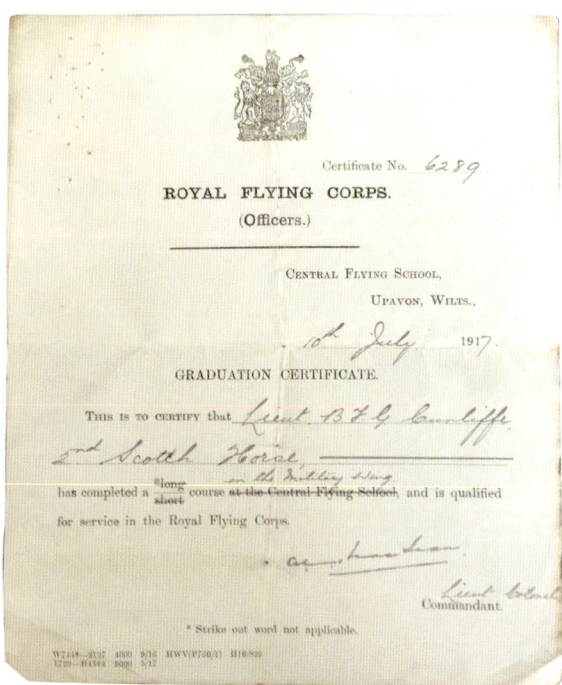

ABOVE: A further example of an RFC logbook (on the right), in this case that which belonged to Lieutenant B.F.G. Cunliffe, who completed his flying course and gained his wings on 10 July 1917. He remained as an instructor and survived the war. Miss Catherine Peake later became his wife and between 1918 and 1919 she served as a Deputy Administrator with the Women's Royal Air Force. Cunliffe left the RAF in 1919 but was temporarily re-commissioned in 1921 for further duty as a flight lieutenant. The card on the left contains details of his training. (Mark Hillier Collection)

LEFT: Lieutenant B.F.G. Cunliffe's RFC graduation certificate, which was issued by the Central Flying School Upavon, Wiltshire, on 10 July 1917. (Mark Hillier Collection)

PAPERWORK AND DOCUMENTS

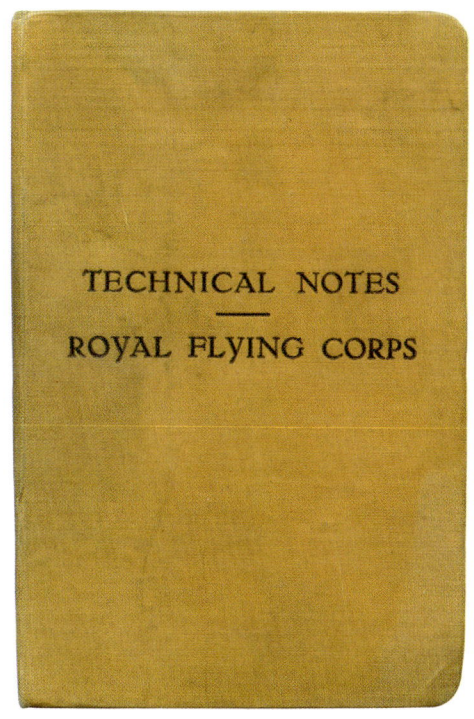

RIGHT and BELOW: RFC technical notes from 1916 containing information about various aircraft, rigging and engines. This example belonged to Lieutenant Vere Nathaniel Faber Surtees who was injured while flying with 9 Squadron on 27 July 1916. He made his own notes throughout the book on the technical aspects of various engines, aircraft and engine handling. (Mark Hillier Collection)

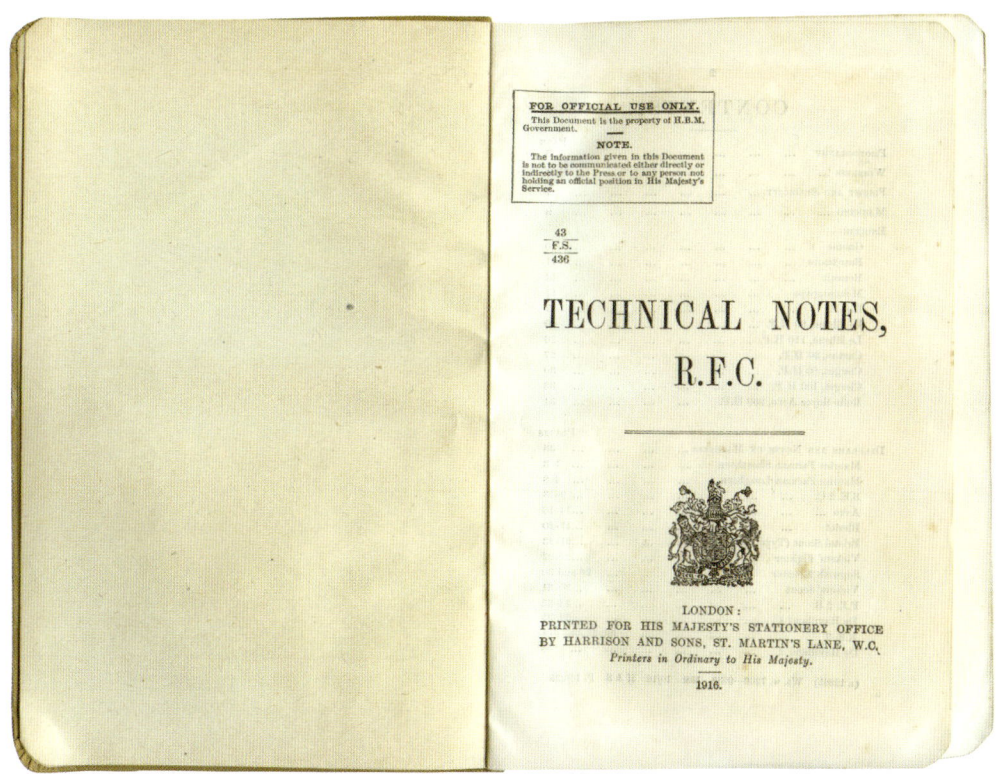

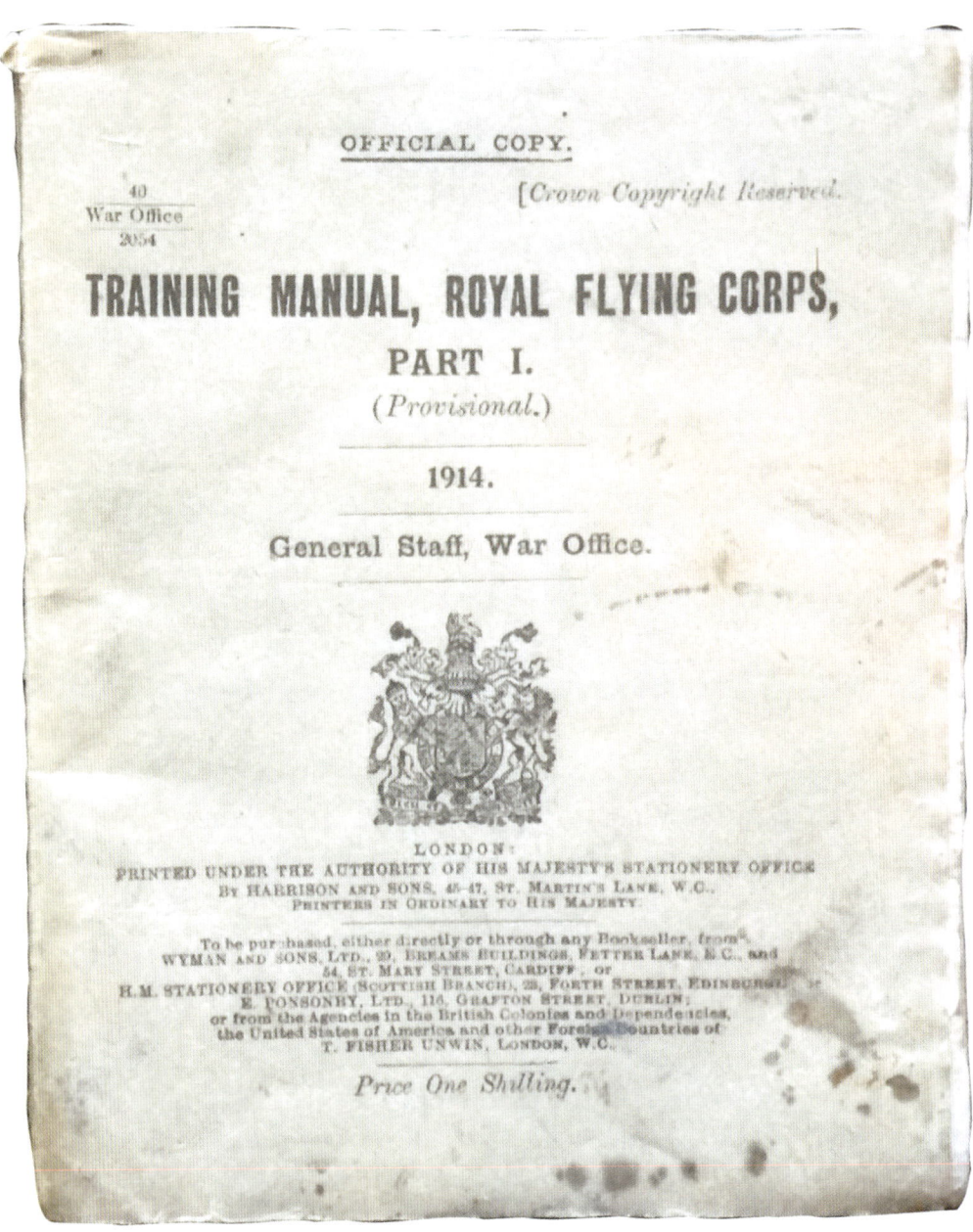

ABOVE: Part I of the *Training Manual RFC*, dated 1914 and published in May of that year. This was the first official RFC publication to be issued. It contains 190 pages of information on topics such as the care of aeroplanes, fabric, care and repair of engines, instruction on flying, basic navigation and meteorology among other subjects. Part II was published in June 1914, and amended in 1915. (Mark Hillier Collection)

PAPERWORK AND DOCUMENTS

RIGHT and BELOW: A soldier's pay book, or Army Book 54, that was issued to 2nd Air Mechanic Davies. It shows his date of joining in 1915 and that he was attached to 8 Squadron RFC. (Scott Rall Collection)

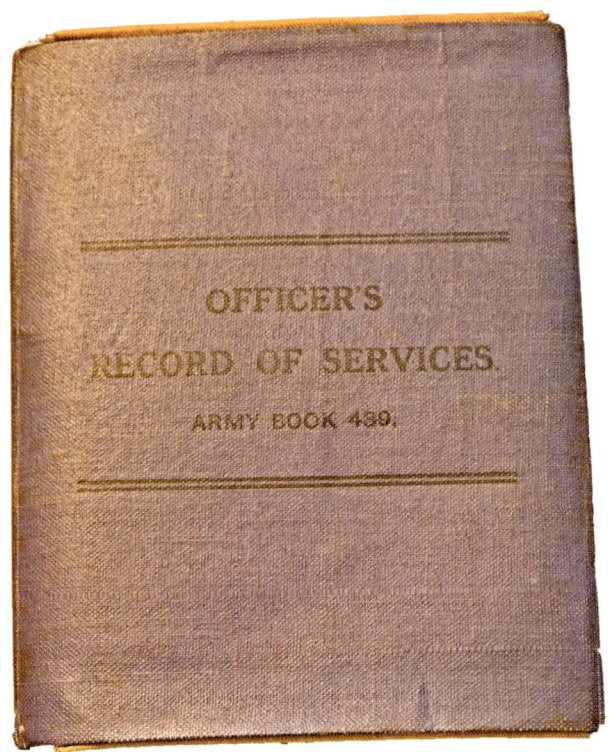

LEFT and BELOW: An officer's record of service book, Army Book 439, belonging to Second Lieutenant James Louis Goss who was originally an observer but was recommended for training as a pilot. He qualified as an observer on 8 May 1918 and was sent to 12 Squadron RAF. (Scott Rall Collection)

PAPERWORK AND DOCUMENTS

RIGHT and BELOW: A government-produced guide containing the silhouettes and outlines of various aircraft to aid recognition both from the ground and from air. This one was produced in 1915 and was issued to training wings. (Scott Rall Collection)

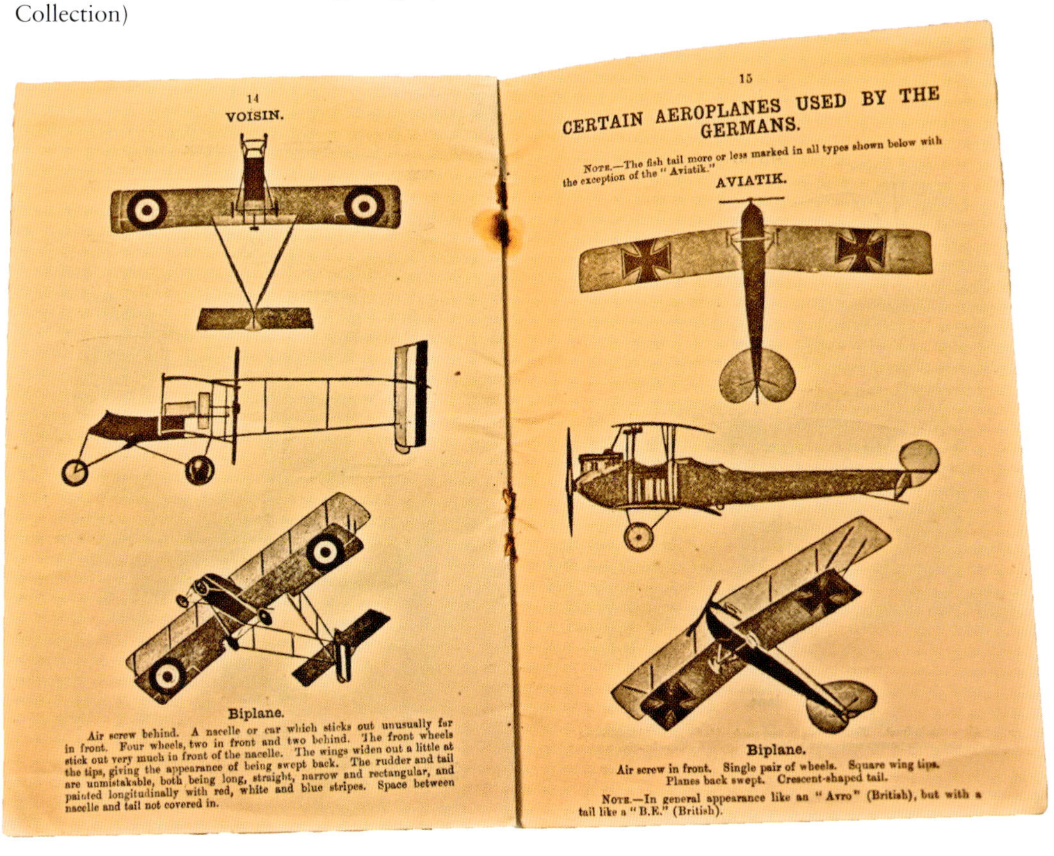

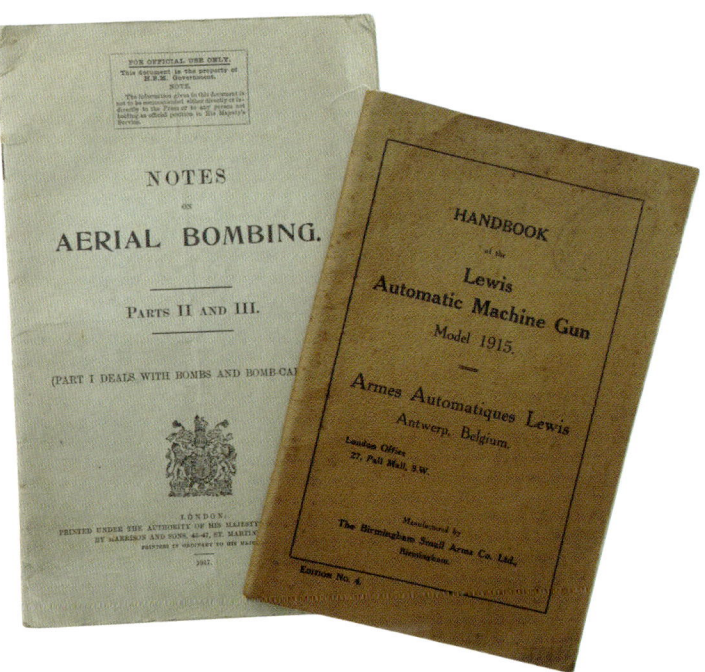

ABOVE: A number of guides were produced to assist training including this one on aerial bombing published in 1917. The one on the right is a guide and handbook for gunners using the Model 1915 Lewis machine gun. (Phil Phillips Collection)

LEFT: An example of a manual for the RAF 1a, which was a British air-cooled, V-8 engine developed for aircraft use during the First World War. Based on a French design, it was produced at the Royal Aircraft Factory and first ran in 1913, although an up-rated version was developed in 1915 and powered the B.E.2, among other aircraft of the period. Many pilots would have had copies of the technical information available as understanding the engine and its functions might have at times saved the day. (Phil Phillips Collection)

No. 1.

ROYAL FLYING CORPS (M.W.)

RIGGING DIAGRAMS

FOR

MAURICE FARMAN

SHORTHORN.

DIAGRAMS NOT TO SCALE.

RESERVE AIRCRAFT PARK,
FARNBOROUGH.

September, 1915.

ABOVE and OVERLEAF: For each aircraft type there was a small booklet for rigging and trueing up of airframes, this one produced by the reserve aircraft park at Farnborough in September 1915 for the Maurice Farman Shorthorn. (Mark Hillier Collection)

MAURICE FARMAN AEROPLANE.
SHORTHORN.

FIG. 5
Side Elevation.
Flying Position.

To bring machine into Flying Position, raise the tail and support in such a position that the Nacelle Longerons are perfectly level. This should bring the engine bearers also level, and the propeller will thus have a perfectly horizontal thrust. When upper longerons are short, use level on engine bearers. Tail Booms must be perfectly straight and correctly adjusted with the diagonals of each bay, (side Bracing Wires) exactly equal in length, and Struts V.W.X. parallel with struts of Main Cell.

FIG. 6
Main Planes and Undercarriage.

Longitudinal Adjustment of Main Cell and Undercarriage.
Erect Main Cell on trestles so that the inter-plane struts are perfectly vertical and a line connecting the leading and trailing edges perfectly level. Measurements taken from this line to the under surface of rear spar should show 40 millimetres throughout the length of the Centre Section. Check by plumbline, straightedge and spirit level as shown. Note that the dimension of 40 m/m applies to the Centre Section only. Under outermost strut on Left Hand Wing dimension would be 40-10=30 m/m. Similarly, under outermost strut on Right Hand Wing, dimension would be 40+10=50 m/m. (See FIG. 3 SHEET No 2.)

Undercarriage Front and Rear Struts, viewed from the front are perfectly vertical and in line with inter-plane struts above. When viewed from the side, the Front Struts incline outwards at the bottom. Measurement from the centre of bottom end of Front Strut to plumbline touching the leading edges of both planes should show 125 millimetres as shown in FIG. 6.

Instead of plumb-line, a large square may be used for getting the struts vertical. The lower limb of the square must touch the under side of Front Spar and TRAILING EDGE, and must be horizontal. Square shown in dotted lines.

FIG. 7.
Diagram showing setting of Tail Plane and Elevator.

With machine in Flying Position place a straightedge with one end touching the under side of rear spar, bring to the horizontal, and adjust Tail Plane to give a measurement of 35 millimetres as shown. Note that this dimension MUST NOT be exceeded. When control bar is in neutral position, Elevator should be set with a droop of about 15 millimetres below the line of rear part of Tail Plane, as shown. This is to allow for the extension of the controls under stress while flying.

ABOVE: 'Air Board Technical Notes issued by Controller – Technical Department', November 1917 and January 1918 print dates. Note the front cover states that the information within is not to be communicated to any person not holding an official position within His Majesty's Service. This book covers engines and has sections on the 90hp P RAF 1.A, 120hp Beardmore, 80hp Gnome, 80hp Le Rhone, 200hp RAF 3.A, 240hp Hawker Siddeley Puma and 110hp Clerget engines. (Historic Flying Clothing)

ROYAL FLYING CORPS KITBAG

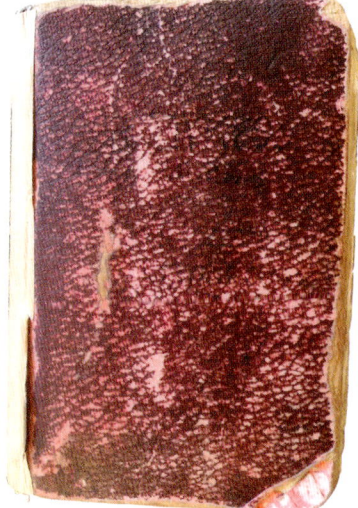
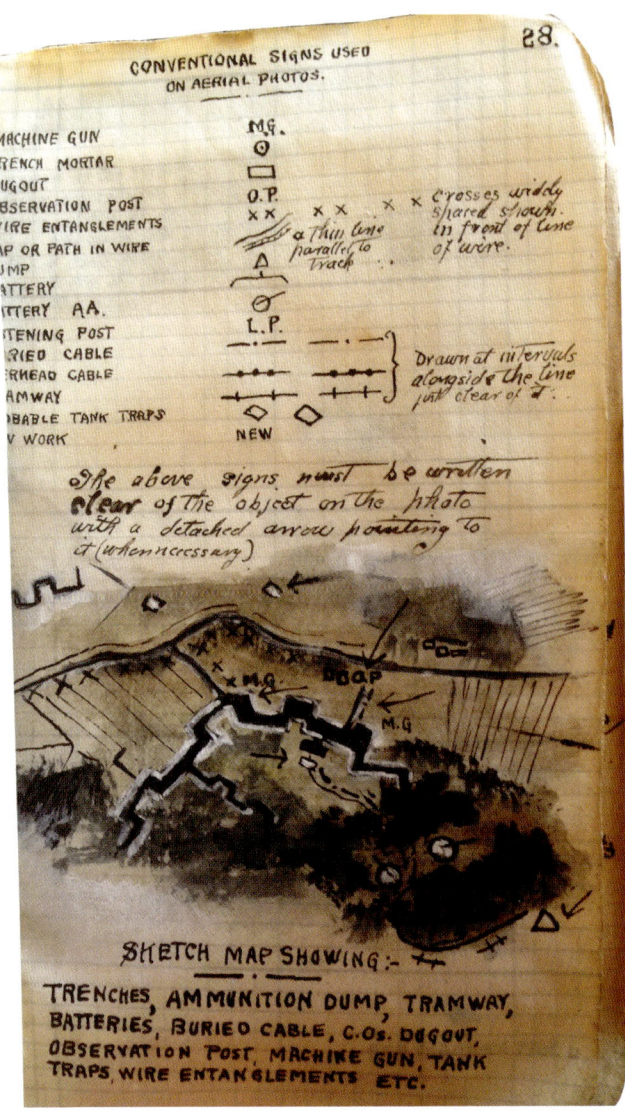

ABOVE, OPPOSITE and OVERLEAF: A notebook maintained by 1st Class Air Mechanic Robert Dykes, who flew as an observer and photographer. At the start of the war Dykes was originally with the BEF in Belgium and France and was commissioned as a second lieutenant into the Queen's Own Cameron Highlanders. Oddly, soon after, in 1916, he is found as a private with the Earl of Surrey's Regiment and Loyal North Lancashire Regiment. He then joined the RFC as an air mechanic 3rd class, working his way up to air mechanic 1st class as a photographer and by December 1916 was in a corps reconnaissance role at St Omer, flying in B.E.2E aircraft until April 1917 and then R.E.8s until end of war. He was active over Bailleul, Menin, Cassel and Wericq. Connected to the RFC School of Photography Training Brigade under Captain Scott at Farnborough, in January 1918 he was attached to RFC 3 Auxiliary School of Aerial Gunnery at New Romney, Kent. He later served in 53 Squadron RAF as an observer. He compiled an aerial photography training manual in 1919. The notebook has over sixty pages of very neatly written notes and diagrams on photography, maps, bomb dropping, gun camera, just a few pages of which are seen here as the book is too fragile to handle extensively and scan. (Mark Hillier Collection)

PAPERWORK AND DOCUMENTS

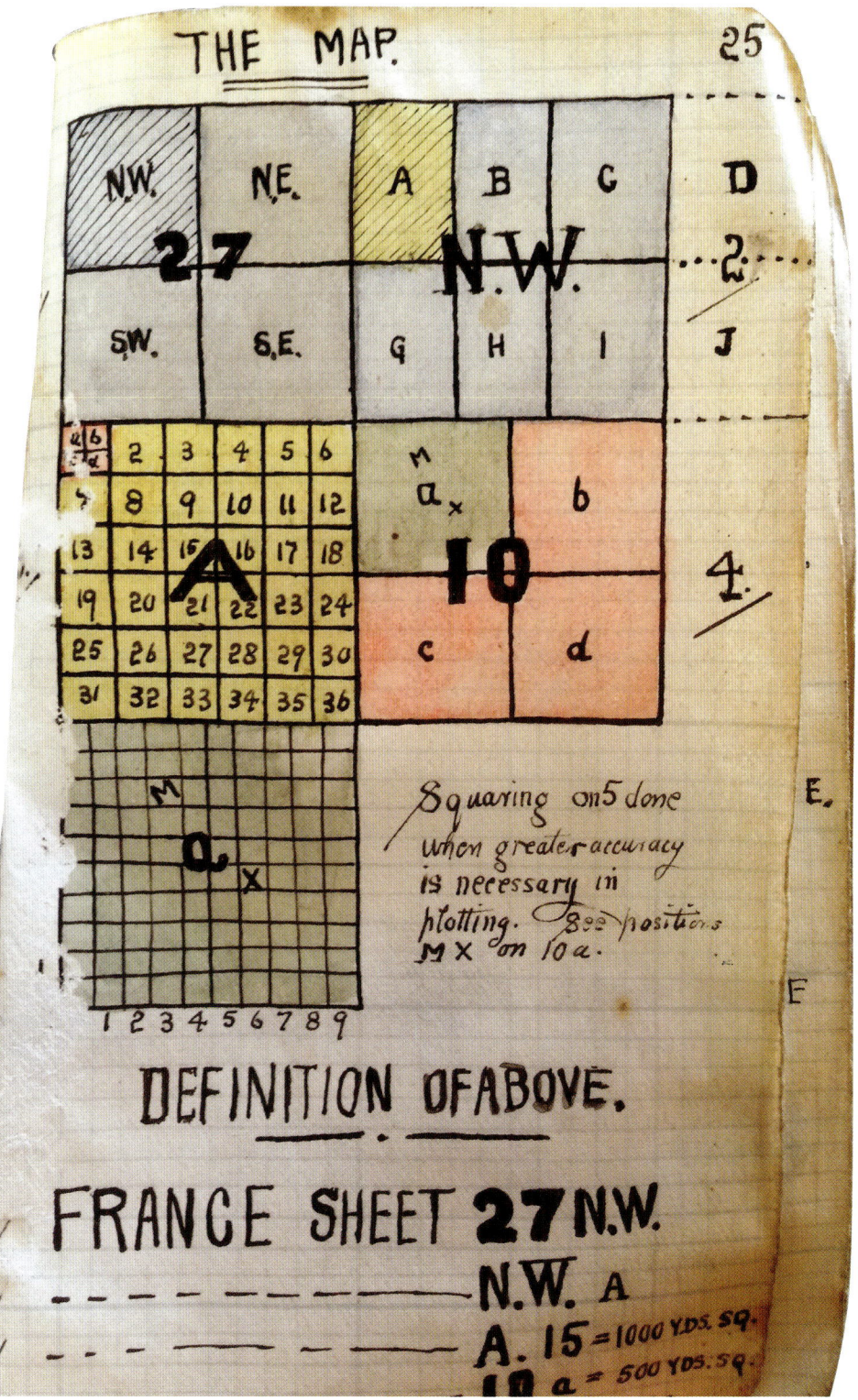

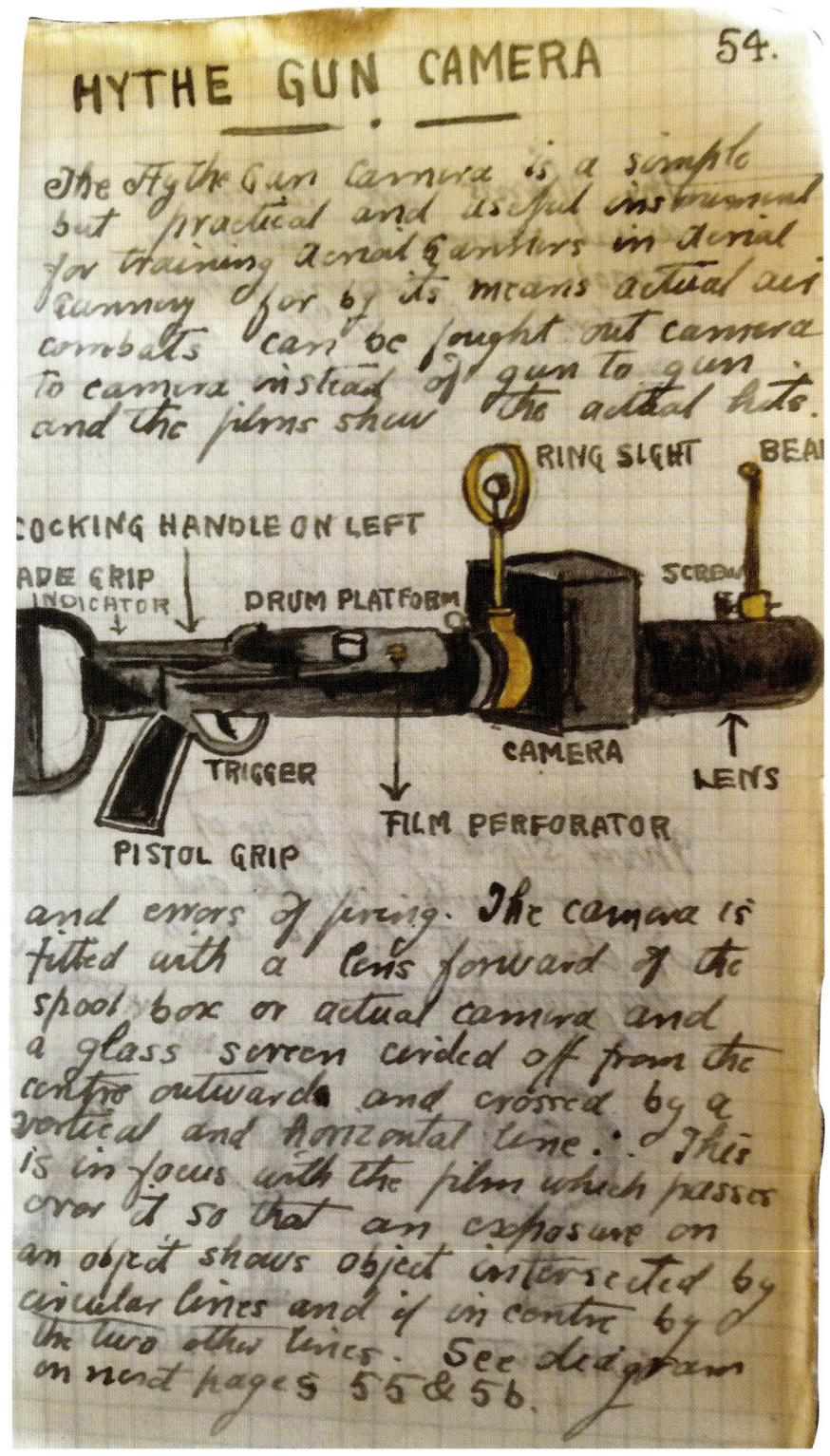

Chapter 6
RFC TO RAF TRANSITIONAL ARRANGEMENTS

Although the predominant focus of this book has been RFC kit and uniform, it is important to look at the period of transition to the new RAF to complete the story. This chapter highlights some of the problems with changing over uniforms and equipment in a time of war and the resultant variation. A representative sample of the different types of kit is included here as the development of uniform and the pace of change at that time deserves a deeper study and a book in its own right.

On 1 April 1918 the RFC ceased to exist and the RAF was born, and an amalgamation of RFC and RNAS badges and rank was decided upon, although the RAF eventually introduced a blue uniform. The transition was slow for a variety of reasons, one of which is mentioned in a letter from Captain Bogart Rogers, dated 9 March 1918, and featured in his book *A Yankee Ace in the RAF*: 'The RFC and Royal Naval Air Service are being combined and are to be called the Royal Air Forces. The uniform is to be different – I'll tell you all about it in the next letter – but most of the fellows are going to stick to what they have got. New uniforms are expensive luxuries these days.'[1]

Many photographs from the period after April 1918 until the end of the war show pilots and observers still in various states of uniform transition, some with maternity tunics, some with RAF khaki and as time moves on into 1919 more RAF blue uniforms.

The extract from *Flight* magazine, dated 4 April 1918, below details the changeover of uniforms for RFC and RNAS personnel:

SUPPLEMENTING the particulars given in our issue of two weeks ago, we are now able to give in full the regulations regarding the uniform of the Royal Air Force. They are as under: —

Khaki will be worn as service dress for the period of the war, after which uniform of the same pattern, but of light blue cloth, will be substituted as early as possible. The blue uniform may be worn by officers during the war as mess kit. The new uniform will not be made compulsory until sufficient time has elapsed for existing uniforms of the R.N.A.S. and R.F.C. to be worn out, unless an allowance is made to officers, when they will be expected to get khaki uniform as soon as possible. Further instructions on the latter point will be issued later. Uniform in khaki and blue may be seen in Room 751, 3rd Floor, North Block, Cecil Chambers, Air Ministry.

Service Dress During the War. Officers. Cap and Cap Badge. —

The cap is the same pattern as that worn by the R.N.A.S. The crown is khaki, and the peak and band are black. The badge is entwined laurel leaves, above which is a reduced facsimile of the metal bird at present worn on the sleeve by the R.N.A.S., the whole being surmounted by a crown.

Rank is denoted as follows: —

2nd Lieuts. and Lieuts. One upright metal bar on each side of the badge.

Captains: — Two upright metal bars on each side of the badge

Field Officers: — One row of gold oak leaves on the peak.

General Officers: — Two rows of gold oak leaves on the peak.

Jacket. —

The pattern is that of the military tunic Service Dress modified as follows: —

(a) — No shoulder straps;

(b) in lieu of 'Sam Browne' belt a cloth belt is sewn on the back of the coat, which fastens in front with a bright buckle of gilt metal;

(c) the buttons are the R.N.A.S. type — i.e., gilt metal with bird surmounted by crown.

Officers transferring from the R.N.A.S., and the R.F.C. will, on supplying themselves with Air Force uniform, wear rank distinction corresponding to that which they hold in their present service, whether their present rank is permanent or temporary.

Badges of Rank. —

Distinction Lace. — The badges of the Royal Navy in khaki braid will be used, with a bird surmounted by a crown, both in gilded metal, in lieu of the executive curl.

Rank is denoted as follows: —

2nd Lieut. No lace, but bird and crown on both sleeves where lace would otherwise be.

Lieut. One row of distinction lace surmounted by bird and crown.

Captain. Two rows of distinction lace surmounted by bird and crown.

Major. Two and a half rows of distinction lace surmounted by bird and crown.

Lieut.-Col. Three rows of distinction lace surmounted by bird and crown.

Col. Four rows of distinction lace surmounted by bird and crown.

Brig.-Gen. One broad row of 2 1/4 in. lace surmounted by bird and crown.

Maj.-Gen. One broad row and one ordinary row of distinction lace surmounted by bird and crown. Lieut.-Gen. One broad and two ordinary rows of distinction lace surmounted by bird and crown. General. One broad row and three ordinary rows of distinction lace surmounted by bird and crown.

Trousers and Breeches. —

As now worn by the R.F.C.

Shirts and Collars. —

Khaki shirts and collars with black ties.

Footgear. —

With breeches—brown field boots or brown boots with puttees or gaiters or brown stockings with shoes for aerodrome and similar wear. With trousers — brown boots or shoes with brown socks.

Greatcoat. —

The usual military type of British warm for mounted services.

Badges of rank will be indicated on the shoulder strap in the same way as on the jacket, by distinction lace surmounted by bird and crown.

Distinguishing Marks. —

For Pilots. —

The 'Wings' of the R.F.C. on the left breast, with the substitution of the letters 'R.FC.' for 'R.A.F.'

For Observers. — The 'Half Wing' with the letter 'O' as at present worn by observers in the R.F.C.

For Medical Officers. — The badge of Caduceus of Mercury on the lapels of the jacket. The cap will be the ordinary cap of the Air Force officer.

Blue Uniform used as Mess Kit. —

The blue uniform is the same pattern as the khaki uniform, except that gold braid is worn instead of khaki braid. White shirts and collars and black ties will be worn, and black boots or shoes.

Warrant Officers, 1st Class. Cap and Cap Badge. —

The cap and cap badge will be the same as for officers, but with no bars on each side of the badge. Uniform (including great coat) will be of the same pattern as for officers, but the cloth will be of the texture issued by the R.A.C.D. Rank will be denoted by a bird surmounted by a crown, both in gilt metal, and worn on both sleeves close to the shoulder. Warrant Officers — 2nd Class, N.C.Os., and Men.

Cap and Badge. —

The same pattern as at present issued to petty officers in the Royal Navy, but with khaki crown and black peak. A bird is substituted for the anchor on the Royal Navy badge. Warrant officers 2nd class and N.C.Os. will wear a gold embroidered badge, and men a worsted embroidered badge.[2]

RAF KHAKI UNIFORM

The 1918 Pattern RAF tunic was intended to replace the RFC cuff-ranked and shoulder-ranked tunics and was introduced at the same time as a sky-blue uniform with Russian gold braid. However, this uniform was initially so unpopular and in short supply that officers were permitted to continue to wear the 1918 Pattern, as mentioned in RAF Orders, well into 1919. The replacement RAF No. 1 blue uniform design has remained largely unchanged apart from the shade of blue to the present day.

On the khaki uniform, each cuff has a two-part, rearward facing eagle and crown sitting above the rank lace. All buttons are gilt featuring the RAF eagle with roped surround. Above the left breast pocket typically is the 1918 Pattern RAF silk, hand-embroidered pilot's wings. Interestingly, many tunics show indications that they have been modified from an earlier cuff-ranked tunic with traces and evidence of cuff-rank lace having been removed. This uniform was not worn with a Sam Browne belt but a khaki cloth belt with a single-prong buckle. The uniform was worn with either khaki trousers or breeches in shades of fawn, as seen during the days of the RFC, along with brown footwear, again the same as RFC dress.

ABOVE: A DH.9 squadron in France, mid-1918. A variety of uniforms, both RAF and RFC, are seen here which is typical of the transitional period. (Tangmere Military Aviation Museum)

LEFT: This 1917 Pattern jacket has been altered to reflect the new requirements with the cuff rank being removed and one row of khaki rank lace added to denote a lieutenant with a bird and crown over. The buttons have been changed to the RAF style with the single-prong belt fastener and cloth belt sewn to the jacket in lieu of the Sam Browne. This jacket has nice early RAF pilot's wings on the left breast, and the shoulder epaulettes have been removed.

It is interesting to note that on the creation of the RAF on 1 April 1918, an order was given to officers that RFC or regimental uniform could continue to be worn for the duration of the war. However, officers were encouraged to adopt the new pattern as soon as practicable, but a large number of officers, not wishing to go to the expense of the purchase of the new pattern, had existing tunics converted, and this appears to be the case with this one. Closer examination reveals collar badges have been worn and the shade of the waist belt is slightly different from the cloth of the jacket. Looking at the wear and colour match and natural fading there is no doubt that this is a 1918 conversion which makes it a rarer than usual example of the pattern. (Mark Hillier Collection)

RFC TO RAF TRANSITIONAL ARRANGEMENTS

RIGHT: Captain Malcolm McGregor of 85 Squadron photographed in front of a Sopwith Dolphin at Hounslow, April or May 1918, just after the formation of the RAF. He is wearing his 1912-style jacket with rank shown by pips on the laced cuff patch with trousers rather than breeches or jodhpurs. He is not wearing a Sam Browne belt, but has RAF wings on the uniform. The jacket should have been belted with a cloth belt, as seen in the archive image and mentioned in the transitional dress arrangements of April 1918. (Mark Hillier Collection)

BELOW: A close-up of the modified jacket showing the new cuff rank for the RAF, this being the rank of lieutenant. (Mark Hillier Collection)

LEFT: An RAF lieutenant pilot wearing RAF uniform but still retaining RFC wings. He also has a one-year overseas service chevron on his right sleeve. (Tangmere Military Aviation Museum)

BELOW LEFT: Another version of the khaki RAF uniform. This is a correctly tailored variant, not a transitional uniform. Note on this example the two-prong belt which was adopted for the RAF blue uniform. The British War Medal and Victory Medal are seen on the left breast above the pocket but under the wings. This rank is for second lieutenant, but initially there was no lace approved only the eagle and crown on the sleeve for this rank. (Phil Phillips Collection)

BELOW RIGHT: An interesting example of the traditional uniform in that the regimental buttons and shoulder rank of lieutenant remain but only the wings have changed to the RAF version. (Phil Phillips Collection)

RFC TO RAF TRANSITIONAL ARRANGEMENTS

RIGHT: An RAF officer's uniform with no rank lace shown at all but it would have had the eagle and crown on the sleeve for the rank of second lieutenant, as first approved for the RAF. (Phil Phillips Collection)

LEFT: This observer is wearing an RFC khaki jacket that has begun the transition to RAF uniform with the addition of RAF buttons, but the shoulder rank is still in evidence for a second lieutenant. The observer wing remained the same. He is wearing fug boots and carries a 'Gor Blimey' cap with an RAF officer's badge. (Mark Hillier Collection)

ROYAL FLYING CORPS KITBAG

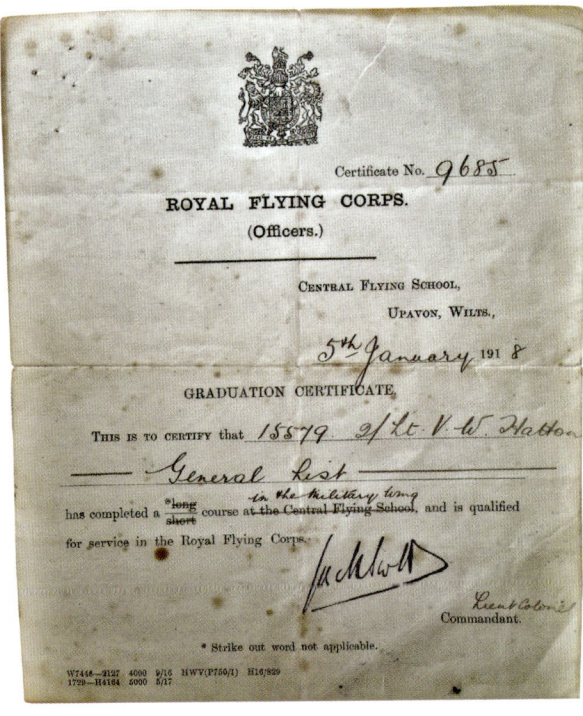

LEFT and ABOVE: Second Lieutenant Victor William Hatton pictured while in the RAF and wearing the uniform seen here. He was born in Wood Green, London in February 1899. Educated at Owen's School, Islington, he duly enlisted in the RFC at South Farnborough in March 1916. Owing to his age, however, he was transferred to the Reserve until recalled in March 1917, at which point he was commissioned as a second lieutenant. Having then attended a training unit at Yatesbury, he qualified as a pilot and was posted to No. 5 Squadron in France in February 1918. Having been being wounded in the air (hence the wound stripe), Hatton was sent back to the Home Establishment. Suffering from 'a nervous disability in the sky', he was eventually discharged. Hatton was placed on the Unemployed List in February 1919. Also seen is his pilot's certificate. Note the eagles on the cuff are pointing the wrong way. (Simon Lannoy Collection)

RFC TO RAF TRANSITIONAL ARRANGEMENTS

LEFT: A captain-rank transitional uniform of an observer with a single-prong belt buckle. Note the very rare BLAV badge above the right breast pocket indicating the wearer was a British Latin American Volunteer. (Phil Phillips Collection)

BELOW LEFT: A close-up of the rare British Latin American Volunteer badge worn on the right breast above the pocket. This badge was introduced late in 1918 by Army Order No. 1067, War Office dated 27 September 1918: '1). The King has been graciously pleased to approve of a special badge to be worn by those officers and soldiers who were residing in South America (inc. Central America and Mexico) at the outbreak of the war and who voluntarily came to this country to join the Army. 2). The badge consists of the letters B.V.L.A. (British Volunteer Latin America) in a diamond worked in yellow on a blue ground. It will be worn on the right breast, immediately above the breast pocket of the service-dress jacket.' (Phil Phillips Collection)

BELOW RIGHT: A typical pair of khaki trousers as worn with the transitional uniform. (Phil Phillips Collection)

RAF PALE-BLUE UNIFORM

Major General Mark Kerr designed the first officer uniform which was largely pale blue with gold braid trimmings. It has been suggested that the pale-blue colour was adopted as the cloth had been intended for use by the Imperial Russian Cavalry and following its disbandment after the Bolshevik Revolution the material became available at a low price.

The pale-blue colour for officers' uniforms was unpopular and impractical and John Slessor, who was later promoted to Marshal of the RAF, described it as 'a nasty pale blue with a lot of gold over it, which brought irresistibly to mind a vision of the gentlemen who stands outside the cinema'. A little over a year after its introduction the pale-blue colour was discontinued. On 15 September 1919, Air Ministry Order No. 1049 replaced it with the blue-grey colour that remains in use to this day.

Captain Bogart Rogers was not impressed when he saw the first examples of the Prussian blue uniform, as he described in a letter home dated 10 May 1918, 'As for the new Air Force uniform it's an awful looking affair, and no one out here is getting it. The old major I told you about saw one the other night and said, "my word, this gentleman looks like a cross between a commissionaire and a P and O boat steward."'[3]

The Air Ministry Order regarding the khaki to blue uniform replacement for officers, dated 4 July 1918, states what was expected and gives an idea of the transition of uniform and badges during this period:

> Important changes in RAF uniform have been approved by A.M. Monthly order No 162 is amended, so far as officers' uniform is concerned, as laid down below.
>
> Officers in possession of khaki uniform of the pattern authorised by the above order may continue to wear same until it becomes necessary to renew it. Light Blue uniform of the pattern laid down below must be then provided.
>
> Light blue uniform already authorised by above quoted order for evening wear, may be taken into use forthwith for general wear, but must first be modified to conform in detail to the patterns described below:-

[the light-blue uniform was initially to be used as an optional mess dress]

No grant in respect of blue uniform will be made

Description of Light Blue Uniform for Officers

Cap
Of the same pattern as the present RAF khaki cap but with light blue crown.

Cap Badge
For all ranks below Major General as at present. Officers of the rank of Major General and above will wear a special Cap Badge, consisting of a wreath of laurel leaves, surmounted by a crown and lion, with gilt metal bird superimposed on the laurel wreath.

Rank Distinction on Cap
The vertical Bars now worn on either side of cap badge by officers below rank of major will not be worn on blue caps.

RFC TO RAF TRANSITIONAL ARRANGEMENTS

Field officers will wear one row of gold oak leaves, and general officers will wear two rows, on peak of cap, as at present.

Jacket
The pattern is the same as that at present authorised for khaki, but the material is of light blue cloth. Buttons the same design as at present authorised but flat, and of gilding metal, without 'rope' edge. Buckles, the same type of buckle will be worn on the belt, but with two prongs instead of one. Badges of rank, the bird and crown at present worn on the cuff is abolished. Badges of rank are as at present authorised, but in gold lace instead of worsted braid. Note second lieutenants will wear the 'half row' of gold lace.

Distinctive badges
Pilot:- Wings of the present pattern but in gold and silver embroidery.
Observer:- Single wing of the present pattern but in gold and silver embroidery.
Service Chevrons:- Will no longer be worn in the RAF.
Wound Badges:- Gold embroidered stripes of the pattern worn in the Navy and Army.

LEFT and BELOW: An RAF pale-blue uniform. This particular piece of uniform was worn by Noel Percy Longdon, who joined the RFC from the Royal Horse Artillery, gaining his commission in February 1918. (Phil Phillips Collection)

Trousers
Of the pattern at present but of blue cloth.

Breeches
Of the pattern at present authorised but of light blue material.

Shirts and Collars
Blue or silver-grey shirts and collars with black ties, may be worn for working wear. White shirts and collars with black ties, may be worn as an option.

Foot Wear
A) With trousers, black shoes or black boots with black socks.
B) With breeches, black boots and light blue puttees or brown boots and brown gaiters or brown field boots. Black field boots may continue to be worn as laid down in A.M W.O 331 of 1918.

Great Coat and Waterproofs
Instructions will be issued later.[4]

ABOVE: Officers serving under Major S. Blackley, for the Director General of Aircraft production, 1918. Most of these men are wearing the transitional khaki uniform apart from the officer second left on the front row, Lieutenant Arthur Whiten Brown, the navigator of the first non-stop transatlantic flight in a Vickers Vimy in 1919. He is wearing the new RAF blue uniform and also sports a wound stripe and the gold and silver wire bullion RAF wings. (Mick Prodger Collection)

RFC TO RAF TRANSITIONAL ARRANGEMENTS

RAF OFFICERS' HATS

The 1918 Pattern RAF Officer's Peaked Cap, with a black mohair band and patent-leather peak with a chin strap, was in khaki ribbed cloth. This originally had an officer's badge of a crown above a gilt metal eagle with laurel leaves under in gold wire. However, a shortage of gold wire lead to the use of an economy version comprising a three-part metal officer's cap badge with either parts made in silver gilt or struck in one piece in gilt brass. This cap was worn with the 1918 Pattern tunic. Early on the RAF officers' cap also had a system of bars used either side of the main badge to identify rank, but this was later dropped.

RIGHT: An early RAF transitional cap with metal parts rather than gilt wire of the approved style badge, as a result of a shortage of gilt wire. This cap, however, appears to be an upgrade on the pattern based on an earlier, perhaps RNAS, cap. Internally the words '*Mes Felicitations*' ('My Congratulations') are printed on the sweatband, which perhaps celebrate a promotion while serving in France. This cap is clearly an early modified example of the RAF officers' hat. (Mark Hillier Collection)

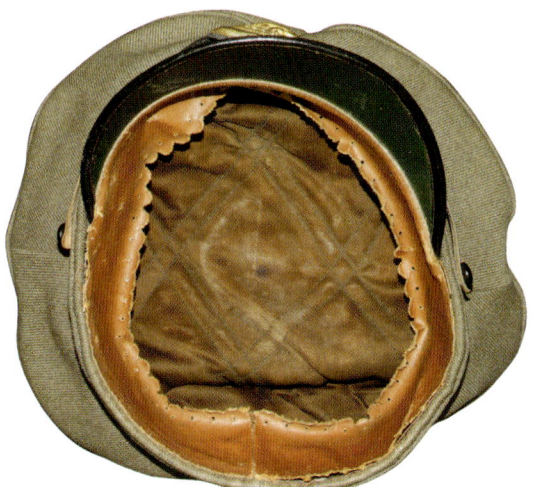

ABOVE LEFT and RIGHT: The inside of the same cap, now showing its age and wear and the sweat protector that would have been in the top long since gone. Also, a close-up of the cap badge. (Mark Hillier Collection)

LEFT: A close-up of a three-part, early RAF officers' cap badge. (Phil Phillips Collection)

BELOW: The second lieutenant or lieutenant (indicated by the two bars either side of the cap badge) who owned this cap was not able to purchase an officer's badge but instead acquired a warrant officer's cap badge as an interim measure, no doubt due to a shortage of gold embroidery. A captain would have had two bars either side to indicate the rank. (Phil Phillips Collection)

LEFT: An RAF officer's khaki cap with a gold bullion, wire cap badge rather than the three-part badge. (Jason Hutton Collection)

RFC TO RAF TRANSITIONAL ARRANGEMENTS

ABOVE LEFT: A well-worn and battered RAF officer's hat in khaki featuring an early cap badge with the crown and wreath in gilt metal rather than bullion wire. There is a black mohair band round the cap and it has a black stiff peak. (Phil Phillips Collection)

ABOVE RIGHT: The officer's hat of Lieutenant Victor William Hatton who joined the RFC initially and was transferred to the RAF. This is a rare example because the bars either side of the cap badge survive as usually these would have been removed. No doubt they have remained as the owner was sent home with medical issues. (Simon Lannoy Collection)

ABOVE: This is a cap belonging to a field officer of the RAF. General officers would wear two rows of gold oak-leaf embroidery. (Phil Phillips Collection)

RIGHT: Lieutenant Peter Rosie, 85 Squadron Engineering Officer, with the squadron goat and dog belonging to Captain Horn, France. He is seen wearing his RAF khaki uniform with belt and arm cuff rank with bird over the braid. Note the RAF cap badge with the two bars, one either side denoting the rank, as mentioned in the extract from *Flight* magazine, 4 April 1918. (Mark Hillier Collection)

ABOVE: Officers of 186 and 187 Squadrons at Retford, 1918. No. 186 Squadron of the RAF was formed on 1 April 1918 at East Retford and provided night pilot training for home defence and on the Western Front. Here a variety of uniforms are seen with some men still wearing RFC hats and maternity tunics. The majority are wearing the khaki transitional uniform and RAF cap badges. What is clear is that there was certainly no uniformity during the war years and into 1919. (Mark Hillier Collection)

BELOW: Three squadron pilots wearing three different uniforms, France, 1918. This photograph was taken after 1 April and the man at the back of the group is wearing the RAF transitional uniform and RAF cap, while the man at front left has the maternity tunic and the officer on the right a cuff-rank tunic, a common sight during the remaining war years. (Tangmere Military Aviation Museum)

RFC TO RAF TRANSITIONAL ARRANGEMENTS

AIRMEN AND OTHER RANKS

At the inception the RAF airmen were wearing examples of the general service Pattern clothing and tunics as well as the maternity jacket. At the time of the change, cap badges were altered, as were shoulder flashes. The approved uniform was a stand and fall collar service jacket with five buttons to close it, in khaki, but the standard general service tunics were prevalent. Ranks were still displayed on the arm including warrant officer 2nd class, flight sergeant, sergeant, corporal and air mechanic 1st class. Pantaloons with boots remained the norm at this stage. The introduction of embroidered cap badges to khaki caps was a key change. Greatcoats remained for those in mounted services and was worn with red shoulder eagles and rank badges on the arm, as per the uniform. In all of the period photographs from 1918 there is a variety of styles seen and very little uniformity.

RIGHT: An enlisted man's maternity jacket dating from post-1914 owing to the shoulder straps and pockets in a hard-wearing, hairy serge material and the rank of corporal worn on the sleeve. This version has an early RAF shoulder insignia under the epaulette which was worn by all ranks of warrant officer 2nd class and below. This uniform continued as it was accepted that until enough stocks of the new uniform were available the old-style uniform would have to suffice. Originally it would have featured the RFC shoulder flash. (Phil Phillips Collection)

ABOVE: RAF transitional cap badges, each colour representing a different rank. Red was for airmen and was worn with khaki. The yellow worsted second from left was for sergeants, although it could be used for warrant officer 2nd class if there was a shortage of badges. Worsted was used because of a shortage of bullion wire. Gold bullion was for the senior NCOs. Blue was for airmen and worn with the blue uniform. White was for the WRAF. The warrant officer 1st class' cap badge is second from right and the officer's cap badge far right. (Phil Phillips Collection)

RIGHT: A close-up of the yellow worsted badge for sergeants, although it could be used by warrant officer 2nd class if there was a shortage of badges. Note this is more typical of the size and style of eagle on original versions. (Mark Hillier Collection)

LEFT: A sergeant observer standing to the left of the propeller of a D.H.9 wearing 1902 Pattern service-dress tunic for other ranks but with RAF badges. He has the other ranks' cap on with new RAF cap badge. He has had a tough war as he wears two wound stripes on his arm. Note still the mix of uniform with the officer next to him wearing RAF transitional uniform and the chap on the right an RFC maternity tunic. (Tangmere Military Aviation Museum)

RFC TO RAF TRANSITIONAL ARRANGEMENTS

ABOVE: An airman wearing a five-button RAF khaki uniform, or serge drab as it was known at this point. He is also wearing an enlisted man's rank service-dress cap with red worsted RAF cap badge. Notice the black peak of the cap rather than khaki cloth. (Mark Hillier Collection)

RIGHT: A very rare RAF version of the other ranks' service-dress jacket, 1918. It is belted with five leather-covered RAF buttons, four pockets with the rank on the sleeve as well as an early RAF eagle. (Phil Phillips Collection)

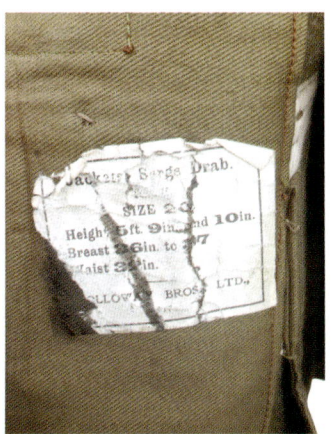

ABOVE: Some of the items of note from this uniform include the label stating 'Jackets, serge drab' and the rank and sleeve insignia in red on a khaki or drab background. Also, a close-up of the leather RAF buttons, five in total and which were brass on earlier examples. (Phil Phillips Collection)

ABOVE: Personnel of 92 Squadron, photographed three days after the Armistice at Bertry, France, in front of their S.E.5 as with CO Major A. Coningham, DSO, MC in the centre, late 1918. Note the variety of uniforms still being worn, some RAF some RFC, and it was not until well into 1919 that consistency began to appear in the form of the new RAF blue. (Tangmere Military Aviation Museum)

APPENDIX I

1914 SCALE OF PROVISION

Royal Flying Corps   A.C.D. R.F.C. 1

Gauntlets, leather, pairs	50}	}	
Goggles, pairs	40}	Per Aeroplane Squadron }	Military Wing
Helmets, Aviation	25}	}	

Coat, leather, per man	1}	For 50 per cent. of }	
Trousers, leather, pair	1}	Establishment. }	Military Wing

Jean clothing, Combination suits, 2 per man, biennially   }   Military Wing

Helmets, Aviation	50}	
Coats, leather	25}	
Trousers, leather, pairs	25}	Will be supplied for use during course of instruction at Central Flying School
Goggles, pairs	50}	
Gauntlets, leather, pairs	100}	

APPENDIX II

ROYAL FLYING CORPS SCALE OF FLYING CLOTHING (AEROPLANES)

Articles	Each pilot or observer or pupil training as such	For mechanics training as observers or gunners per service squadron	Pilots' Aeronautical Inspection Department
Boots, thigh R.F.C. pair.	1	6	–
Caps, fur-lined (summer).ˣ	1	6	–
Caps, fur-lined (winter).#	1	6	5
Gauntlets (observers only), pairs.	1	6	–
Gauntlets (pilots only), pairs.	1	–	5
Gloves, chamois leather, pairs.	–	12¢	–
Goggle mask, leather with nose piece and without glasses (for winter use).	1	6	10
Goggle mask, leather without nose piece and glasses (for summer use).	1	6	10
Glasses, Triplex, for goggles (light tinted for pilots, dark tinted for observers) pairs.	1	6	10
Glasses, Triplex, non-tinted (in case) pairs.	1	6	–
Helmets, aviation.*	–	6	5
Jackets, leather.	1	6	5
Overshoes, gaitered.	1	6	–

ˣ Egypt, Mesopotamia and East Africa only.
Not for Egypt, Mesopotamia or East Africa.
¢ For use in cold weather by men doping wings in the open.
* 25 Helmets, aviation will be held on charge by each of the following establishments for use of Officer pupils: Central Flying School, School of Aerial Gunnery, Service Squadron and Reserve Squadron.

APPENDIX II

N.B. The articles in column 2 above, on issue to pilots or observers, etc., will be written off charge and subsequent free replacements will only be made on production of the unserviceable equivalents.

Pupils at the Schools of Military Aeronautics at Reading and Oxford will be supplied with the articles on departure from the Schools to join Squadrons for further instruction.

If the pilot or observer etc., ceases to be employed by the Royal Flying Corps, the articles will be returned to store, retaken on charge and cleaned and re-issued to another pilot or observer, etc.

Jackets life saving will be supplied as follows for the use of pilots flying overseas:

Jacket, life saving:

No. 1 (Boddy) for pilots under 5 feet 9 inches in height.
No. 2 (Read) for pilots 5 feet 9 inches and over in height.

The articles in column 2 above, on issue to pilots and observers, will be written off charge and subsequent free replacement will only be made on production of the unserviceable equivalents.

If the pilot or observer ceases to be employed by the Royal Flying Corps, the articles will be returned to store, retaken on charge and cleaned and re-issued to another pilot or observer.

APPENDIX III

'Stock', 'Due in' & C. of Clothing and Necessaries for the RFC   31.12.17.

Articles.	Stock on 31.12.17	Under inspection	Arrears	Due In Firm Block	Due In Firm per week	Under Provision Block	Under Provision Per week	Due Out
Caps, Field, R.F.C.	7795	21685	73314	–	6952	–	–	1045
Combination suits, R.F.C.	25002	21904	65417	–	4500	–	–	7455
Coats, great, R.F.C. with embroidered titles.	4220	3036	22618	x 24	1975	–	4220	5164
Coats, W.P. fur-lined, Pilots, R.F.C.	161	75	1773	–	–	–	–	–
Jackets. Service Dress, R.F.C.	20106	3819	10067	x 18	1710	–	8660	10323
Pantaloons, cord, R.F.C.	–	9384	18470	x 44	2450	–	–	18162
Badges, Cap, R.F.C.	154183	20500	–	20000 of sorts	–	–	–	–
Boots, thigh, R.F.C.	6291	–	6517	–	–	–	560	–
Caps, fur-lined, Summer.	507	580	1372	–	256	–	–	250
Caps, fur-lined, Winter.	–	1222	11232	261	1900	–	–	482
Gauntlets, Pilots and Observers N.P.	–	543	2946	–	1800	–	–	–
Gauntlets, Observers only.	5486	300	2527	–	–	–	–	–
Gauntlets, Pilots only.	3672	140	2395	–	–	–	–	–
Gloves wool linings for gauntlets.	1336	12	3600	–	–	–	3600	–
Gloves chamois leather.	1391	–	120	–	60	–	–	–

APPENDIX III

Item									
Gloves silk.	12	–	21	–	–	–	–	–	–
Goggle mask leather with nose piece and without glasses (for winter use).	1	–	219	–	–	–	–	–	–
Goggle mask leather without nose piece and glasses (for summer use).	1	250	430	–	–	–	–	–	–
Gloves, rubber.	1201	–	300	–	100	–	–	–	–
Glasses, Triplex for goggles (light tinted for Pilots).	–	–	–	2073	–	–	–	–	–
Glasses Triplex for goggles (dark tinted for observers).	–	7	–	–	–	–	–	–	–
Glasses Triplex non-tinted (in case).	–	3200	1999	–	–	–	–	–	–
Helmets, aviation.	9911	1825	3289	200	–	–	–	–	–
Jackets, leather.	–	2075	6179	46275	–	–	–	341	–
(Sidcot) Suits Aviation R.F.C.	–	1050	798	450	–	–	450	–	–
Overshoes, gaitered.	12936	–	–	–	–	–	–	–	–
Overalls, cloth, drab, R.F.C.	43	900	267	–	–	–	–	–	–
Jackets, life saving No. 1 (Boddy).	1525	–	–	1650	–	–	–	–	–
Jackets, life saving No. 2 (Read).	71	–	600	2400	–	–	–	–	–

X Factory

NOTES

Introduction
1. Duncan Grinnell-Milne, *Wind in the Wires* (London: Hurst and Blackett, 1933), p. 19.
2. https://www.aerosociety.com/media/4847/a-brief-history-of-flying-clothing.pdf.
3. *Training Manual RFC*, Part II (Military Wing), p. 82.
4. A.J.G. Whitehouse, *Hell in the Heavens* (London: W. & R. Chambers Ltd, 1938), p. 16.
5. Dr Graham Rood, 'A Brief History of Flying Clothing', Farnborough Air Science Trust, Paper No. 2014/01.
6. Norman Macmillan, *Into the Blue* (London: Duckworth, 1929), p. 49.

Chapter 1
1. The National Archives (TNA), Air 2/3/87/687.
2. Donal MacCarron, *Letters from an Early Bird, The Life and Letters of Denys Corbett Wilson 1882–1915* (Barnsley: Pen & Sword, 2006), p. 87.
3. Ibid., p. 123.
4. Grinnell-Milne, *Wind in the Wires*, p. 110.
5. Arthur Gould Lee, *Open Cockpit* (London: Grub Street, 2012), p. 54.
6. Leonard H. Rochford, *I Chose the Sky* (London: Kimber, 1977), p. 101.
7. Elliot White Springs, *War Birds, The Diary of a Great War Pilot* (Barnsley: Frontline Books, 2016), p. 65.
8. Cecil Lewis, *Sagittarius Rising* (London: Folio Society, 1998), p. 11.
9. Peter Lord, 'Written Memories of William Urquhart Dykes' (1999; author's collection).
10. TNA, Air 2/3/87/687.
11. Andrew Cormack, *British Air Forces 1914–18* (Oxford: Osprey Military, 2000), Vol. I.
12. Alan Bott, *An Airman's Outings by Contact* (Edinburgh and London: William Blackwood and Sons, 1917).
13. https://historicgosport.uk/gosport-tube/.
14. James T.B. McCudden, *Flying Fury* (London: Hamilton, 1930), p. 81.
15. Macmillan, *Into the Blue*, p. 74.
16. Bogart Rogers, *A Yankee Ace in the RAF* (Lawrence, KS: University Press of Kansas, 1996), p. 73.
17. Bott, *An Airman's Outings*, p. 158.
18. Lewis, *Sagittarius Rising*, p. 101.

19. Bott, *An Airman's Outings*, p. 221.
20. Whitehouse, *Hell in the Heavens*, p. 37.
21. Bott, *An Airman's Outings*, p. 221.
22. L.A. Strange, *Recollections of an Airman* (London: John Hamilton Ltd, 1935), p. 103.
23. McScotch, *Fighter Pilot* (London: Newnes, n.d.), pp. 202, 203.
24. Whitehouse, *Hell in the Heavens*, p. 256.
25. TNA AIR 1/818/204/4/1311.
26. ibid.
27. ibid.
28. ibid.
29. ibid.
30. Whitehouse, *Hell in the Heavens*, p. 256.
31. TNA, Air 1/1294/204/11/119.

Chapter 2
1. https://www.greatwarforum.org/topic/201639-list-of-army-forms/.
2. TNA, AIR 1/823/204/5/68.
3. *RFC Manual 1914*, p. 94.
4. ibid., p. 95.
5. ibid., p. 109.
6. ibid., p. 111.
7. Strange, *Recollections of an Airman*, p. 129.
8. Whitehouse, *Hell in the Heavens*, p. 25.
9. *RFC Manual 1914*, p. 112.
10. Imperial War Museum (IWM), Department of Sound, 23151.
11. https://www.flightglobal.com/FlightPDFArchive/1963/1963%20-%201728.PDF.
12. Bott, *An Airman's Outings*.
13. Macmillan, *Into the Blue*, p. 92.
14. Lord, 'Written Memories of William Urquhart Dykes'.
15. Grinnell-Milne, *Wind in the Wires*, pp. 243, 244.
16. Joshua Levine, *On a Wing and a Prayer* (London: Collins, 2008), p. 107.
17. Personal account, courtesy of Mrs Roberta (Bobbie) Webb, granddaughter.
18. I. Jones, *King of the Air Fighters* (London: Greenhill Books, 1989), p. 169.
19. Lord, 'Written Memories of William Urquhart Dykes'.
20. General Staff, War Office, Field Artillery Training, 1914, p. 239.
21. Lewis, *Sagittarius Rising*, p. 73.
22. Lord, 'Written Memories of William Urquhart Dykes'.

Chapter 3
1. TNA, Air 2/3/87/687.
2. ibid.
3. I. Jones, *Tiger Squadron* (London: W.H. Allen and Co. Ltd, 1955), p. 53.
4. Lord, 'Written Memories of William Urquhart Dykes'.
5. Lewis, *Sagittarius Rising*, p. 14.
6. TNA, Air 2/3/87/687.
7. Strange, *Recollections of an Airman*, p. 31.
8. *Regulations for the Clothing of the Army, 1914* (Uckfield: Naval & Military Press, n.d.), p. 84.

9. TNA, Air 2/3/87/687.
10. Lewis, *Sagittarius Rising*, p. 14.
11. TNA, Air 2/3/87/687.
12. MacCarron, *Letters from an Early Bird*, p. 156.
13. Whitehouse, *Hell in the Heavens*, p. 19.

Chapter 4
1. TNA, Air 2/3/87/687.
2. ibid.
3. TNA, Air 1/818/204/4/1306.
4. TNA, Air 2/3/87/687.
5. ibid.
6. TNA, Air 1/1301/204/11/158.
7. C.G. Jefford, *Observers and Navigators and Other Non-pilot Aircrew in the RFC and RNAS* (London: Grub Street, 2014), pp. 4–5.
8. ibid.
9. Whitehouse, *Hell in the Heavens*, p. 17.
10. TNA, Air1/785/204/558.
11. TNA, Air1/1301/204/11/158.
12. http://www.researchingww1.co.uk/ww1-wound-stripes.
13. TNA, Air 2/15.
14. Cormack, *British Air Forces 1914–18*.
15. https://salisburyinquests.wordpress.com/1916-2/battye-cyril/.

Chapter 6
1. Rogers, *A Yankee Ace in the RAF*, p. 72.
2. *Flight* magazine, 4 April 1918.
3. Rogers, *A Yankee Ace in the RAF*, p. 104.
4. TNA, AIR 1/29/15/1/141/3.

BIBLIOGRAPHY

Bott, Alan, *An Airman's Outings by Contact*, Edinburgh and London: William Blackwood and Sons, 1917

Carroll, Warren, *Eagles Recalled*, Atglen PA: Schiffer Military History, 1997

Chambers, Stephen J., *Uniforms and Equipment of the British Army in World War 1*, Atglen PA: Schiffer Military History, 2005

Cole, Christopher (ed.), *Royal Air Force Communiques 1918*, London: Tom Donovan, 1990

Cooksley, Peter, G., *The Royal Flying Corps 1914–1918*, Stroud: Spellmount, 2004

Cormack, Andrew, *British Air Forces 1914–18*, Vols I and II, Oxford: Osprey Military, 2000

Cunningham, G., *Mac's Memoirs, The Flying Life of Squadron Leader McGregor*, Wellington, NZ: A.H. and A.W. Reed, 1937

Douglas, S., *Years of Combat*, London: Collins, 1963

Franks, Norman and Saunders, Andy, *Mannock, The Life and Death of Major Edward Mannock, VC, DSO, MC, RAF*, London: Grub Street, 2008

Grinnell-Milne, Duncan, *Wind in the Wires*, London: Hurst and Blackett Ltd, 1933

Hobart, Malcolm, *Badges and Uniforms of the RAF*, Barnsley: Pen & Sword, 2013

Hobson, Chris, *Airmen Died in the Great War*, London: J.B. Hayward & Son, 1995

Jefford, C.G., *Observers and Navigators and Other Non-pilot Aircrew in the RFC and RNAS*, London: Grub Street, 2014

Jones, I., *Tiger Squadron*, London: W.H. Allen and Co. Ltd, 1955

Jones, I., *King of the Air Fighters*, London: Greenhill Books, 1989

Kilduff, Peter, *Billy Bishop VC, Lone Wolf Hunter, The RAF Ace Re-examined*, London: Grub Street, 2014

Lee, Arthur Gould, *Open Cockpit*, London: Grub Street, 2012

Levine, Joshua, *On a Wing and a Prayer*, London: Collins, 2008

Lewis, Cecil, *Sagittarius Rising*, London: Folio Society, 1998

MacCarron, Donal, *Letter from an Early Bird, The Life and Letters of Denys Corbett Wilson 1882–1915*, Barnsley: Pen & Sword, 2006

McCudden, James T.B., *Flying Fury*, London: Hamilton, 1930

Macmillan, Norman, *Into the Blue*, London: Duckworth, 1929

McScotch, *Fighter Pilot*, London: Newnes, n.d.

Oughton, Frederick, *The Personal Diary of 'Mick' Mannock, VC, DSO (2 Bars), MC (1 Bar)*, London: Spearman, 1966

Philpott, Ian, *The Birth of the Royal Air Force*, Barnsley: Pen & Sword, 2013

Pollendine, Chris, *Campaign 1914, Volume 1*, Hitchin: Military Mode Publishing, 2013

Prodger, Mick, *Vintage Flying Helmets: Aviation Headgear Before the Jet Age*, Atglen PA: Schiffer Military History, 1995

Rawlings, John, *Fighter Squadrons of the RAF and Their Aircraft*, London: MacDonald, 1969

Regulations for the Clothing of the Army, 1914, Uckfield: Naval & Military Press, n.d.

Rochford, Leonard H., *I Chose the Sky*, London: Kimber, 1977

Rogers, Bogart, *A Yankee Ace in the RAF*, Lawrence, KS: University Press of Kansas, 1996

Shores, Christopher, Franks, Norman and Guest, Russell, *Above the Trenches*, London: Grub Street, 1990

Skennerton, Ian D. (ed.), *List of Changes in British War Materiel, Volume IV 1910–1918*, Ashmore, Australia: Ian D. Skennerton, 1993

Springs, Elliot White, *War Birds, The Diary of a Great War Pilot*, Barnsley: Frontline Books, 2016

Strange, L.A., *Recollections of an Airman*, London: John Hamilton Ltd, 1935

Vaughan, David K., *Letters from a War Bird, The World War I Correspondence of Elliot White Springs*, Columbia, SC: University of South Carolina Press, 2012

Whitehouse, A.J.G., *Hell in the Heavens*, London: W. & R. Chambers Ltd, 1938

Williamson, H.J., *The Roll of Honour RFC and RAF 1914–1918*, Dallington: Naval & Military Press, 1992

INDEX

Abeale, Belgium 212
Africa 196, 212, 258
Alberta 96, 142
Aldershot 1, 129
Amiens 142
Anderson and Son of
    Edinburgh and London 145
Armstrong-Whitworth 106
Arras 60, 161
Australia 201, 266
Avro 76, 216

Balfour, Second Lieutenant
    Harold 2
Barclay, Second Lieutenant
    James 186, 187, 222
Battye, Lieutenant Cyril
    Wynyard 211–13
Bayes, 1st Class Air Mechanic
    Albert Horace 199
Belgium 185, 212, 234
Berkshire 212
Béthune 109
Birmingham 121
Bissegem (Bisseghem) 38
Bleriot helmet, 3
Bodley, Second Lieutenant
    W.G. 28
Borgel watches 113, 115
Bournemouth 9, 215
Bristol 21, 143, 157, 163
Brooklands 23, 184
Browne, Sam, belt 29, 120,
    122, 130, 139, 147, 148,
    151, 157, 185, 238–41
burns 93, 131

Cadbury, Flight Lieutenant
    Egbert 29

Cairns, Captain W.C. 118
Calthrop 10, 11
Cody, Samuel 21
Cordeaux, Air Mechanic
    Charles Albert 212
Courcelles 79, 153, 204, 211
Courtrai 38
Crespigny, Major Hugh Vivian
    Champion de 38
Cunliffe, Lieutenant
    B.F.G. 224

Davies, 2nd Air
    Mechanic 227
Doncaster 170
Dowsett, Second Lieutenant
    Thomas 59, 152
Drummond, Lieutenant
    M.D.G. 220
Dunhill 89
Dykes, William Urquhart 11,
    113, 122, 125, 129, 185,
    234, 262, 263

Edinburgh 145, 262, 265
Egypt 258
Evans 90

Falmouth 100
Farman, Maurice 13, 192,
    218, 231
Farnborough 14, 15, 21, 98,
    184, 231, 234, 244, 262
Farnsworth, David 20, 33, 53,
    54, 81, 87, 89, 100
Farrer, Sergeant Fred 192
Fownes-style mittens 67
Fraser, Captain 92
Fulford 154, 170

Gallipoli 201, 220
Geneva 129
Gieve's tailors 22, 100
Gnome 233
Gosport 33, 36, 39, 99, 129
Goss, Second Lieutenant
    James Louis 228
Gotha 169
Gower, Lieutenant 131
Grange 36, 99
Gribben, Captain Edward 151
Grider, John McGavock 10
Grinnell-Milne, Duncan 5, 113,
    262, 263, 265

Hall Brothers of Oxford 139
Hamilton 185, 262, 263,
    265, 266
Hampshire 162
Handley Page 42
Harrods 5, 84
Hatton, Victor William
    244, 251
Hawker, Major Lanoe 5, 69,
    84, 233
Hellyer, Captain 212, 213
Henderson, General Sir David
    183, 196
Hendon 20, 39, 44, 51, 130
Hythe 182, 183, 196

India 212
Ireland 175
Italy 220

James-Williams, Captain 38
Jefford, Wing Commander
    C.G. 194, 264, 265
Jones, Ira 118, 128, 263, 265

ROYAL FLYING CORPS KITBAG

Kelly, Lieutenant 145
Kent 212, 234
Kerr, Major General Mark 246
Kingston 215, 216
Knibbs, Gunner George 70
Krebs, Fritz 161

Laing, Second Lieutenant
　Thomas Harr 50
Lannoy 24, 25, 29, 30, 34, 49,
　52, 59–63, 65, 67, 82, 88, 91,
　105, 121–4, 126, 133, 134,
　137, 146–8, 152, 156, 162,
　190, 210, 212, 220, 244, 251
Lanoe, Simon 5, 69, 84
Longdon, Noel Percy 247
Lorraine 21

McCudden, James T.B. 44, 45,
　262, 265
Macdonald, Lieutenant
　Wilfred Ferguson 199, 266
McElroy, Captain George 85
McGregor, Captain Malcolm
　241, 265
McKeever, Major Andrew
　Edward 143, 144
Macmillan, Captain Norman
　45, 112, 262, 263, 265
Malta 212
Mametz 125
Mannock, Major Edward
　Corringham 'Mick' 25, 37,
　62, 85, 118, 265
Maubeuge 106
Menin 69, 234
Mesopotamia 258
Mexico 245
Miller Manufacturing
　Company 40
Milton 212
Montauban 125
Montrose 142

Neilsen-Jones,
　Lieutenant H.F. 157
Netheravon 23, 28, 68, 76,
　184, 195, 198, 206, 207,
　211, 212
Norfolk 29, 108

Omer 234
Oxford 128, 139, 196, 215,
　259, 262, 265

Pacific 201
Parfield, E.S. 30
Park, Major, later Air Chief
　Marshal Sir Keith Rodney
　157, 192, 231
Parker, Air Mechanic William
　Percy 24, 36, 39, 52, 61
Patterson, Sergeant David 192
Peake, Miss Catherine 224
Pentland, Alexander Augustus
　Norman Dudley 201
Perrin, Paul 99
Perrin-Auliff 100
Phillips, Phil 18, 27, 35, 43, 45,
　57, 64–6, 75–8, 83, 86, 87,
　90, 99, 116, 119, 120, 132,
　136, 139, 145, 146, 155,
　158, 165–8, 170, 171, 173,
　176–80, 186–9, 196, 197,
　200, 204, 205, 209, 210,
　222, 230, 242, 243, 245,
　247, 250, 251, 253–5
Poperinghe 106
Popham, Brigadier General
　Robert Brook 89, 91, 92
Pratt, Captain 6
Pulling, Flight Sub Lieutenant
　Edward L. 29
Puma 233

RAAF 201
Rabagliati, Lieutenant
　later Lieutenant Colonel
　Cuthbert Euan Charles 106
RAMC 212
Rayner, C. 213
Retford 252
Rochford, Leonard H. 9, 262,
　266
Roe, A.V. 42

Salisbury 1
Salonika 152, 220
Sansom, Major G.S. 86
Saunders, Sergeant Samuel
　23, 118, 198, 265
Scotland 142
Seagrave, Lieutenant 213
Seeporah 147
Shepard, Captain G.S. 194, 198
Sidcot 10, 51, 69, 75, 77,
　89–93, 96, 261
Siebe-Gorman 43
Slessor, John 246

Smith-Barry,
　Robert Raymond 36
Smithie, Second Lieutenant
　James Deardon 60
Solent 39
Somme 70
Sopwith 9, 45, 151, 161, 201,
　220, 241
SPADs 201
Spence, Howard 53
Spencer parachutes 10, 117
Spuy, Kenneth van der 118
Stallwood & Son, military
　outfitters 84
Stohwasser leggings 2,
　157, 179
Surtees, Lieutenant Vere
　Nathaniel Faber 225
Sutcliffe, Lieutenant John 162
Sykes, General
　Sir Frederick 183

Tangmere 4, 40, 50, 51, 53,
　58, 80, 83, 92, 93, 135, 142,
　147, 150, 153, 155, 157,
　163, 166, 172, 174, 175,
　177, 190–3, 202, 208, 209,
　240, 242, 252, 254, 256
Thompson, Air Mechanic
　Harold 169
Trenchard, Major Hugh, later
　Marshall of the RAF 137
Trethowan, Mr F. H. 212

Upavon 130, 137, 192,
　218, 224
Urvillers 109
Urwick, Henry 61
USA 133

Vickers 117, 212, 248
Voss, Werner 199

Warner, Captain 145
Washington, Second
　Lieutenant F.W. 68
Wilson, Denys Corbett 4, 21,
　175, 262, 265
Wiltshire 224
Windsor 212

Yates, Sergeant 11
Yatesbury 244
Ypres 109, 219